Fear
at
Work

DATE DUE

Richard Kazis
Richard L. Grossman

Fear at Work

Job Blackmail, Labor and the Environment

The Pilgrim Press

New York

Library of Congress Cataloging in Publication Data

Kazis, Richard, 1952–
    Fear at work.

    Includes index and bibliographical references.
    1. Environmental policy—United States—Cost
effectiveness. 2. Environmental protection—United
States—Cost effectiveness. 3. Costs, Industrial—
United States. 4. Unemployment—United States.
I. Grossman, Richard L.   II Title.
HC110.E5K39   1982   331.13′7042′0973   82–9829
ISBN 0–8298–0600–8 (pbk.)

Excerpts from *The Zero Sum Society: Distribution and the Possibilities
for Economic Change* by Lester C. Thurow are copyright © 1980 by
Basic Books, Inc. Used by permission of Basic Books, Inc., Publishers,
New York. Excerpts from *Workers' Control in America* by David
Montgomery are copyright © 1979 by Cambridge University Press and
used by permission.

The Pilgrim Press, 132 West 31 Street, New York, New York 10001

Contents

Acknowledgments

It is impossible to acknowledge all the people and organizations that have made this book possible. Our primary debt is to the many activists within both the labor and environmental movements who have stood up to job blackmail and refused to accept the false choice of "jobs versus the environment."

This book has grown out of the work of Environmentalists for Full Employment (EFFE), founded in 1975 by Peter Harnik, Hazel Henderson, and Byron Kennard. We are grateful to them for their important contributions to its genesis and to labor-environmental cooperation.

We are grateful also to the many friends and colleagues who helped us shape our experience and ideas into this book. George Kohl, Leonard Rodberg and Gail Williams merit special thanks for their careful criticism of successive drafts. Their enthusiasm, along with the assistance and encouragement of EFFE board members, Claudia Comins and Harriet Barlow, were most important to us.

We appreciate the critical comments of: Cliff Aron, Jordan Barab, George Coling, Barry Commoner, Gail Daneker, David Dickson, Brock Evans, Joe Frantz, Elliott Gilberg, Debbie Goldman, David Gordon, Brian Gorman, Samuel Hays, Mark Hertsgaard, Lorin Kerr, William Klinefelter, Charles Komanoff, Cindy Matsakis, Tony Mazzocchi, Stuart Newman, Rice Odell, Mike Olszanski, David Plotke, Mitt Regan, Sheldon Samuels,

Margaret Seminario, Harley Shaiken, Cathy Sunshine, William Tabb, Tom Turner, Elias Vlanton, Frank Wallick, Rob Wolcott, John Yolton, and Jeffrey Zinsmeyer.

Preparing a manuscript for publication is an awesome task. M.E. Warlick and Judy Linsky patiently and efficiently typed draft after draft. Jan Simpson, our office manager, kept both the manuscript and its authors in order. We thank them for their work and for their good cheer throughout a long and demanding process.

We appreciate as well the many organizations and individuals that provided financial support. Jay Harris enabled us to revive the idea of writing this book. With Maryanne Mott, Herman Warsh, Wade Greene, and David Hunter, he helped us see it to completion.

We also thank the following for their support: the Public Concern Foundation, the Stern Fund, the Center for Community Change, the National Rural Center, the Natural Resources Defense Council, Friends of the Earth Foundation, the Center for Renewable Resources, the United Steelworkers of America, the United Auto Workers, the International Association of Machinists, the National Football League Players Association, W. H. and Carol Ferry, Lawrence Latto and John Steiner.

Naturally, while we appreciate the assistance and support of so many fine people and organizations (including the inevitable one or two we have omitted), responsibility for opinions or errors in this book rests entirely with us.

Finally, we would like to thank Suzanne Chollet, Mary MacArthur, Alyssa Grossman, and our other friends and family for their encouragement, patience, and understanding during the many months that this book absorbed so much of our time and energy.

Richard Kazis
Richard Grossman
Washington, DC

Preface

An occupational health physician in Washington tells of a man suffering from mercury poisoning who was visited by his company doctor. Entering the hospital room, the doctor glared at the patient, then snapped angrily, "What are you trying to do, shut down the plant?"

Control over jobs gives employers the power to intimidate. They can close plants and offices, move to other states and countries and leave people without jobs. Intimidation by employers takes place outside the workplace as well. Communities are led to believe they must accommodate long lists of corporate demands to keep existing jobs in their area or to attract new jobs. The public is offered only two options: to give corporations what they want or face higher unemployment.

This is *job blackmail*. It is a tactic used by business and government leaders to manipulate public opinion on issues as varied as military spending, civil rights, tax reform, urban development and public health. Whenever national investment priorities are debated, the public is warned that policies restricting corporate freedom or profits will cost jobs.

This book is about one particularly insidious form of job blackmail: *environmental job blackmail*. Citizen activism in the past fifteen years resulted in new environmental, safety and health laws. These laws were enacted to protect people on the job and in their communities by limiting the ability of employers to pollute at will and use resources indiscriminately. Many business and government leaders have responded to their new environmental obligations by claiming that these regulations have been killing the economy, making growth next to impossible, throwing people out of work and interfering with the creation of new jobs. Charging that people must choose between jobs and environmental quality, they have played on fears of unemployment to alienate members of organized labor from their counterparts in the environmental movement.

This strategy has met with some success. "Environmentalists Are Polluting Our E-C-O-N-O-M-Y!" read one bumper sticker popular in the mid-1970s. Trade unionists and environmental activists have lined up on opposing sides of many bitter confrontations, such as the Alaska Pipeline, the SST, nuclear power, the Tellico Dam, clean air laws and the expansion of Redwoods National Park. Despite frequent labor-environmental cooperation in the past decade, highly publicized conflicts have led to the perception that environmentalism and unionism do not mix.

This book intends to change that perception. Jobs and environmental quality are not mutually exclusive. Both are basic requirements of a just society—and both should be recognized as basic rights of all citizens. Environmental protection is essential to labor. Pollution hurts workers and destroys jobs. A toxic chemical which harms people in their communities is certainly a threat to workers in the plant where it is produced. And a nation which fails to ensure wise use of its natural resources and their protection for future generations endangers its own economic future. Similarly, secure and decent jobs for all who want to work—full employment—is essential to environmental protection. Without jobs, most Americans are unable to support themselves and their families. And as long as people remain afraid of losing their jobs, they will be vulnerable to job blackmail. Out of fear, they may support programs and policies which are not in their best interest.

Today, with so many people out of work, vulnerability to all kinds of job blackmail has increased dramatically. In his first State of the Union address, President Reagan rationalized his support for a weakened Clean Air Act by claiming that his amendments would be good for jobs. Vice President Bush and other administration officials have charged repeatedly that environmental regulations have been a significant factor in the past decade's high unemployment. After Solidarity Day brought more than 250,000 working Americans to Washington to protest the first year of Reagan's economic and regulatory policies, White House spokesman David Gergen tried to argue that there were "many areas of agreement" between the administration and organized labor. To make his point, he claimed that both were opposed to "environmental extremists" who stand in the way of jobs.

The Reagan administration and its allies have been capitalizing on today's economic crisis to widen the split between labor and environmentalists over "jobs," while cynically attacking rights and protections that have been won by both movements. The assault on labor and environmental protections will intensify. As in the past, "jobs" will be the rationalization for new antiworker, anti-environmental policies. In order to defend and broaden environmental, health and job rights, the labor and environmental movements will have to make a conscious effort to work together to resist and overcome job blackmail. Antagonism between the two constituencies should be replaced by commitment to a society where jobs and environmental quality are preeminent as national goals and public rights.

PART I

Whipping Workers into Line

The Power of
_____Job Blackmail

At 11:00 A.M. on 29 September 1980, James L. Marvin, president of the Anaconda Copper Company, opened a press conference which Montana residents had been anxiously awaiting. Atlantic Richfield Co. (ARCO), the Denver-based energy multinational which bought Anaconda in 1977, was finally prepared to announce its decision on the future of its Montana copper operations.[1]

Marvin got right to the point:

> Anaconda Copper Company, a unit of Atlantic Richfield Company, announced today it is suspending operations indefinitely at its smelter in Anaconda, Montana, and its refinery in Great Falls. The closings, which do not affect the company's operations at the Berkeley Pit in Butte, are expected to impact 1,500 employees.

The reason for the shutdowns? "The company has determined by in-depth studies that the existing plant cannot be retrofitted to satisfy environmental standards and become cost competitive with modern large-scale smelters."

3

Marvin assured the citizens of Montana that the company made its decision only after "exhausting every option available" to bring the smelter in Anaconda into compliance with state and federal environmental and occupational health standards.

The announcement left most residents of Anaconda in shock, including the 1,000 smelter workers suddenly unemployed. Just one day earlier a pensioner who had worked more than 35 years at the smelter told a reporter, "Ain't no way the company's ever gonna abandon this place. They got every damn thing they need. Water. Everything. That's just a scare tactic is all that is." Many people agreed: to think otherwise was to accept the death of their town, a small isolated community of 12,000 where 8 of 10 jobs depended directly or indirectly on the smelter.

Following the company's lead, many workers and local residents directed their anger at environmental activists and governmental bureaucrats. The day after the shutdown, a group of workers meeting with the governor's staff carried signs that read, "Our Babies Can't Eat Clean Air." Workers complained about "all these kids that work for the Environmental Protection Agency (EPA) and the Occupational Safety and Health Administration (OSHA)," who "don't know how to make a living the hard way."

Others, however, cursed the company. At a rally of over 300 people in Great Falls two days after the shutdown, James Kelliher, who had worked at the refinery for 31 years, said, "We didn't get any warning or anything. It was ARCO—they don't care about us." Glen Sanders, another refinery worker, carried a placard with two rhyming messages: "Work Like a Nut for a Kick in the Butt" and "After 26 Years, Nothing But Tears."

The day after ARCO made its announcement, EPA Regional Administrator Roger Williams challenged the company's claim that air pollution regulations were the primary reason for the smelter shutdown. He said the company could have asked for extension of Clean Air Act compliance deadlines through January 1988—a grace period of nearly eight years which the EPA allowed all firms in the copper industry. "So far," Williams explained, "the company has chosen not to discuss this option with EPA nor to seek our approval."

Dr. John H. McGregor, chairman of the Montana State Board of Health, felt that ARCO's singling out environmental regulations was "just an excuse" for closing operations during the existing copper surplus. He noted that ARCO never addressed any complaint or special request to the Board. "We would never close down a business in Montana because of pollution," he said. "I don't think the Board is that stupid."

Union officials reacted angrily. "We don't believe what the company said," asserted Robert C. Murdoch, president of United Steelworkers of America Local 16-A in Anaconda.

> We don't believe it closed down because of the air quality standards. We believe it closed because it was unwilling to pay the cost of supporting the workers and communities of this country. ARCO knew the pay scales and working conditions of American copper workers. It knew the smelter needed to be modernized.

"How many times in the past have they threatened to close down because of the unions?" asked Howard Rosenleaf, business manager for Local 88 of the United Brotherhood of Carpenters and Joiners of America. "Now they say it is because they don't want to clean up the air for workers and their children." Rosenleaf believed the company's decision had nothing to do with air quality standards: "They want all the U.S. laws scrapped which require irresponsible companies to provide a healthy workplace and living wage for their employees. And they want to be rid of the unions."

Democratic Governor Thomas Judge told a group of workers that he had offered ARCO a virtual blank check from the state government in an effort to keep the smelter and refinery open, but the company had refused every offer. Democratic gubernatorial candidate Ted Schwinden called a news conference: "It is apparent that the decision . . . is really the result of the Anaconda Company's failure to reinvest a portion of the billions it has earned in Montana over the years. For years, the company took the money and ran." Columnist Tom Kotynski agreed: "It is apparent," he wrote, "that someone long ago in the Anaconda hierarchy made the decision not to upgrade the antiquated smelter and it was allowed to deteriorate. The result of that decision is manifest now."

By the end of the week, few people still believed ARCO's claim that environmental regulations had forced the shutdown and that the company had done all it could to keep the smelter and refinery open. A reporter from one Montana newspaper uncovered some revealing testimony by Robert O. Anderson, ARCO's chief executive officer and board chairman. At a 1977 federal court hearing on whether ARCO should be allowed to buy the Anaconda Company, Anderson had pledged capital investments in Anaconda's Montana holdings of "two to three hundred million a year over the next four or five years"—a billion dollars in five years. "A tremendous amount" of that money, according to Anderson, was to go toward improving smelting techniques and meeting EPA and OSHA standards. To most observers Anaconda's actual expenditures of only $65 million between 1972 and 1980 on state- and federally-mandated health and environmental clean up reflected less than a full commitment to the facilities, the company's employees, and their families.

JOBS VERSUS THE ENVIRONMENT?

ARCO's management tried to make the Anaconda and Great Falls shutdowns just another case of "jobs versus the environment," of faceless government bureaucrats and "elitist" environmentalists cleaning the environment by closing industry and throwing local residents out of their jobs. This is not unusual. Employers often claim that the economic burden of government regulations forces them to close factories, mines, and mills, and lay off workers. They also maintain that environmentally-related citizen opposition leads to cancellations and delays of major projects, resulting in the elimination of thousands of proposed new jobs.

The implication of these employers' claims and threats is clear: our nation cannot afford both *jobs* and *environment*. If the public wants careful resource use and a clean, protected environment, that must come at the expense of working people. And if workers want to keep their jobs and be assured of future jobs, they must live and work with health hazards and accept environmental damage.

Consider these examples:

- In January 1971, in one of his first acts as administrator of the new Environmental Protection Agency, William Ruckelshaus ordered the Union Carbide Company to comply with air pollution clean up deadlines at its Marietta, Ohio, metals plant. The company announced that it could reduce the plant's sulfur dioxide and particulate emissions only by shutting down two boilers and laying off over 600 workers.[2]

- In September 1971 Federal District Court Judge Allan B. Hannay ordered the Armco Steel Corporation to stop dumping highly toxic cyanide, ammonia, sulphide, and phenol wastes into the already heavily-polluted Houston Ship Channel. C. William Verity,

Jr., Armco's president and an influential Republican
contributor, fired a letter to President Nixon in
which he claimed that the court order to stop
dumping hazardous wastes had "eliminated about
300 jobs in one stroke of the pen" and that its
application to other plants "would shut down not
only all steel plants but also all chemical, oil and
many other industries." An Armco lawyer explained
to the press that the company went to the White
House for help because "jobs were involved."[3]

• In the 1960s the federal government and the aerospace industry began developing a supersonic transport plane—the SST. The aerospace companies, led
by Boeing, claimed that 200,000 new jobs would be
created and that the SST would enable them to
maintain their competitive edge over European
firms. But many scientists, engineers, and environmentalists opposed the SST. They argued the plane's
sonic booms would disrupt an area 50 miles wide for
over 2,000 miles between New York and California.
They also believed the SST would cost too much and
waste fuel, while benefiting only a small number of
wealthy people. When funding for the project
bogged down in Congress, John A. Volpe, President
Nixon's Secretary of Transportation, argued for
continuation. If the SST were not built, he claimed,
"then in six or seven years you would have tens of
thousands of employees laid off and an aviation
industry that would go to pot."[4]

• In April 1974 after the discovery of liver cancer
among workers at B.F. Goodrich's vinyl chloride
plant in Louisville, Kentucky, OSHA issued an
Emergency Temporary Standard for vinyl chloride
exposure and began to develop a permanent standard. When the proposed permanent standard of a
zero-to-1-part-per-million (ppm) exposure ceiling
was announced, vinyl chloride and polyvinyl chloride (PVC) producers—dominated by Shell, Dow,
Goodrich, Firestone, Union Carbide, Conoco, and
other petrochemical giants—released studies claim-

ing they could not meet the standard. One study by Foster D. Snell, Inc., predicted the cost of trying to reach 1 ppm would cause PVC prices to rise about 80 percent (assuming the companies made the necessary investment rather than close). The study concluded that, even with a 50 ppm standard, as much as one-fourth of the PVC production capacity would be lost. General Motors, which used PVC in many car parts, warned that a PVC shortage might force the layoff of 450,000 GM workers and eliminate another 1.8 million jobs throughout the economy. Arthur D. Little, Inc., predicted the loss of between 1.7 and 2.2 million jobs and a GNP decline of 65 to 90 billion dollars if the standard were set at 1 ppm.[5]

• California citizens qualified an initiative for the June 1976 ballot to empower the state legislature to decide whether nuclear power safeguards in California were adequate. The Nuclear Safeguards Initiative, as Proposition 15 was called, met with stiff opposition from utilities, banks, and practically every other industry in California. Former California Governor Edmund G. "Pat" Brown, Sr., was a leader in the fight against the initiative. He argued that jobs were at stake: "We must act now, with nuclear power plant developments which are planned and about to begin, to minimize unemployment in California." Brown predicted layoffs of over 1,000 workers employed by nuclear plants then under construction and the loss of thousands of other jobs in nuclear facilities planned for the future. He warned that without continued development of nuclear power, the economy of California would crumble: "The general unemployment resulting from a severe energy shortage will be drastic."[6]

In each of these instances employers and government officials blamed threatened or actual job loss on efforts to protect workplace and natural environments. A tradeoff between jobs and the environment was made to appear unavoidable. The apparent inevitability of such a conflict has set labor and environmentalists against each other at various times in the past two decades. In 1967 the Sierra Club announced its opposition to the SST. Other national environmental organizations followed, including the National Audubon Society, Friends of the Earth, and the Environmental Defense Fund.[7] Against these groups stood the federal government, the aerospace industry —and the AFL-CIO, the Air Line Pilots Association and the International Association of Machinists.

The 15 unions which comprise the Building and Construction Trades Department of the AFL-CIO have been unswervingly in favor of nuclear power while most environmental organizations have been just as staunchly opposed. The successful drive to defeat the Nuclear Safeguards Initiative in California had the support of virtually all California labor organizations. Sigmund Arywitz, executive secretary-treasurer of the Los Angeles County Federation of Labor, wrote to all local unions and councils advising against "giving in to extremist environmentalists who must have their own way on every issue without regard to the number of jobs it will cost."[8]

On a variety of both local and national issues, workers and environmentally-concerned citizens—and the organizations which represent them—have been on opposing sides. But conflict is not as frequent or inevitable as workers, environmental activists and the public often assume. ARCO hoped to shift the anger of employees and the public from itself when it decided to curtail its Montana operations and eliminate 1,500 jobs. Wanting people to believe environmental protection costs were to blame, the company announced that regulation forced the shutdown—even though management knew it was bending the truth. In fact, in each of the above "conflicts," industry—and often government—has been wrong about the tradeoff between jobs and the environment:

- Union Carbide retreated from its threatened layoffs when the company met with strong resistance in Marietta from workers, the Oil, Chemical and Atomic Workers International Union which represented them, and local citizens. The plant switched to low-sulfur coal, met the pollution-control deadline, and did not fire a single worker.[9]

- The 300 Armco Steel workers referred to by William Verity in his letter to President Nixon had been laid off several weeks before the court order, when part of the plant was shut down for routine maintenance and repairs. According to EPA Regional Enforcement Director Tom Harrison, any decision as to whether the Armco workers would be rehired or not had nothing to do with the court's pollution-control order and everything to do with the slumping steel market.[10]

- The aerospace industry and the taxpaying public should be glad the SST was never built. France and England, which jointly financed and built the *Concorde* SST, have found no buyers and have lost money. The 200,000 jobs which Boeing and other firms claimed would be created would never have materialized, regardless of the environmental impact of frequent transcontinental flights. Money invested in building the SST would not have been available for designing and producing the newer, more fuel-efficient planes which have become the backbone of Boeing's commercial fleet.

- On 4 October 1974 OSHA promulgated a permanent standard for vinyl chloride only slightly more lenient than the one initially proposed. Once the major producers lost their legal challenges (the Court of Appeals advised the industry to have "more faith in [its] own technological potentialities"), they began introducing technologies for meeting the new exposure ceilings. By April 1975, when the standard went into effect, small and large companies admitted they could operate without curtailing production, and the standard appeared "not to be a serious operating or cost problem." Not one of the threatened plant closings occurred. No jobs were lost. By the end of December the industry announced that any future closings of PVC plants would not be related to OSHA or EPA compliance. A September 1976 *Chemical Week* headline trumpeted: "Polyvinyl Chloride Rolls Out of Jeopardy, Into Jubilation."[11]

• Although the nuclear industry contends nuclear power plants are essential to economic growth, energy independence, and jobs, the evidence indicates otherwise.[12] Nuclear plants have become increasingly expensive and uneconomical.[13] California utilities, which warned in 1976 that passage of the Nuclear Safeguards Initiative would be catastrophic for the state's economy, have abandoned plans for construction of new nuclear power plants and turned to energy conservation and renewable energy resources. A 1981 study published by the Solar Energy Research Institute (SERI) found improved energy efficiency and increased use of renewable energy resources could, over the next decade, help the country to "achieve a full employment economy and increased worker productivity, while reducing national energy consumption by nearly 25 percent."[14] Although nuclear power has been promoted as the key to energy independence, the SERI report concluded that "a strategy built around energy efficiency and the widespread use of renewable resources could result in the virtual elimination of oil imports."[15] Such a strategy would also put people to work: the Industrial Union Department of the AFL-CIO has estimated that 600,000 new jobs could be created by 1990 in the conservation and solar industries.[16]

JOB BLACKMAIL: A POWERFUL WEAPON

In each of these cases the focus on jobs was intentional. Employers made calculated tactical decisions, unrelated to whether the new regulation or the canceled construction would in fact eliminate jobs. The companies and industries involved—and in several instances the federal government—wanted public support for their decisions and actions. They did not want workers, local citizens, or the public suggesting alternatives. What better way to win the active backing (or at least to silence the criticism) of workers and other citizens than to threaten them with unemployment? Since all but a very few Americans must work for a living, threatening people's jobs is the same as threatening their livelihood. It is very effective.

The presidents of ARCO and of Armco Steel knew they were not telling the truth when they blamed job losses on environmental protection requirements. It is likely that corporate managers and government officials involved in the other examples were not sure of the job impact. But they all chose to exploit workers' fears of unemployment. In each instance jobs were the selling point used by business and government. Perhaps the threat of disastrous unemployment would be true and perhaps it would not: that was secondary to employers. Most important was winning workers to their side and slowing the momentum for increased environmental or public health protection by pitting jobs versus the environment and workers against environmental activists.

This strategy is nothing less than blackmail—*job blackmail*. As William W. Winpisinger, president of the million-member International Association of Machinists, told Hawaiian labor and environmental activists in 1978, " 'Either support industry or lose your jobs' is the ultimatum that is often thrown down."[17]

In the cited examples, the ultimatum was thrown down over environmental or occupational safety and health protections. But the use of job blackmail is not limited to these conflicts. In the name of "jobs," employers can —and do—propose almost anything: from wage cuts to reductions in social spending to destruction of entire neighborhoods.

For as long as workers have tried to organize unions, employers have used job blackmail to frustrate their efforts. In 1964, for example, workers at the Monroe Auto Equipment Company in Hartwell, Georgia, tried to organize a United Auto Workers (UAW) local. The company resisted. Inside the factory, Monroe hung huge pictures of its former plant in Hillsdale, Michigan, which management *had* closed in order to move south in search of cheaper labor. Plastered across each picture of the closed factory was a big "X" and the words, "It can happen here."[18] Articles in local newspapers repeated the warning. Workers voted against the union, 466–147.

A few years ago J.W. Marriott, Jr., president and chief executive officer of the Marriott Corporation, opposed ending tax deductions for three-martini lunches and other business expenses. Arguing his case to the public, he focused on how the tax change might hurt his employees: "Our country's hotels and restaurants draw a substantial portion of their patronage from expense account customers. Do you know what this so-called 'reform' would do to our employment?"[19] General Motors and the City of Detroit joined in 1981—in the name of 6,000 prospective jobs at a proposed Cadillac plant—to displace 3,500 residents and to destroy 1,021 homes and apartment buildings, 155 businesses, 12 churches, several schools, and a hospital in the integrated neighborhood of Poletown. In July 1981 the Mobil Corporation charged in a full-page advertisement in the *New York Times* that new state taxes intended to help New York City's ailing subway system would force business and jobs from the city.

On one issue after another employers use jobs as the public justification for their position. Steve Max, a community organizer who has participated in and observed many campaigns to organize and win rights in both the workplace and in the community, has written:[20]

> Over and over we hear: "Lifeline will cost jobs, tax reform will cost jobs, occupational safety will cost jobs. Don't oppose redlining because it gives the banks more money to invest in new housing which creates more jobs. Affirmative action will cost jobs, welfare spending will raise taxes and cost jobs. Nuclear reactors are good for us—more jobs."

By focusing on jobs employers accomplish two goals: they make the pursuit of their own private interest synonymous with the public's interest in more and better employment opportunities; and they scare workers into thinking they have no alternative but to support their employers' proposals. The lure of jobs and the threat of unemployment are powerful persuaders.

The promise of jobs—and therefore of income and sustenance—has prompted people to make great personal sacrifices and to violate ethical principles. In 1941, in an action which has been repeated in different cities, different industries, and different eras, the Ford Motor Company hired unemployed black workers to replace striking white UAW members at the mammoth River Rouge plant in Detroit. One of the strike breakers was so upset by what he was doing he called his pastor to apologize: "I know I am doing the wrong thing," he said, "but I haven't had a job for a long time. I am getting $15 a day and something to eat."[21]

The fear of unemployment is equally powerful. Fear forces people to stay in jobs they know are hurting them, their families, and their communities. Linnie Mae Bass had to retire in 1975 from her job in a Burlington Industries denim factory in Erwin, North Carolina. She had worked 20 years in the mill, knowing her breathing was getting progressively worse. She chose to ignore the signs of brown lung disease until it was too late and she could no longer breathe while working. "Mill workers are scared," she explained. "They are scared of losing their jobs. They are even scared to admit that they are sick."[22]

Because people are afraid they will not be able to get another job, they take jobs they know they do not want. Then they struggle to keep their jobs—often at great personal cost—because they feel they have no choice. It is this harsh reality which has led Machinists' president Winpisinger to conclude, "In a free society, job blackmail represents economic bondage."[23]

But are the threats of job loss always a bluff? Is there evidence that environmental and occupational health regulations do cost jobs and that the "jobs versus the environment" tradeoff is inescapable? These questions are addressed in chapter 2.

2

Setting the Record Straight: Environmental Protection
_____and Jobs

In 1971 the Department of Commerce warned that environmental regulations would cause such severe economic dislocation and unemployment that major new relief programs would have to be created.[1] Speaking before the National Petroleum Council, Commerce Secretary Maurice Stans asked:[2]

> Are the environmental dangers so imminent, so critical, that we have to throw thousands of productive people out of work? Are the dangers so great, so immediate, that whole communities must be run through the economic wringer?

A decade after that speech the evidence is clear: health and environmental protections have been good for employment and for society. Few jobs have been lost. Several hundred thousand jobs have been created as a result of the legislated shift toward wiser use of resources,

17

a cleaner environment, and safer workplaces. Many jobs which were threatened by continued environmental degradation and resource misuse have been preserved.

WHAT ARE THE FACTS ON JOB LOSS?

Despite all its complaints of layoffs and job loss due to environmental and occupational health and safety regulation, the business community has generated no data to substantiate its claims.[3] One national trade association economist expressed his frustration with industry's indifference to factual evidence:[4]

> As an economist, I find it irritating that [industry] will spend a million dollars on public relations, putting some editorial in the newspaper, and not one penny on collecting any hard data. They call me up all the time and want some hard numbers, but they won't pay for gathering the statistics.

The *McGraw-Hill Survey on Pollution Control Expenditures* is the only regular survey conducted by industry of environmental spending and its economic impact. The Tenth Annual *Survey* reported that corporate executives in the nation's major industries attributed less than 1 percent of plant capacity shut down during the years 1976–78 to environmental and safety regulation.[5] In more recent surveys McGraw-Hill has stopped asking executives about environmentally-related shut downs and job loss: there was not enough response to warrant continuing the question. Major firms and business associations, such as the U.S. Chamber of Commerce, the National Association of Manufacturers, and the Business Roundtable, rely on the Environmental Protection Agency for figures on plant closings and job loss due to environmental standards.

For over 10 years EPA has tabulated plant closings and curtailments which could be attributed to environmental regulations. Between January 1971 and June 1981, the

EPA Economic Dislocation Early Warning System (EDEWS) identified 153 such closings or curtailments in firms of 25 or more workers. During the 10-year period 32,611 workers in those 153 companies were alleged to have lost their jobs: an average of about 3,200 workers a year in a workforce of roughly 100 million people (or .003 percent). Close to three-fourths of the reported layoffs were in four industries: chemicals, paper, primary metals, and food processing.[6] The only other government survey of environmental-related plant closings—the Commerce Department's Bureau of Economic Analysis (BEA) Plant Closing Survey—confirms the EPA findings. Conducted for the years 1972–78 the BEA study included firms with fewer than 25 employees and still found no greater environment-related layoffs than did EPA.[7]

The EPA figures exaggerate the number of jobs lost as a result of environmental regulations. Its surveys include many plant closings for which environmental regulation was one of the least compelling of many reasons to suspend operations. Employers rarely close a facility solely because of pollution control requirements. In most cases obsolescence, declining sales, problems with raw materials, more efficient competitors, and increased energy costs are much more important.

A 1976 study prepared by the Oil, Chemical, and Atomic Workers International Union found that, at worst, environmental protection requirements merely hastened plant closings which were already imminent. The union examined the condition of 21 plants which closed between 1970 and 1976, leaving 1,700 members without work, and found that all the facilities were quite old, averaging 39 years. Plants were described as a "bucket of bolts," or "serviceable, but technologically obsolete." The union's report concluded:[8]

> It is our experience that environmental considerations are generally not the overriding factor in the decision to close a plant facility. Too many other economic

factors seem to be involved. At best, environmental regulations assume the character of the "straw that broke the camel's back." Removal of environmental restrictions would, in our opinion, have only delayed the inevitable in the vast majority of cases.

The EPA surveys support the union's conclusions.[9] For example:

Ideal Cement Co., San Juan Batista, California: Closed in 1973; 148 workers. The cement plant was having trouble meeting federal air pollution standards for dust. It was 60 years old, economically obsolete, and had been operating at a loss for several years. At the time of closure it was responsible for only 2.5 percent of the company's cement production.

Concel Inc., Clayville, New York: Closed in 1972; 80 workers. According to the EPA, "Plant was marginal operation and the firm declined to spend $10,000 designated as their share of the municipal sewage treatment plant." Any firm which cannot spend $10,000 is not far from bankruptcy.

Rockwell International, Newton Falls, Ohio: Closed in 1976; 920 workers. The company, which manufactured automobile bumpers, cited the cost of 1977 water pollution control compliance. EPA argued that declining demand for large automobile bumpers was a major factor in the decision.

N.J. Zinc Division, Gulf and Western Industries, Austinville, Virginia: Closed in 1981; 300 workers. In 1979, the company maintained that procedures for reducing emissions of dust, smoke, and cyanide into the air would cost $116,700 in capital expenditures and $61,000 in annual operating and maintenance costs. EPA found the mine was more than 100 years old and that its ore would be depleted by 1983.

Simpson Timber Co., Shelton, Washington: Closed in 1974; 235 workers. The company argued it would need to spend $2.34 million to comply with state air and water pollution regulations. EPA noted the operation was a "marginal plant profitable in only 2 of 27 years" and cited escalating operating costs and the depressed state of the construction industry as additional reasons for closure.

Georgia-Pacific Sawmill, Oliver Springs, Tennessee: Closed in 1977; 100 workers. The sawmill had one year of economic operating life left when the state air pollution regulations required an end to open burning of scrap materials.

Each of these examples, and others like them, are included in the EPA figures. It is questionable whether they should be counted at all. John Sheehan, legislative director for the United Steelworkers of America, agrees that few if any facilities are shut down solely because of environmental regulations. He asserts that an employer's decision to fight pollution control requirements is often a sign the company is already thinking about closing the facility:[10]

> As far as we're concerned in the Steelworkers, we don't know of any single facility that had to shut down because of environmental clean-up. Indeed, it's just the converse. . . . We experienced it at the Johnstown, Pennsylvania, plant; we experienced it at the Lackawanna plant of the Bethlehem Steel Corporation; we experienced it at the United States Steel Corporation in Duluth, Minnesota. When they began to say that they were refusing to abate and comply with the laws, that was an early warning sign that they intended to discontinue production activity at those facilities.

Sheehan's views on environment-related job loss in the steel industry—an industry which is one of the top

spenders on pollution control—are confirmed by economist Robert W. Crandall, Senior Fellow at the Brookings
Institution:[11]

> I doubt you'll find very many cases of jobs lost because
> of environmental policy. I don't think, in the end, that
> the steel industry is particularly worried about envi-
> ronmental regulations and jobs. There is a lot of
> rhetoric, but no real worry about it.

There is a second reason why EPA's figure on
environment-related job loss is an overestimate. The EPA
survey does not account for any rehiring of laid off
workers by the same or other firms. For example, when
the American Smelting and Refining Company (ASA-
RCO) closed its Amarillo, Texas, zinc facility in 1975
rather than comply with state air pollution laws, EPA
counted 300 lost jobs. Forty-five of the workers, however,
were eligible for retirement and began receiving pension
payments. Another 200 were rehired by the company for
work in a new copper smelter it built in Amarillo. It is
difficult to estimate the extent of rehiring among the
32,611 workers reported by EPA to have lost their jobs,
but a 1976 Department of Labor study found that approximately 40 percent of those whose layoffs employers
claimed were due to environmental regulation in 1975–76
were rehired by their original companies.[12]

Neither business nor government has analyzed the
impact on national employment of occupational health
and safety regulation. The Inflation Impact Statements
commissioned by OSHA for its coke oven emissions,
inorganic arsenic, benzene, and noise standards included
estimates of the potential jobs impact of those specific
regulations. But as University of Wisconsin economist
Robert Haveman and two colleagues warned the Congressional Joint Economic Committee, each estimate was
flawed and "any effort to extrapolate from the few studies
which are available to the entire [OSHA] program would

be highly misleading."[13] There is no reason to believe OSHA requirements cause significant layoffs. Environmental regulation does not—and industry spends six times as much on pollution control as on health and safety protections.

In September 1975 the Industrial Union Department of the AFL-CIO released a study of plant closings between 1970–74 that were blamed on either environmental or occupational health and safety regulations. The report concluded that of more than 1,400 plant closings during that period, only 39 companies even alleged that closings were due to environmental and/or health and safety regulation compliance costs. In none of those 39 cases did local union representatives feel health and safety or environmental regulation was the "primary" cause of the shutdown.[14]

Given the frequency and intensity with which corporate leaders claim regulation is throwing people out of work, it is surprising they have such little evidence to back their charges. Only 32,000 people have allegedly been laid off during a decade of major new regulatory activity. Some of these were quickly rehired. Many were laid off at plants which closed for economic reasons unrelated to environmental regulations.

This figure, small as it is, appears even smaller in the context of job losses resulting from other recent corporate and government policies. A study commissioned by the State Department, for example, estimated that between 1966 and 1973 over a million Americans lost their jobs because multinational companies chose to shift investments overseas.[15] Between 1974 and 1977 American Telephone and Telegraph installed new computer technologies and reduced its workforce from a million to 900,000.[16] And, according to the AFL-CIO, the Reagan administration's 1982 budget cuts alone threw over a million people out of work in both private and public sectors.[17]

Environment-related job loss during the past decade looks almost irrelevant in comparison. The outcry is clearly not in proportion to the problem.

WHAT ABOUT JOB CREATION?

The number of jobs lost as a result of environmental and occupational health regulations has been small. At the same time the past decade's environmental initiatives have created many new jobs—far more than have been eliminated.

EPA funding for the construction of sewage treatment plants (under the Construction Grants section of the 1972 Clean Water Act amendments) has created tens of thousands of jobs.* In 1976, a year in which $3.34 billion of EPA money was spent in building wastewater facilities, a payroll count identified 46,000 workers employed on-site by EPA-funded construction projects. EPA estimated that another 46,000 people were employed off-site (in manufacturing, construction, transportation, mining, and services) because of the program. A 1980 computer simulation model developed by EPA wastewater program analysts projected 54,000 on-site jobs on Construction Grants projects.[18]

The vast majority of jobs created by environmental legislation have been in the private sector. Pollution control requirements have forced private firms to buy and install new equipment to meet emissions limits. A dynamic new industry of nearly 600 companies has been created.[19] New research and development firms have been formed to provide legal and technical services. Other

*The job-creation estimates cited in this chapter were all prepared before the Reagan administration's cuts in environmental spending took effect. Reagan's economic and environmental policies will eliminate many thousands of new and existing jobs in both public and private pollution control. Cutbacks in the Construction Grants program will also mean fewer construction, maintenance, and operating jobs in sewage treatment.

companies design, manufacture, and install pollution control hardware: air pollution control equipment, such as electrostatic precipitators, baghouses, wet scrubbers, and ventilation systems; water pollution filtration technologies, such as clarifiers and screening systems; solid waste disposal and processing facilities and equipment; noise reduction equipment; technologies and equipment for handling, processing, and disposing of toxic waste.

Once a pollution control system is in place, skilled personnel are needed to operate and maintain the equipment. To control coke oven emissions adequately, for example, steel mills must invest in new equipment. But effective emissions control also requires hiring more workers. According to Michael Olszanski, chairman of the Environmental Committee of Steelworkers Local 1010 at Inland Steel's plant in East Chicago, Indiana, "The way to clean up is to put more workers on the coke oven battery. The pollution comes from fugitive emissions around doors. The doors must be cleaned. Workers must be allowed more time. Bigger crews are needed."[20] David Kee, Chief of Enforcement for EPA's Region Five told Local 1010 in 1976, "It's going to take a helluva lot of people." He added, "They're not going to be able to do that work with existing crew sizes. . . . Those devices . . . have to maintained."[21]

Approximately 85,000 people were employed in private industry in 1974 as a result of mandated air and water pollution controls, according to the National Research Council: 27,000 in consulting; 24,000 in equipment manufacture; 34,000 in the operating and maintenance of industrial equipment.[22] A 1978 Arthur D. Little study estimated 35,850 jobs in equipment manufacture and projected an increase to 44,000 by 1983—a 23 percent jump between 1974 and 1983.[23] A similar expansion of job opportunities in consulting and in the maintenance and operation of pollution control equipment would increase' employment in the private pollution control industry to approximately 106,730 by 1983. This figure does not include jobs created in construction of private pollution control facilities or jobs controlling public and worker exposure to radiation, toxic chemicals, and other hazardous materials.

At a February 1981 conference on environmental workforce needs, Walter Gilbert of EPA's National Training and Operational Technology Center stated that a "conservative" estimate of total employment in water pollution control was around 220,000 jobs: 80,000 to 100,000 in municipal wastewater treatment facility construction and operation; 15,000 in federal government research, planning, analysis, and operations; 10,000 in state agencies; 95,000 to 115,000 in the private sector. Private sector jobs include: 30,000 engineers and 24,000 technicians working as consultants; 6,000 scientists and 18,000 technicians involved in planning, design, and manufacture; and at least another 11,000 people operating and maintaining private wastewater treatment facilities.[24]

At the same conference Robert Goldberg of the Department of the Interior's Office of Surface Mining estimated that over 120,000 people were employed in air pollution control. In 1974, according to Goldberg, 22,000 air pollution professionals were employed in private industry, 16,400 at state and local government levels, and at least 10,000 in the federal government: "If one were to count maintenance workers, technicians, construction workers, etc., in the private sector also involved, the number would be well over 100,000—a not inconsiderable workforce."[25] (These figures, like those of the National Research Council, do not include employment generated by legislation controlling hazardous materials and toxic substances.)

In 1975 the President's Council on Environmental Quality sponsored a study which estimated total private and public employment in pollution control to be 1.1 million.

The estimate was made by multiplying 70,000 (a rounded-off Bureau of Labor Statistics' estimate of jobs created per billion dollars of pollution control spending) by $15.7 billion (the approximate pollution control spending for 1975).[26] This figure was cited frequently in the mid-1970s, but few people actually trusted it. The authors failed to differentiate between pollution control jobs which would have existed without environmental legislation and jobs specifically generated by the new laws. They also did not address the question of job losses.

The Council on Environmental Quality and EPA have tried to achieve a more accurate estimate of the employment impact of environmental legislation by looking at the "net" (rather than the "total") number of jobs created because of environmental protections. The first study of this kind was published in 1975. *The Macroeconomic Impact of Federal Pollution Control Programs: 1981 Assessment,* was released in July 1981. These studies do not simply examine the number of jobs created by a given level of expenditure for pollution control in the private and public sectors; rather, they analyze the interaction between pollution control spending and other factors, such as inflation, unemployment, interest rates, and growth (as measured by rate of change in the GNP).[27] They examine whether jobs in the new pollution control industry are created at the expense of jobs in other industries and whether environmental protection spending slows economic growth.

The 1981 assessment, conducted by Data Resources, Inc. (DRI), concluded that for the entire period 1970-87, environmental legislation has created and will continue to create a net increase in jobs. As the report states:[28]

> Employment is stimulated throughout the 1970-1987 period. Jobs are created in the pollution control equipment industry and in all industries to operate and maintain pollution equipment and facilities. The

unemployment rate is on average 0.3 percentage
points lower over the period. By 1987, there is a net
increase of 524,000 additional jobs as a result of
pollution controls.

Environmental protection creates jobs. It also *saves*
jobs. Fishing, forestry, tourism, agriculture, and the
growing leisure and outdoor recreation industries are all
important sources of jobs which depend directly upon
clean water, clean air, and wilderness for their continuation and growth. Although neither industry nor government has tried to estimate the number of jobs saved as a
result of the preservation of environmental quality, it is
likely that many jobs would have been eliminated in these
industries had the environmental legislation of the past
decade not been enacted and enforced.

FLIGHT, DELAYS AND CANCELLATIONS

Environmental regulations have not caused extensive
unemployment, yet threats and claims of job loss persist.
Intense battles still rage, with labor and environmentalists
often on opposing sides. The most heated confrontations
generally involve a charge which is difficult to disprove
statistically: some critics of regulation claim that the
biggest problem with environmental protection is not the
loss of *existing* jobs but the elimination of *potential* jobs.
Relying only on anecdotal evidence, these observers point
to industrial relocation outside the United States, cancellations, and long delays as "proof" that regulation has
indeed been a serious obstacle to employment growth.

Industrial Flight: There is some evidence that individual firms in "dirty" industries have been spurred by
pollution control requirements to close domestic facilities

and move to countries with less stringent regulations. The American asbestos firm, Amatex, for example, closed a modern asbestos yarn mill in Pennsylvania in 1972 and began importing asbestos textile from two plants which the company owned just across the border in Mexico. According to a study on industrial flight conducted by Jeffrey Leonard and Christopher Duerksen of the Conservation Foundation, however, heavy industry is not being driven overseas to any significant extent by strict pollution controls.[29]

National and multinational firms are, of course, moving production overseas. They have been doing so for years. In 1969, before enforceable environmental laws were passed, about 3,400 American firms had invested $71 billion abroad, producing more than $200 billion of goods and services annually.[30] However, variations in the regulatory climates of different nations have far less influence on foreign investment decisions than do traditional determinants like the cost of labor and natural resources.

Multinational firms cannot afford to base major international investment decisions on environmental considerations: regulatory requirements change too quickly and unpredictably. As nations experience severe pollution problems first-hand, they often change their minds about being international "pollution havens." In the early 1970s Ireland pursued the "dustbin" strategy of industrial development, purposely trying to attract hazardous industries. In recent years, however, Ireland has tightened environmental regulation and channeled financial incentives to high-technology industries.

Only when an industry is in decline, technologically inefficient, or dependent on already depleted domestic raw material sources will pollution control spending become a factor in a decision to move production overseas. As the Oil, Chemical and Atomic Workers' study of plant closings concluded, environmental regulations are, at

worst, "the straw that broke the camel's back." Jeffrey
Leonard summarized, "I know of no example of a healthy,
technologically-competitive industry being driven out of
the United States by environmental regulation."[31]

Cancellations: Claims of substantial losses of potential jobs due to environment-related cancellations and
delays can be quite persuasive. Since there is no accurate
way to count jobs which have never existed, it is difficult
to refute the charge that more jobs could be created if
regulations were less stringent. Moreover, because cancellations and delays usually involve specific jobs on
specific projects, employers are often able to mobilize the
political support of workers who hope to get those jobs.

Government and business officials encourage the premature counting of nonexisting jobs. They intentionally
publicize the number of jobs which might be created
—long before any groundbreaking ceremony. Once the
"creation" of jobs is announced, business interests can
repeatedly refer to jobs which will be "lost" and workers
who will be "losers" if the project is not built. The public
is told there is only one option: these specific jobs or no
jobs at all.

Cancellation of a proposed project does not necessarily
mean that jobs are lost. The money that would have been
invested in designing and building the SST was invested in
other areas and in the construction of other planes.
Almost any investment of capital creates jobs.

In 1977, Dow Chemical decided not to build a $500
million plastics plant in California's agricultural Sacramento Delta. The company claimed it scrapped the plant
because of bureaucratic delays and complex state environmental permits. Dow's decision not to build in California
meant 1,000 manufacturing jobs and 3,000 construction
jobs were not created there. Building trades workers, who
rely on large-scale projects for long-term employment,
were angry. But this was not a case of net job loss. Six

weeks after Dow abandoned the California location, it began construction of the same plant at its huge chemical complex in Freeport, Texas. The jobs were not "lost": they were "gained" in Texas.*

This deceptive argument about jobs that are never created is often made in relation to the cancellation of nuclear power plants. James R. Sheets, research director for the Laborers International Union, has claimed that nearly 20,000 potential construction jobs have been lost because of such cancellations. This estimate is pure conjecture.† It is also misleading. A utility company which does not build a nuclear plant might build a coal- or gas-fired facility, creating new jobs in construction, operation, and maintenance. Or the company may create jobs by investing in energy efficiency or solar energy systems. Its energy strategy may or may not create the *same* jobs as would nuclear plant construction—and that is a legitimate concern of unions in the building trades which must worry about jobs for *their* members. But conservation and renewable energy investments do create jobs; more jobs, in fact, than does nuclear power.

Delays: One of the major reasons construction unions oppose sections of the Clean Air Act and resist certain environmental regulations is their concern that environmental legislation causes extended delays and leaves their members without income while they wait for construction to resume. As J.C. Turner, president of the

*As it turns out, pollution and health problems were also "gained" in Texas. Chemical workers in Freeport have twice the rate of brain tumors than in the general public.[32] It is not surprising that, while the building trades unions were supportive of the Sacramento plant, the Oil, Chemical and Atomic Workers, which would have represented workers at the plant, were less enthusiastic. Dow repeatedly refused to tell the union to which toxic substances workers and local residents would be exposed. So the union opposed construction, choosing not to accept jobs at any price and under unhealthy conditions set by the employer.

†Sheets provided no data. When asked for the source of his estimate, Sheets replied, "Just quote me." Of course, it is easy to exaggerate estimates of this kind. It should not be assumed that just because a company promises to create a certain number of jobs it will actually do so.

International Union of Operating Engineers, has explained:[33]

> We have had cases where dams were being built and where our members have gone a thousand miles to go on the job. They've put their kids in school in September and then in December there has been an injunction. The injunction means the shutting down of the dam or whatever the job is, and, of course, they have usually used up whatever money they had to get there and get going. Then they find themselves in the middle of the school term with no job and no income.

Obviously, delays penalize affected workers. But environment-related delays are not nearly as frequent or as long as is commonly believed—and many delays result in better planning and reduced environmental damage.* According to the Council on Environmental Quality's (CEQ) 1979 annual report, fewer than 10 percent of federal proposals for which environmental impact statements (EIS) were issued faced challenges in court. And injunctions to stop projects temporarily were issued for only 2 percent of all EIS's prepared—217 projects in nine years.[36] In a study of the effect on proposed power plants and other energy projects of the National Environmental Policy Act (NEPA) (which requires federal agencies to prepare environmental impact statements for major projects using federal money), CEQ concluded that "NEPA litigation and preliminary injunctions have not presented a significant obstacle."[37]

---

*It is important to note that projects are delayed for specific reasons. As the Council on Environmental Quality's 1979 annual report explained, "During the past decades, environmental impact statements have many times served as the focus of public debate and led to improvements in decisions on such diverse issues as major energy pipelines, water resource projects, nuclear power plants, and land management."[34] In the case of the Trans-Alaska Pipeline, according to CEQ, "Virtually all parties involved agreed that the intensive environmental review of this project prompted important design changes and other improvements in routing and construction techniques."[35]

Charges of unreasonable construction delays related to Clean Air Act compliance are also exaggerated. According to David Doniger of the Natural Resources Defense Council, "The average permit goes through in less than a year."[38] Longer delays are often the result of the government's decision to give companies additional time to improve grossly inadequate applications. Many environment-related construction delays could be reduced if companies would take their responsibility seriously from the outset. A company which forthrightly addresses potential environmental problems when a project is still in the design stage—by consulting with unions, local residents, environmental groups, and government agencies—is much less likely to have unanticipated construction delays due to environmental protection requirements.

Environmental groups are frequently blamed for blocking federal development planning through long court battles. In fact, citizen lawsuits and mandatory court enforcement actions represent less than 15 percent of all lawsuits filed against EPA. Of the approximately 750 lawsuits pending against EPA at the end of 1978, roughly two-thirds were industry challenges to existing or proposed regulations.[39] Industry-initiated litigation has caused long delays not only in the formulation of policy and in industry compliance with the law, but also in beginning some projects and in the creation of jobs.

Finally, merely because firms (and sometimes labor unions) blame environmental laws for construction delays, it should not be assumed that environmental protection requirements are the primary cause of a delay. Just as plant closings are often attributed to environmental regulation when there are other causes, there are many reasons why delays can—and do—occur. Construction delays can result from poor planning, insufficient capital, material shortages, strikes, and even purposeful stonewalling by companies looking for ways to avoid potentially-costly compliance with environmental laws. Large-scale industrial and construction projects are inherently complex and difficult to coordinate. Environmental regulations often serve as an easy and politically convenient scapegoat.

AGGREGATE STATISTICS, INDIVIDUAL WORKERS

While regulation has been good for employment and the economy, some workers *have* paid with their jobs for cleaner air and water. Walter Reuther, former president of the United Auto Workers, once said that workers do not want to know what will happen to them in the abstract. From the perspective of a worker whose job has just been eliminated, there is little comfort in knowing that he or she is the exception rather than the rule. When Dow Chemical chose not to build its chemical complex in California, for example, some workers lost jobs they had hoped to get. No explanation of *why* the facility was not built changes that fact. Similarly, it is not very reassuring to workers who have been laid off because of regulation-related plant closings that, while they have lost their jobs, thousands of other people have found new employment opportunities manufacturing pollution control equipment. Gus Tyler, assistant president of the International Ladies Garment Workers' Union, put it well in referring to another kind of job loss:[40]

> When the head of a railroad union writes that "in the 17 year span from 1947 to 1964, railroad employment in the U.S. was just about sliced in half—from 1,500,000 to less than 700,000 workers," he is talking not only of declining membership but of a major calamity to hundreds of thousands who saw in railroading the way to a good life. To the railroader, there is little balm in the knowledge that, in the same years, the number of workers employed in truck and air transport may have picked up by 700,000 or more.

Advocates and supporters of environmental regulation cannot afford to take comfort in the fact that very few jobs have been lost as a result of compliance with environmental laws. Any job loss results in financial and psychological hardship. And because of the general job insecurity of American workers, even slight job loss due to environmental regulation provides anecdotal evidence and credibility for employer use of job blackmail.

3

"Hell, That's Market Performance": Unemployment and Pollution

It is a myth that workers must sacrifice their jobs for a clean environment and safe workplaces. This myth, however, has a life and power independent of the facts. As Leonard Woodcock, former president of the United Auto Workers, explained in 1976:[1]

> Environmental blackmail has been going on for years
> . . . It's frequently a false conflict, but to a worker
> confronted with the loss of wages, health care benefits
> and pension rights, it can seem very real.

Why do employers resort to this kind of threat? What is the political motivation behind their use of job blackmail?

A basic tenet of American economic wisdom is that the pursuit of profits in the marketplace provides the public with the "good life." The result of the corporate pursuit of profit is the "provision of goods and services of the highest possible quality, to the largest number of people, at the lowest price," as Irving Shapiro, former head of both the Du Pont Corporation and the Business Round-table, once explained. Together, the nation's several million individual firms provide "sufficient jobs and reasonable profits"—the greatest good for the greatest number.[2]

There is a problem with this appealing scenario, as many Americans know first-hand: industry's private interest is *not* consistent with the public interest. While the pursuit of ever-increasing profits has inspired people to channel great energy into producing and distributing goods and services, it has failed to spark business planners to satisfy certain basic human needs. *Specifically, business has never provided—and cannot provide—a job to everyone or fair wages to all. Nor can the pursuit of profits by individuals and by corporations guarantee safe workplaces or a clean and healthy environment.*

Employers use job blackmail to compensate for these basic failings. By threatening their employees with a "choice" between their jobs and the environment, or their jobs and their health, employers seek to make the public believe there are no alternatives to "business as usual." Job blackmail, as Machinists' president William Winpisinger has explained, is "a tactic used by corporate America to whip American workers into line."[3]

THE BUSINESS OF BUSINESS

Corporations are not in business to provide jobs, to protect the environment, to insure worker health and safety, or even to produce particular goods and services. As former General Motors' boss Alfred P. Sloan said, "The primary purpose of the corporation was to make money, not just to make motor cars."[4] Making money comes before any concern corporations may have about providing sufficient jobs, safe workplaces, or clean air and water. In fact, making money often conflicts with these goals. The Committee on Economic Development (CED), an influential business organization, has noted, "Corporations are necessarily limited by various constraints on what and how much they can do to improve society." According to CED, "No company of any size can willingly incur costs which would jeopardize its competitive position and threaten its survival."[5]

Economist Lester Thurow of the Massachusetts Institute of Technology has written:[6]

> We need to face the fact that our economy and institutions will never provide jobs for everyone who wants to work. They have never done so, and as currently structured, they never will. . . . Private enterprise is incapable of guaranteeing jobs for everyone who wants to work.

There is good reason for this. Employers want to keep costs down, including labor costs. Whether a firm is large or small, in a competitive or a concentrated industry, management will try to keep wages low and employ as few people as possible. Businesses try to hire workers who have historically been underpaid, such as women, minorities, and undocumented workers, and to locate in low-wage states or countries which have weak unions. They continually try to find ways to save money by substituting machinery for people. The director of Southern Airways explained in 1978, concerning the company's decision to fire 500 people so that it could afford to buy $65 million in planes, "One of the quickest ways to reduce expenses is to reduce people."[7]

From the employer's perspective it is advantageous to have a certain percentage of the population out of work at all times. When there is a "long line of men at the gate," as utilities magnate Samuel Insull recommended at the turn of the century, employers can more easily withstand demands for higher wages and better working conditions. The long line helps discipline workers and weaken unionization efforts. It sets one group of workers against another: employers can point to the large pool of jobless workers who would be glad to work at existing wages and under existing conditions.

Just as the business community cannot provide enough jobs for American workers, it cannot and does not protect the natural environment or the health and safety of workers and their families. Alfred Kahn, chairman of the Council on Wage and Price Stability under President Carter (and a man not known for environmental "extremism"), put it bluntly:[8]

> No one in his or her right mind could argue that the competitive market system takes care of protecting the environment—it does not.

Consider a textile mill whose workers are exposed to cotton dust fibers. Installing vacuum equipment in the mill lowers the amount of airborne cotton dust and reduces the likelihood that workers will contract brown lung disease. But it is a rare firm that would install the equipment and make health and safety improvements voluntarily. The cost of brown lung—shortened worklife, difficult breathing, and early death—are borne primarily by the workers themselves. It is in the company's narrow financial interest to keep its costs down by letting workers pay with their health. These costs (which economists call "externalities") are not entered on the corporate balance sheets. But the costs of installing pollution control equipment are.

When the public demands and the government requires companies to reduce workplace or community pollution levels, firms must begin to pay production costs which they had previously forced workers, consumers, and local residents to absorb. A 1977 report by the federal General Accounting Office explained:[9]

> Compliance with OSHA regulations involves the shift of a cost of production from the workers (the unexpected loss from injury and illness) to the firm (the cost of removing the hazard).

Employers resist internalizing these costs. Paying for pollution control and occupational health protections (like paying higher wages and benefits) threatens short-term profits. There is, however, another reason employers resist taking responsibility for providing secure jobs, safe workplaces, and a clean environment.

THE BATTLE FOR CONTROL

In many instances the cost to business of environmental health and worker protections can be passed to consumers without affecting profits. The extra cost of a seat belt is routinely added to the price of a new car. The added cost of cleaning up a refinery usually finds its way into the price charged for oil and gasoline. One year's wage increase usually becomes part of the next year's price hike.

But environmental, health, and worker protections do more than increase costs. They also alter the balance of power between employers and the public by increasing worker and public involvement in the production and investment decisions of private corporations.

"The last thing a good manager would think of doing would be to make his policies of shop management the subject of a referendum," President John Calder of the Remington Typewriter Company said in 1912.[10] Calder was articulating a basic principle of employer-employee relations. Management vigorously defends its prerogative

—its sole right to determine what is produced and how, what plants are to be built and where, how much capital is invested, what machinery is installed, when workers are hired, transferred, pensioned, or laid off, and when plants are closed or moved.

But strong, independent unions and enforceable environmental and public health laws threaten management prerogatives. In 1892 the Carnegie Steel Corporation used Pinkerton men and the state militia at its Homestead Plant to destroy the Amalgamated Association of Iron and Steel Workers. After the union was defeated, the company offered to rehire only those former employees who had not taken part "in the attempts which have been made *to interfere with our rights to manage our business.*"[11] Before workers finally forced the federal government to recognize and uphold their right to organize in the 1930s, employers treated *any* attempt by workers to join together as a challenge to the basic rights of management. The structure of industry, of unions, and of work itself has changed dramatically since Carnegie's day; but corporate insistence on preserving control over critical workplace decisions has not. In a 1979 discussion about automation, United Auto Workers member Pete Kelley said, "This thing ultimately comes down to the management prerogatives clause. As a vice-president of General Motors once said to UAW President Walter Reuther at one set of negotiations, 'If you want to touch *that* clause, you'd better go get your army.' "[12]

Environmental laws provide increased opportunities for the public to participate in plant siting and other decisions, to suggest alternatives, and to pressure industry to reduce pollution. Economist E.J. Mishan has written:[13]

> [Anti-pollution laws] have the most dramatic effects on private enterprise. . . . What is being proposed . . . [by such laws] may be regarded as an alteration of the legal framework within which private firms oper-

ate, in order to direct their enterprise towards ends
that accord more closely with the interests of modern
society.

Occupational health and safety laws also enable people to
know more about the dangers they face and to take a
more active role in making their workplaces safe. Sheldon
Samuels, director of Health, Safety and Environment for
the Industrial Union Department of the AFL-CIO, has
explained:[14]

> What businesses are really complaining about is the
> basic thrust of the [Occupational Safety and Health]
> act, which gives workers rights that enable them to
> participate in the determination of their own level of
> risk. . . . All this is driving management to the wall
> because it amounts to worker participation in an area
> where management believes it has the sole preroga-
> tive.

Management understands that when it opens itself to
public scrutiny, participation, and accountability, its own
power is diminished. People begin to see there *are* alternatives, there might be better ways to organize the work
process, produce particular goods, and allocate capital,
resources, and labor. Demands for greater democracy in
the workplace, for jobs, for safe and healthy workplaces,
for strong protection of public health and the environment, and for a say in natural resource use are also
demands that corporations accept limits on their power
and their freedom from accountability.

With so much at stake corporate management does all it
can to maintain control and defend its "right to manage."
Employers keep trying to shift production costs onto
workers and the public and to resist those who challenge
their ability to do so. Although business leaders rarely
acknowledge, much less detail, the costs of their private
pursuit of profit, the result has been a legacy of hardship
and tragedy: joblessness, pollution, destruction of irre-

placeable resources, disease, and premature death. These "social costs of private enterprise," as economist K. William Kapp described them in 1950, may not exist on the corporate balance sheets, but they are very real for a great many Americans.

UNEMPLOYMENT, UNDEREMPLOYMENT, AND POVERTY

"Recurrent unemployment" has been the "one basic flaw in the profit system almost from its inception," according to Nobel Prize-winning economist Kenneth Arrow.[15] The American economy has never created enough jobs for everyone who needs work, and it has certainly never provided enough "good jobs"—jobs with adequate wages and benefits, decent working conditions, stability and security, and opportunities for advancement.[16]

Unemployment and underemployment in America are not simply problems affecting an unlucky (or, as some would charge, "lazy") few at the bottom of the economic ladder. Official government unemployment figures indicate that 8.9 percent of American workers were unemployed at the end of 1981—9,462,000 people. For minority workers the percentage was almost double the national figure—16.1 percent. And for minority youth, official unemployment in 1981 was just under 40 percent.[17] Although these numbers are high they do not include people who have become discouraged and have stopped looking for work, people who want to work full time but have to settle for part time jobs, people who work full time but do not earn living wages, people who are in the military or in prison, and people whom census-takers overlook.[18] Nor do these statistics reflect the number of people working at jobs for which they are overtrained and overqualified.

Labor economist David Gordon, using the 1975 official estimate of 8.5 percent unemployment, calculated that the true level of unemployment and underemployment in 1975 was at least 16 million people (17 percent of the labor force) and possibly as high as 35 million.[19] Figures for 1981 would be comparable.

Official unemployment statistics are also deceptive because they count only people unemployed at any one time, not the total number who are out of work for some period during the year. Although there were 7 million officially unemployed Americans in 1980, over 21 million —nearly 1 of every 5 people who work—were without jobs at some time during that year. In 1977 labor economist Eli Ginzburg estimated that 24 million potentially employable Americans were out of work.[20] David Gordon has concluded that between one-third and one-half of all Americans who must work encounter employment problems from time to time which adversely affect their way of life, health, and economic well-being.[21]

Unemployment and underemployment waste our nation's greatest resource—the talents and initiative of its people. Dr. Harvey Brenner of Johns Hopkins University has shown direct links between unemployment and stress, depression, alcoholism, child abuse, marital problems, suicide, homicide, heart attacks, liver disease, infant mortality, and deteriorating physical health.[22] Some people actively endanger the public welfare when they are without work: homicides, robberies, larcenies, and narcotics arrests all increase when unemployment rises.[23] Steven Sheffrin of the University of California at Davis estimates that our failure to maintain even the 1956 unemployment rate of 4.1 percent cost $2.3 trillion (1976 dollars) in lost production in the twenty years between 1956 and 1976.[24]

Each 1 percent of unemployment—approximately a million jobless workers—costs society $25 to $30 billion in lost tax revenues and added government expenses for unemployment compensation, welfare, food stamps, and other services.[25] The National Advisory Council on Economic Opportunity concluded in its 1980 Report to the President:[26]

> Unemployment is still a personal catastrophe, for individuals and families, and a source of expensive social disruptions for the country as a whole.

Persistent underemployment and unemployment are the cause of widespread poverty. This has been the conclusion of countless analyses and studies, including the Kerner Commission investigation of the 1968 urban riots.

Observers such as President Reagan's first domestic policy advisor Martin Anderson maintain that poverty in America has virtually disappeared, since the number of Americans living below the official poverty level dropped from 22.1 percent in 1960 to 11.8 percent in 1977. But in fact, the poverty population has been increasing in recent years. In 1980, *before* the Reagan administration began eliminating jobs and social programs, the number of Americans categorized as "poor" by the federal government had reached 13 percent.[27] Moreover, like its unemployment figures, the government's official poverty statistics are unrealistically low. The food budget used to determine poverty is based upon diets designed only for "temporary and emergency" use, not for year-round nutrition.[28] The reality is that a large number of Americans live a spare, hard existence. Members of families earning less than the Bureau of Labor Statistics' lower four-person family budget—millions of whom work full time but for inadequate wages—have difficulty maintaining a nutritionally balanced diet. Yet, close to 1 of every 3 Americans lives in a household which falls short of this income line.[29]

Approximately 20 percent of the people in this country

own little more than their clothes, furniture, and miscellaneous items. Another 20 percent own a used car and some more furniture. Amidst great wealth, 40 percent of the people (about 67 percent of ethnic minorities) are essentially without property. In addition, even though the GNP has quadrupled since World War II, the gap between the 40 percent at the bottom and the 2 percent of Americans at the top who own most of the property and share most of the wealth has hardly changed.[30]

Unemployment, underemployment, and poverty are not marginal problems. Fifty years ago, the Catholic bishops of the United States issued this statement:[31]

> Unemployment is the great peacetime physical tragedy of the nineteenth and twentieth centuries, and both in its cause and in the imprint it leaves on those who inflict it, those who permit it, and those who are its victims, it is one of the great moral tragedies of our time.

The tragedy persists. Between 1960 and 1980 official unemployment averaged 5.6 percent. In this decade it promises to rise even higher. The increase in overseas production by American multinational firms, the reversal of the postwar trend toward expanded government employment, and the new era of automation spurred by breakthroughs in computer technologies are combining to bring America into what could be an extended period of "jobless growth"—economic expansion accompanied by fewer jobs. The private sector continues to be inadequate to the task of putting people to work and eliminating poverty.

WORKPLACE AND ENVIRONMENTAL DAMAGE

Like unemployment and underemployment, environmental damage, occupational disease, and accidents are far more widespread and destructive than business concedes and than most Americans would like to believe. Between 6 and 8 million Americans are injured on the job each year, including 2.5 million disabled and 14,000 killed. Approximately 100,000 people die each year from job-related diseases, according to the National Institute for Occupational Safety and Health (NIOSH).[32]

Occupational health and safety problems are a fact of working life for most Americans. At least 1 of every 5 Americans has had contact at work with hazardous substances regulated by OSHA. A 1968 study by the Chicago Institute of Medicine found that workers in 73 percent of Chicago's workplaces were exposed to one or more potentially hazardous materials.[33] Thirty-eight million Americans work with substances which can cause respiratory diseases such as silicosis, black lung, brown lung and asbestosis.[34] Between 10 and 15 million workers suffer from excessive noise on the job—which can cause deafness, stress, and high blood pressure.[35]

As many as 390,000 people contract new cases of occupation-caused diseases each year, according to U.S. Public Health Service estimates. A 3-year study by the Toxic Substances Strategy Committee appointed by President Carter concluded that the projected cancers among workers exposed to just six substances—asbestos, arsenic, benzene, chromium, nickel, and petroleum distillates —constitute 20 percent of the estimated 600,000 cases of cancer reported each year.[36] Over 1.5 million American workers inhale arsenic at work: they are dying of lung and lymphatic cancer at 2 to 8 times the average national rate.[37] Of the 4 million living workers heavily exposed to asbestos since World War II, at least 1.6 million (35–44 percent) will die of asbestos-related cancers.[38] The Toxic Substances Strategy Committee study concluded that between 22 and 38 percent of all cancers may be job-related.[39]

Sooner or later workplace health hazards become community health problems. According to Pam Woywod of the Amalgamated Clothing and Textile Workers Union,[40]

> There are very few cases where industry is producing carcinogens, toxins, whatever, that are spilled out into the air or the water, that don't first endanger the people who are working in the plant.

Spouses and children of asbestos workers have died of cancer because they were exposed to asbestos carried home on work clothes. So have people living near asbestos plants and even laundry workers who have cleaned asbestos-covered work clothes.

A disproportionate share of industrial pollution falls on the poor—particularly the urban poor. The Environmental Protection Agency found that urban areas have dirtier air and drinking water, more wastewater and solid waste problems, and greater exposure to lead and other toxic heavy metals, than nonurban areas:[41]

> Suburbanites are exposed to less than half of the environmental health hazards inner city residents face. . . . The inner city poor—white, yellow, brown, and black—suffer to an alarming degree from what are euphemistically known as "diseases of adaptation." These are not healthy adaptations, but diseases and chronic conditions from living with bad air, polluted water, and continued stress.

Economist A. Myrick Freeman estimated that in the early 1960s the air in suburban Scarsdale, New York, had only one-fifth the carbon monoxide, one-half the sulfates, and one-tenth the benzoapyrene (a known carcinogen) as that of Herald Square in Manhattan.[42]

Environment-related diseases are certainly not restricted to the urban poor. The 1.2 billion pounds of pesticides sprayed on American farms and forests each year jeopardize the health of some 5 million farmworkers, causing as many as 21,400 cases of pesticide poisoning annually.[43]

Airborne pesticides and herbicides also affect people living nearby, since they often drift off-target and settle on land and in water supplies. Some of these chemicals cause cancer and genetic damage. Dieldrin and aldrin, ranked sixth in sales among insecticides until their use was banned in 1976, caused afflictions ranging from insomnia and nightmares to convulsions and brain damage.[44]

Toxic wastes endanger the lives of millions, many of whom do not even know they are being exposed to carcinogens, mutagens, and other hazardous substances. Victims can live anywhere: in cities, suburbs, or rural areas. Love Canal—Hooker Chemical Company's abandoned dump site in upstate New York where cancer-causing chemicals have percolated into basements, playgrounds, and backyards—is only the tip of the iceberg. The EPA has estimated that between 32,000 and 50,000 disposal sites containing hazardous wastes exist in the United States. Between 1,200 to 2,000 of these may pose significant risks to human health or the environment.[45] And 29 or more are considered by the EPA to be at least as dangerous as Love Canal.[46]

Radioactive uranium mill tailings piled high near mill sites blow with the wind, leach into the soil and water supplies, and threaten workers and local residents with cancer and genetic problems.[47] Mill tailings constitute only a small part of the 3 billion cubic feet of radioactive wastes stored across the country. Little of the radioactive material from commercial nuclear reactors, the manufacture of nuclear warheads, and shut down nuclear facilities is safely contained.

The natural environment is fragile. When resources are abused, the harm is often irreparable. In farm states prime agricultural land is disappearing, and irreplaceable topsoil is eroding. Agricultural land in the United States is being gobbled at a rate of nearly 1 million acres each year.[48] Inadequate conservation and wasteful farming techniques have accelerated topsoil erosion: 14.1 tons of topsoil per acre of cropland is lost each year in Tennessee, 11.4 tons in Missouri, and 10.9 tons in Mississippi.[49]

Strip mining of coal, copper, and other minerals has polluted rivers and streams in Appalachia and the West, ruining them for fishing, drinking, swimming, and agricultural and industrial use. As hills and valleys have been reshaped, natural drainage patterns have been altered, causing frequent flooding and mudslides. People in some Appalachian towns have been forced out of their homes permanently because of repeated flooding.

Pollution of coastal fishing areas has caused serious deterioration of seafood stocks. The Chesapeake Bay, the country's largest estuary and one of the world's richest, now produces far smaller harvests of oysters, shad, and striped bass than in previous decades.[50] And as resort and vacation communities encroach on coastal wetlands, key fish-spawning grounds and animal habitats are threatened.

Acid rain, a by-product of industrial and automobile air pollution, is damaging lakes and ground water supplies hundreds and even thousands of miles from the pollution source. A survey of high-altitude lakes in New York's Adirondack Mountains found that one-half had no fish because of acid rain.[51] In Canada, where the prevailing winds blow from the industrialized northeast and midwest United States, acid rain could destroy fish in an estimated 50,000 lakes by the year 2000.[52] The economic impact is significant, not only for fishing but also for the tourist trade in the Adirondacks and other wilderness areas. Moreover, according to the National Academy of Sciences, there is "clear evidence of serious hazard to human health and to the biosphere" from acid rain.[53]

Significant progress has been made in curbing some pollutants in the past decade. But many problems persist and new environmental hazards are continually being created and discovered. The health impact of indoor air pollution and of the steady use of new office computer technologies are two problems about which data have been collected only recently. Two thousand new chemicals are introduced each year. Environmental and occupational health problems remain serious, costly, and pervasive. And, like unemployment and poverty, their intractability is a direct result of the priorities which guide management decisions. As economist Daniel R. Fusfeld has written:[54]

> Problems of pollution, corruption, discrimination and inequality are produced by business decisions made in the marketplace. Market failure—hell, that's market performance.

Employers are aware of the public toll caused by their market performance. They know they are responsible for pollution and employment problems. So they look for ways to keep people from challenging their priorities and control. They turn to job blackmail—the threat of layoffs and economic hardship. But, as was shown in chapter 2, regulations which improve environmental and workplace quality eliminate few jobs and create many more. This being the case the question must be asked: if the costs of inadequately-controlled production have been great and the number of regulation-related layoffs small, why is job blackmail so effective?

4
"What Else Can We Do?": Why Job Blackmail Persists

When David Packard, chairman of the Hewlett-Packard Company, and Robert Wilson, president of Memorex Corporation, testified before the California State Energy Commission in 1979, they presented commission members with a simple choice: speed up licensing of the Diablo Canyon nuclear power plant or kiss thousands of new electronics jobs goodbye. Packard was the first to speak:[1]

> If the Diablo Canyon [nuclear facility] is not brought on stream this year, our company will clearly have to re-evaluate its decision to build a major facility in Roseville. . . . Our company's current plans call for the creation of 15,000 to 20,000 additional jobs in the decade of the '80s. These jobs will be lost to the state if energy problems force us to divert this growth outside California.

Wilson provided the global perspective:[2]

> If the United States continues in its infinite wisdom to strangle itself on energy problems, we'll have to go elsewhere. We need to look not only between states, but between countries.

The two industrialists were offering a lesson in corporate power. They reminded the state and the public that while employers can create jobs, as both companies had already done in California, they can also eliminate jobs. If the state wanted to put people to work, it had better listen carefully to its business leaders.

The power to hire and fire, to expand operations or close them, to move jobs around the country or around the world is the basic source of corporate domination over the lives and fortunes of most Americans. Employers control the jobs. Political leaders, workers, and the public do not. For this reason both the public and its elected officials are vulnerable. Steve Max has explained:[3]

> As long as corporations are free to move to any part of the country or the world where they can pay the lowest taxes and wages, they can successfully use the jobs argument to set the terms of our good behavior.

Whether they actually move or not, and whether they move for reasons related to environmental and public health requirements or not, they *can* move. The threat is credible.

This leverage is reinforced by other advantages which employers have over workers and the public: tremendous economic power; control over corporate information; the ability (with the help of their supporters in government, academia, and the media) to define public debate on national priorities.

ECONOMIC POWER

David Packard made sure to tell the Energy Commission that Hewlett-Packard was planning to create 20,000 new jobs and that he represented a county manufacturers' organization whose members already employed 127,000 people. The larger the company the more effective the job blackmail. And, over the years, this nation's employers have grown phenomenally. In the 1890s none of the largest companies employed more than 15,000 people. In 1980 American Telephone and Telegraph had over 1 million employees; General Motors more than 800,000.[4] Although there are over 14.5 million business enterprises in the United States, sales of the 500 largest industrial corporations account for well over 50 percent of the nation's total GNP. The trend has clearly been toward increased concentration: in 1955 the contribution of the top 500 industrials to GNP was 40 percent.[5] The top 100 manufacturing firms have increased their share of total manufacturing assets from about 33 percent in 1925 to roughly 50 percent today.[6] These companies are huge, and they are getting bigger. Their size gives them great power not only over their own industries but also over the economic activity of the nation—over prices, products, and jobs. In 1956 sociologist C. Wright Mills observed:[7]

> The economy—once a great scatter of small productive units in autonomous balance—has become dominated by two or three hundred giant interrelated corporations, which together hold the keys to economic decisions.

Economic power translates into political power and influence. Government officials know which corporations contribute to whose political campaigns and to which local charitable organizations. They understand who pays taxes, who generates business for other local employers —and who provides jobs. Elected officials and political appointees know corporations have access to investment capital. Corporations can transform ideas into reality. They can turn proposals into products, jobs, and local revenue. And government officials know there is more practical political advantage in doing favors for people with clout than for the weak, unorganized, and disenfranchised. The result, in the words of social scientist Ralph Miliband, is that:[8]

> No interest other than business, anywhere, has the same ease of access to the most important organs of executive power, and none enjoys the same familiarity with its agents. Nor is any other interest group able to wage, when required, the kind of pressure campaign which business interests can undertake.

CONTROL OF INFORMATION

Corporate America understands the art of persuasion. Large corporations devote significant resources to public relations. They use sophisticated, high-visibility newspaper and television advertising campaigns to sell not just their products but also their political opinions. At the same time, however, corporate managers zealously restrict worker and public access to information which is needed to make independent, reliable assessments of employer claims and threats. Asked to prove they cannot afford a particular action, corporate leaders generally resist. When the Ford Motor Company demanded in late 1981 that workers at its Dearborn Stamping Plant change their work rules to become more competitive with other Ford stamping plants, the United Auto Workers local asked Ford to open the company books and prove Dearborn Stamping was inefficient. The company flatly refused.[9]

Similarly, when Union Carbide threatened 600 layoffs at its Marietta, Ohio, metals plant, in response to a 1971 order for the company to comply with the Clean Air Act, the firm did not have to open its books and prove it could not afford required pollution controls. Few firms do. EPA occasionally investigates the claims of corporations which threaten to close a facility because of environmental-protection costs (17 were conducted between 1977–80). But the corporate financial information provided to EPA is kept confidential.[10] It is not made available to the public or affected workers. The Clean Air Act, Clean Water Act, and other major environmental laws of the past decade include provisions, lobbied for by the Steelworkers and other unions, which give workers laid off because of an environment-related plant closing the right to request an EPA investigation and public hearing. EPA has some subpoena power, but firms need not divulge proprietary information. Financial or technical data which might affect a company's competitive position are considered confidential.[11] More importantly EPA is empowered to conduct these investigations (of which there have been only two) only after the closing has already been announced.

Employers also try to keep workers ignorant of on-the-job dangers and hazards. The predicament of Marvin Gaddy, an employee for more than 20 years at Olin Corporation's film division near Brevard, North Carolina, is typical. Gaddy's job was to add carbon disulfide (CS_2) to huge rotating vats so raw wood pulp could be broken quickly into a liquid mixture. He knew—even though the company never told him—the process was harming his fellow workers: "People would act real unusual, get headaches and think they were getting the flu. After a few overdoses, the nightmares would start coming on them."[12] When Gaddy and his co-workers complained to the company, management's response was "We don't need you. If you don't enjoy your job, then go home."[13] Management did not tell Gaddy or any of the other workers that exposure to high levels of CS_2 could cause nerve damage—even though the health hazards were known in France as early as 1851 and in the United States for at least a generation.[14] Olin is not an exception. As a worker at a California tannery explained, "They tell you to add this and to add that—they don't tell you what can happen or whether it's dangerous."[15]

By keeping a tight lid on corporate information which might help workers and other citizens distinguish between what is possible, what is necessary, and what is blackmail, employers are able to manipulate both the government and the public. In 1976 Leonard Woodcock, who was then president of the United Auto Workers, explained how industry uses its control of information to resist both worker and community environmental standards:[16]

> First, an industry will claim that it can't comply with a proposed standard, because the technology to do so does not exist. Next, the industry will claim that the cost will drive it out of business. Finally, companies announce that they can, but that it will cost everybody plenty.

Corporations can keep changing their tune in this way because they restrict access to the information which could prove them right or wrong.

Employers try to deny for as long as possible that environmental or health problems exist. Coal owners called black lung disease "miners' asthma" for years. And black lung was not officially recognized under worker's compensation as an occupation-caused disease until 1969. As recently as 1978 byssinosis—brown lung disease —which has killed or crippled over 84,000 textile workers, was labeled a "myth" and a "misnomer invented purely for its emotional impact" by Joseph L. Lanier, chairman of the Safety and Health Committee of the American Textile Manufacturers Institute.[17]

Employers and their supporters also try to downplay independent or government-sponsored studies which link serious health or environmental threats to production processes. At General Motors' Fisher Body plant in Warren, Michigan, workers have been developing intestinal and rectal cancers at almost three times the national and Detroit area rates. But, according to the *New York Times*:[18]

> The scientists involved—working for GM, the University of Michigan, the Memorial Sloan-Kettering Cancer Center, which gets funds from GM, and Cornell Medical College—have cautioned that the sample is too small and the period of study too brief to prove that the higher incidence of cancer can be attributed to chemicals in the work place. [According to one report,] "Although this result may be statistically significant, it cannot be accepted in isolation but must be further analyzed. . . ."

If the momentum for change does not slow, employers can always resort to their ace-in-the-hole: they can threaten to lay off workers and close plants. At the Fisher Body plant, workers on the shop floor, far from public relations' specialists and the public eye, receive a standard reply when they complain about working with hazardous substances. "The answer's always the same," according to one worker. "We say, 'Get rid of the [suspected material],' and they say, 'What are you trying to do, run the job out of here?' "[19]

The lack of accurate information and the difficulty of getting employers to acknowledge the validity of alternatives insure that any debate between employers and environmentally-concerned citizens will be based largely on emotion and fear. "Forget the facts once in a while," recommended the manager for special projects for the Public Service Company of New Hampshire (builders of the Seabrook nuclear power plant). "Counter the activists not with facts but with closed factory gates, empty schools, cold and dark houses and sad children."[20]

Corporations manipulate the public's sense of possible alternatives. This is key. As social scientist E. E. Schattsschneider wrote, "The definition of alternatives is the supreme instrument of power."[21]

SETTING THE TERMS OF THE DEBATE

In January 1974 Billy Williamson, a Texas state representative, told reporters:[22]

> I don't need some bunch of do-gooder nuts telling me what's good to breathe. . . . I think we are all willing to have a little bit of crud in our lungs and a full stomach rather than a whole lot of clean air and nothing to eat.

Williamson was trying to justify his opposition to legislation which would allow citizens to sue state agencies and public officials who failed to administer state environmental laws properly. Williamson had good reason to oppose such a law. Tyler, a town which he represented, had been the site of a Pittsburgh Corning Corporation asbestos plant. For years workers at the plant and local residents had been exposed to high concentrations of cancer-causing asbestos fibers. The result was above-average rates of asbestosis and lung cancer among the 895 people who had worked there. In 1972 the company closed and dismantled the plant rather than install new equipment to protect workers. While the plant was still in operation, Williamson never spoke against the company. After it was closed he did not want to be held personally liable for failing to represent the interests of his constituents. So he shifted the debate from the question of whether elected officials should be held accountable.

First he ridiculed those people in his town and in the state who expressed concern about such "do-gooder" things as clean air and public health. Then he trivialized the health problem by dismissing asbestos, a known carcinogen, as "a little crud." Finally he resorted to the classic "jobs versus the environment" argument, conveniently ignoring that for the people of Tyler, Pittsburgh Corning's decisions meant both more disease *and* fewer jobs.

Williamson was manipulating definitions, a common practice among business and government leaders trying to resist demands for accountability and public participation. How problems are defined greatly influences what people think can be done about them. If people can be made to believe their problems are not too serious, or that there are no alternatives, they will be less likely to demand any changes. This requires that a number of problems and contradictions (including the employment, health, and environmental problems discussed in the previous chapter) be ignored, trivialized, or defined away.

Alan Greenspan, chairman of Gerald Ford's Council of Economic Advisors, expressed concern in 1976 that the official unemployment rate was getting too high. He did not, however, propose creating millions of new jobs. Instead, Greenspan argued that the definition of unemployment be changed. Official statistics would be more palatable to the public, he contended, if "we exclude a great deal of the very difficult pockets of unemployment which are essentially structural."[23]

The Bureau of Labor Statistics announced in October 1981 that the Consumer Price Index (CPI), the most widely used measure of inflation, would be changed by replacing the home ownership component with a rental equivalence measure. This will result in a lower official rate of inflation during periods of high interest rates. Inflation will appear less severe, but will not have changed. As Machinists vice-president George Poulin has told his members, "Tinkering with the way inflation is measured does not change the impact of rising costs on American workers."[24]

Queens College economist William K. Tabb calls this "methodological predestination": if you don't want something to count, then don't count it. Another good example is the Carter administration's National Energy Plan, in which unemployment was defined away entirely:[25]

An individual is unemployed when he or she is looking for work, but cannot find a suitable job at that moment. In the long run, an individual will adjust to this situation by either working, e.g., by acquiring suitable job skills, or taking a lesser job; or by not working, e.g., retiring, living on welfare, etc. In either instance, the worker is no longer unemployed. Unemployment, in short, is a disequilibrium phenomenon where workers are between one of two possible equilibria, namely, working or non-working.

Minimizing environmental and occupational health hazards, as Billy Williamson attempted, is also quite common. The president of the National Academy of Sciences, Dr. Philip Handler, tried to downplay the health hazards involved in pesticide use in a 1971 interview with the U.S. Chamber of Commerce's magazine, *Nation's Business*. Handler referred patronizingly to "his nature-loving friends" and their concern for the "handful of bird species that seem to be endangered"; but he did not mention the genetic damage, cancer, and other diseases which can and do strike people exposed to certain pesticides.[26] The Pacific Gas and Electric Company, analyzing its successful campaign to defeat the 1976 Nuclear Safeguards Initiative in California, acknowledged that its strategy consisted of avoiding the whole question of nuclear dangers. As one official explained, "We did not allow ourselves to be sidetracked into a debate over nuclear safety (which is an argument we would not have won)."[27] Instead the utility and other major corporations convinced labor unions and the media to focus on one simple theme: no nukes means no jobs.

President Reagan's Environmental Protection Agency has been systematically redefining environmental problems, banning words which the administration feels might arouse the public. Near the top of the list is "cancer-causing." According to EPA public relations chief Byron Nelson, "We edit our press releases so they don't sound alarmist. . . . We want to avoid the kind of scare tactics engaged in by maverick scientists, environmentalists and public interest groups."[28]

As has already been noted poverty and unemployment are officially defined in ways which exclude millions of people who are poor and unemployed. The GNP, a principal yardstick of national welfare, does not differentiate between economic activity which contributes to national welfare and that which causes harm. GNP is calculated by totaling the prices of all goods and services bought and sold in a year. It does not matter if the expenditures are needed to remedy social ills which should have been avoided in the first place, such as the hundreds of millions of dollars needed to clean up after the nuclear accident at Three Mile Island. If pollution, accidents, occupational disease, and the mismanagement of resources result in more goods and services, they are counted as additions to the GNP—even though they are clearly personal and social losses. Russell Peterson, former chairman of President Nixon's Council on Environmental Quality and current president of the National Audubon Society, is one of many who has criticized GNP:[29]

> If we produce a million dollars worth of carcinogens, this weighs as much on the GNP scale as a million dollars worth of antibiotics. If we hire a housekeeper, this counts on the GNP, but when one's spouse manages the house, it doesn't count. Teaching counts, but learning doesn't. GNP gives no measure of the hungry, the unemployed, the sick, the ill-housed, the illiterate, the oppressed, the frightened, the unhappily employed, or those who have reached the highest level of fulfillment. Furthermore, it does not measure the waste of resources, the spending of our natural capital such as oil, or the befoulment of our life support systems.

Gross National Product is clearly an inadequate measure.* But GNP serves an important purpose: it elevates the private goals of business—production, sales, and profits—into national goals. And it defines the resultant pollution, workplace accidents, and unemployment as irrelevant.

Using GNP, with all its built-in biases, as a key indicator of national well-being and guide to national investment priorities, business propagandists can appear quite reasonable in their opposition to environmental protection. Consider the *Wall Street Journal*'s explanation of why pollution control spending is a drain on the economy:[31]

> . . . expenditures on pollution control equipment also represent lost opportunities to invest in *productive* ventures which could *materially* improve our standards of living with inputs of new jobs and services. (emphasis added)

The *Journal*'s editors imply that improvements in health and environmental quality due to reduced pollution levels are nonproductive and nonmaterial changes—because they are not quantifiable as part of GNP. By this definition, pollution control spending produces nothing of value. And it prevents other investment which, while it may increase pollution, is the only way to *material* well-being and, of course, more jobs.

Definitional sleight-of-hand enables business and government leaders to sidestep fundamental discussions of what is produced and how it should be produced. Critics of environmental regulation can get away with a remarkable logic. First they declare "quality of life" goals to be of no economic significance. Then they attack people who

---

*Some economists have tried to develop alternative measures of national welfare which do discriminate between positive and negative expenditures. Paul Samuelson has suggested a Net Economic Welfare measure. James Tobin and William Nordhaus have developed a Measure of Economic Welfare (MEW) which adds non-market items and values such as housework and leisure and which subtracts expenditures related to reducing the "disamenities of urbanization."[30]

contend public health and environmental regulation are important goals by criticizing them for noneconomic thinking. British economist John Maddox has written, "In general, economics is not the strong point of environmentalists."[32] Harvard Professor Gottfried Haberler has gone a step further:[33]

> The hostility that the capitalist market economy encounters in many quarters is to a large extent of an irrational nature or is at least based on non-economic reasoning.

Employers' ability to control definitions is strengthened by their ability to shape public perceptions of whose ideas matter and whose do not, whose are "serious" and whose are "irrational." When Billy Williamson ridiculed the "do-gooders" who wanted to protect people from asbestos-caused diseases, he joined a long tradition of speakers who belittle and isolate those who challenge the status quo of wealth, power, and political values.

Another example was provided by nationally-syndicated columnist Joseph Kraft when he contrasted productive "Big America" with obstructionist "Little America." Kraft defined Big America as the "major industrial producers—the makers of steel, chemicals, autos, rubber, ships and many other such items." Little America consists of "those primarily interested in fair employment, the environment and the consumer."[34] Little America made some gains during the 1970s—resulting in the overregulation of Big America. This was particularly disastrous, according to Kraft, because Little America is unable to provide the jobs and products which the nation needs: "The health of the economy is, in the long run, bound up with the revitalization of industry."[35] Kraft thus reinforced the notion that it is not possible for the nation to be concerned with both strong industry and secure, decent jobs; with economic revitalization of industry and environmental protection; with industrial innovation and consumer protection. Some day perhaps, when

Big America has made the country wealthy enough, the interests of Little America can be addressed. But if the millions of people Kraft writes off as Little want to see that day, they had better give corporate America free rein.

Employers have always been eager to limit or at least shape the boundaries of democracy. Sometimes they are not very subtle. In a 1980 discussion of what "reindustrialization" would require, *Business Week* asserted that business, labor, and academia would have to develop a new social contract: "The drawing of a social contract takes precedence over the aspirations of the poor, the minorities, and the environmentalists."[36] In 1946 Auto Workers president Walter Reuther challenged General Motors to prove it could not afford the 30 percent wage increase the union was demanding. He told Howard Cohen, GM's assistant director of personnel, "If you can prove that you cannot give us 30 percent, hold prices and still make a nice profit, we will settle for less than 30 percent." Cohen made it clear that Reuther was overstepping his bounds:[37]

> Why don't you get down to your size and get down to the type of job you're supposed to do as a trade union leader and talk about money you would like to have for your people and let the labor statesmanship go to hell for a while. . . . It's none of your damn business what GM does about prices.

Business and government have a long history of labeling people who champion Little America as dangerous and untrustworthy. People who fought for the 8-hour day, the minimum wage, Social Security, and the right to unionize were called anarchists, socialists, communists, and un-American troublemakers—anything to challenge their credibility without responding to their analyses and demands. Today there are business leaders, government officials, elected representatives, academics—even some labor leaders—who use similar terms to describe environmentalists. Environmental activism, according to one economist, is "marked by strong undertones of anti-Americanism."[38] A New York businessman writing in a union magazine labeled environmentalists "leisure class elitists, counter-culture dreamers and hard core radicals."[39] The public relations campaigns of national business organizations are designed to convince the public that environmentalists, unlike corporate executives, represent narrow, special interests which conflict with the "national interest." Powerful corporations represent themselves as suffering populists handcuffed by an elite of environmental activists. Consider the complaint of Mobil, the fourth largest U.S.-based corporation, which was ready to drop $6 billion in cash to buy Marathon, the world's seventeenth largest oil company:[40]

> We feel the need to express, from time to time, our belief that those who object to economic development on ecological grounds may often be expressing mere rhetoric and couching their real elitist motives in terms they see as popular and effective.

Employers and their supporters have been quite effective in restricting national economic and political debate to a fairly narrow set of "alternatives" which do not challenge the primacy of business priorities, prerogatives, and power. They have convinced large segments of the public that there are *no* alternatives. People's beliefs can be shaken when they are told repeatedly that change is impossible, that their ideas are impractical. And they can be persuaded to "be realistic" when employers make it clear that to persist might cost them their jobs. For this reason people often accept the choices put forward by their employers as the only alternatives: we accept "jobs versus the environment," rather than insist on "jobs *and* the environment." As one Fisher Body worker told a *New York Times* reporter, "If that's a guy's livelihood, and they say it's the only way to do it, what's a guy going to do?"[41]

PART II

"Regulatory Relief": The New Job Blackmail

5
"One-Sided Class War": The Corporate Campaign Against Labor _____ and Environment

Gould, Inc., is an electronics company with nearly 30,000 employees and annual sales over $2 billion. In 1978 Gould ran a full-page advertisement in the *Wall Street Journal* featuring a drawing of the Statue of Liberty with a rope around her neck. The ad read:[1]

> As the noose of overregulation tightens, it threatens to strangle creativity and invention—and, therefore, productivity and increased employment. To discourage risk and investment in capital expansion. To discourage increasing investment in research and development. To erode our standard of living. And, ultimately, to stifle progress.

At roughly the same time, the National Cotton Council published its own full-page advertisement blaming gov-

ernment regulation for high prices and inflation.*
Amway, the country's fiftieth largest privately-owned
company, launched an advertising campaign suggesting
that only across-the-board budget cuts for all regulatory
agencies would eliminate the "dead wood" and put a halt
to "regulatory overkill."[2]

These ads emphasized the need to "put regulation back
in perspective" while they contended that the economy
would be more productive—and would create more jobs
—with less regulation. They belittled and ignored the
serious problems environmental and health protections
were designed to address. They did so by presenting
regulation as if it were simply some unfair, irrational idea
which hurts consumers. The aim of each was to persuade
the public that the corporations' interest in getting the
government off their backs was identical to the public
interest in lower prices, higher wages, more jobs, and a
higher standard of living.

Business propaganda of this kind has frequently succeeded in obscuring the basic conflict between business
and the public interest. In fact, the battle over government regulation has always been one between competing
interests—the profit-oriented priorities of business and
the very different interests of those who suffer from
industry's failure to provide adequate jobs and income,
protect the environment and public health, and preserve
natural resources. Throughout the nation's history,
Americans have turned to government for protections
they could not provide for themselves. At the same time
business leaders have also turned to government for help.
As the federal government has become more powerful,
the conflict has intensified. "More than ever before,"
writes social scientist Ralph Miliband, "[people] now live
in the shadow of the state. . . . It is for the state's

*The National Cotton Council has another antiregulation ad which reads, "You
might never get to wear cotton again. Not if the government has its way." The
ad features four men nattily attired in business suits—but without shirts.

attention, or for its control, that [they] compete; and it is against the state that beat the waves of social conflict."[3]

It is not a very even fight. The business community, with its great wealth and economic power, has a distinct advantage. John Quarles realized this during his term as deputy administrator of the Environmental Protection Agency under Presidents Nixon and Ford:[4]

> Left alone, our government will not always look after the public interest. In the environmental area, there is a natural built-in imbalance. Private industry, driven by its own profit incentives to exploit and pollute our natural resources, uses its inherent advantage to exert political pressure to resist environmental requirements. The machinations of industry explain at least in part why the abuses of pollution became so severe before steps were taken to establish controls.

Although corporate leaders and their supporters contend too much government is the problem, business has always sought government intervention on its behalf. And, more often than not, government has obliged. Governmental intervention in national economic life is directed far more frequently toward assisting business enterprises than restricting them.

"RIGHT" AND "WRONG" KINDS OF REGULATION

In the early 1900s steel magnate Andrew Carnegie was one of many business leaders who argued that business needed government protection against the risky ordeal of naked price competition: "It always comes back to me," Carnegie explained in his book *Problems of Today*, "that government control, and that alone, will properly solve the problem."[5] It was up to business "to help shape the right kind of regulation," Samuel Insull told a gathering of fellow industrialists in 1909.[6]

The record shows a long history of business pressure for

favorable tax, resource development, and other governmental policies to protect them from uncertainty and
competition. According to one historian, leading corporate policy makers "did not merely pervert and take over
the [early] regulatory agencies—they planned and developed them."[7]

It was largely at the insistence of the major railroad
companies that Congress created the Interstate Commerce Commission in 1887 as the first federal agency with
the power to set prices and place conditions on entry into
the industry. The railroads wanted to stabilize prices in
their young and expanding industry and to prevent companies from destroying one another. When Congress
created the Federal Trade Commission in 1914 to fight
against deceptive and fraudulent sales practices, President
Woodrow Wilson noted "that the businessmen themselves desire nothing so much as a trade commission."[8]
Industries from meat packing to trucking to banking also
turned to the government. Historian John Roche described the industrialists who built their empires and
amassed great fortunes between the Civil War and the
New Deal:[9]

> This elite lived at the public trough, was nourished by
> state protection, and devoted most of its time and
> energy to avoiding Adam Smith's individualistic in-
> junctions. It demanded and applauded vigorous state
> action in behalf of its key values, and denounced state
> intervention in behalf of its enemies.

This same attitude prevails today. America's most
powerful business leaders do not hesitate to seek favorable regulation or government assistance. William E.
Simon, Treasury Secretary under President Nixon, was
dismayed by what he saw during his years as a public
servant:[10]

> During my tenure at Treasury, I watched with incre-

> dulity as businessmen ran to the government in every crisis, whining for handouts or protection from the very competition that has made this system so productive. I saw Texas ranchers, hit by drought, demanding government-guaranteed loans; giant milk cooperatives lobbying for higher price supports; major airlines fighting deregulation to preserve their monopoly status; huge companies like Lockheed seeking federal assistance to rescue them from sheer inefficiency; bankers like David Rockefeller demanding government bailouts to protect them from their ill-conceived investments; network executives like William Paley of CBS fighting to preserve regulatory restrictions and to block the emergence of competitive cable and pay TV.

Today's economists generally differentiate between two types of federal regulation: economic and social. The major purpose of economic regulation is to "insure the smooth functioning of the economy through controls on monopoly, discrimination, unfair business practices and denial of service."[11] The Interstate Commerce Commission, the Civil Aeronautics Board, and the Federal Communications Commission are economic regulatory bodies. These agencies, as Carnegie and Insull understood, are relatively easy for firms in the regulated industries to "capture" and influence.

Social regulation is quite different. The primary concerns of social regulation include product quality, health, safety, and environmental protection. Social regulations try to prevent businesses from causing harm to people and the environment and to force them to pay the full costs of production. While economic regulation may not always be welcomed by business, social regulation is more often resisted. It is this latter kind of restriction on corporate autonomy which Samuel Insull was concerned about when he warned fellow industrialists that failure to fight for the "right kind" of government regulation would lead to having "the wrong kind forced on [them]" by an angry public.[12]

Winning the "wrong kind" of protections in the face of intense corporate opposition has generally been a difficult task. For example, it took 35 years and hundreds of deaths before the first federal safety legislation, regulating boiler use on steamboats, was enacted over the opposition of steamboat owners and lawmakers.

After the maiden voyage of Robert Fulton's steamship, the *Clermont,* on 17 August 1807, entrepreneurs on all major rivers moved quickly to beat competitors into the steamship business. In their enthusiasm, they paid little attention to public safety. During the first six months of 1817, 30 people were killed in seven separate boiler explosions. Citizens began demanding protection, but Congress was reluctant to act. In 1836, when 496 people were killed in 14 different explosions (roughly equivalent, given today's population, to 7,000 airplane fatalities in one year), public pressure mounted. Congress passed legislation in 1838 which required licensing and inspection of steamboats and which assigned liability to owners and to negligent employees. The law established the first federal regulatory body, the Steamship Inspection Service. However, it included no enforcement provisions and few owners complied.

Stiffer legislation was not introduced until 1851, a year in which boiler explosions killed another 407 people. During Congressional debate Senator Robert F. Stockton of New Jersey denounced the bill vigorously:[13]

> What will be left of human liberty if we progress on this course much further? Can a man's property be said to be his own, when you take it out of his control and put it in the hands of another, though he may be a Federal officer?

But another senator computed the damage and cost of boiler explosions between 1818 and 1848: 2,563 deaths, 2,097 injuries, and property losses of $3 million. He responded:[14]

> I consider that the only question involved in this bill
> is this: whether we shall permit a legalized, unques-
> tioned and peculiar class in the community to go on
> committing murders at will, or whether we will make
> such enactments as will compel them to pay some
> attention to the value of life.

The legislation passed, resulting in fewer boiler explosions. For the first time elected federal representatives
had accepted responsibility and acted decisively to protect
citizens from corporate negligence.

Thirty years later, in the 1880s, rapid expansion of the
railroad system precipitated a similar safety crisis—and a
similar response from industry. Accidents due to faulty
link-and-pin railroad car couplers were causing extensive
injuries and deaths to railroad passengers and crews.
Faced with the prospect of federal legislation to correct
the problem, the same industry which welcomed regulation by the ICC stubbornly resisted safety regulation,
using remarkably contemporary arguments.

First the companies blamed the high accident rate on
workers and their unions. Erie Railroad officials claimed
there was a "growing disregard of personal safety mani-
fested by the rank and file."[15] Colonel H.S. Haines,
president of the American Railway Association, blamed
the workers' "lack of unquestioning obedience to authority."[16] Then the companies argued that safety regulations
would destroy the industry and throw thousands of people
out of work. Haines claimed the proposed Safety Appli-
ances Act, which would require railroads to equip their
cars with air brakes and automatic couplers, would "petri-
fy the art of railroading." The pending legislation, he
said, was an unnecessary and unwarranted intervention
into private industry affairs.

The law passed in 1893 and gave the railroads five years
to comply. In 1897 (prefiguring the auto industry's resistance to air pollution standards 80 years later) the railroads

sought another 5-year extension, arguing they could not afford to pay the increased cost while the nation was in the throes of a serious industrial depression. The following year, however, after the economy bounced back, the industry contended that business had become too brisk to allow the removal of cars from active service for installation of the required couplers. When this rationalization failed, the railroads tried to delay enforcement by repeated court challenges. They also continued to blame railroad workers. An article in the railroad industry's trade journal even suggested improved safety equipment would only increase accidents by encouraging workers to be more careless and lazy.[17]

Clearly the railroad companies saw the creation of the ICC as the "right kind" of regulation—and the passage of railroad safety legislation as the "wrong kind." From the industry's perspective, the good thing about the ICC was that it stabilized prices and profits—without challenging corporate power. As U.S. Attorney General William Olney assured the president of the Burlington Railroad in 1893:[18]

> The [Commission] . . . is, or can be made, of great help to the railroads. It satisfied the popular clamor for a government supervision of the railroads, at the same time that the supervision is almost entirely nominal. Further, the older such a commission gets to be, the more inclined it will be to take the business and railroad side of things. It thus becomes a sort of barrier between the railroad corporations and the people and a sort of protection against hasty and crude legislation hostile to railroad interests.

Railroad safety legislation, on the other hand, threatened corporate profits and prerogatives by encouraging more democratic participation in major corporate decisions.

THE BUSINESS OFFENSIVE OF THE 1970s

Conflict between corporate and public goals has been a constant factor in regulatory politics. Vigorous public pressure in the 1960s and the early 1970s forced the passage of important federal laws regulating the use of natural resources, air and water pollution, the use and disposal of toxic substances, and workplace health and safety. By requiring business and government to accept responsibility for the destructive effects of production, these laws changed the relationship between business and the public as dramatically as did the labor laws of the 1930s. In the 1940s and 1950s the business community fought to undo worker gains of the 1930s. In the past decade there has been a similar corporate push to reverse environmental protections and worker and consumer rights. Ronald Reagan did not initiate this effort. The Reagan administration's attacks on regulation are in fact the culmination of a sophisticated, decade-long campaign. This campaign began to take shape as soon as the first environmental, health, and workplace protection laws of the 1970s were passed.

In 1970 President Nixon created the National Industrial Pollution Control Council (NIPCC). The 200 member companies—a *Who's Who* of big polluters—took an active role in advising federal, state, and local agencies on environmental issues.

In 1970 and 1971 a number of companies, including Armco Steel and Union Carbide, threatened to close plants if they were forced to comply with new environmental regulations. Commerce Secretary Stans, along with other business and government officials, issued public warnings that the wave of new environmental and occupational health protections would throw large numbers of people out of work.

In 1972 opposition directed from the highest echelons

of the business community became more aggressive. Industry trade associations, corporate law firms, and individual companies rushed to hire anti-environmental lobbyists and other Washington-based staff. They realized that their traditional style of Washington lobbying—based on influence-peddling and personal friendships with legislators—was inadequate in the face of a rapidly-growing environmental movement. They realized too that widespread public pressure for changes in the behavior of *all* polluting industries called for a new strategy. Previously, companies within an industry had united to influence that industry's regulatory body. But the creation of new regulatory agencies with authority over all industries —such as EPA, OSHA, the Consumer Product Safety Commission, and the Equal Employment Opportunities Commission—made it necessary for firms in all major industries to pull together. As economist Murray L. Weidenbaum (first chairman of President Reagan's Council of Economic Advisors) explained, the broad scope of these new social regulatory agencies made it "impractical for a single industry to dominate these regulatory activities in the manner of the traditional [single industry] model."[19]

The NIPCC's effectiveness was limited because its organizational roots were in the Nixon White House. So in 1972 the chief executive officers of America's largest corporations met to form a new group and to plan a coordinated campaign to reestablish business primacy in federal decisionmaking. The Business Roundtable, as the business leaders called themselves, was intent on stemming the tide of environmental, safety, and health laws. It was also committed to winning concessions from labor. One of the Roundtable's first actions was to absorb two older business groups, the Labor Law Study Committee and the Construction Users Anti-Inflation Roundtable, which had been formed to combat union wage and work rule demands, particularly in the construction industry.[20]

The Business Roundtable has grown in size and influence since 1972. Comprised of 196 chief executive officers, the Roundtable now counts among its members the heads of the top 10 corporations in the 1980 *Fortune 500* list, 70 of the list's 100 largest U.S. firms, and 131 of the top 500.[21] The Roundtable's policy priorities include "regulatory reform" (as the Roundtable and other business organizations call it), energy and environment, and labor policy. In conjunction with a reinvigorated U.S. Chamber of Commerce, the National Association of Manufacturers, and a long list of trade associations and lobbying groups, the Roundtable has spearheaded an intense campaign against both recently-won environmental and health rights and older labor protections.

The business offensive has been relentless. Looking back over the 1970s former Congressman Paul G. Rogers (D-FL) noted in 1978 that American industry had[22]

> fought every inch of the way against every environmental health requirement. Every dollar invested to reduce deadly coke oven emissions, to control radiation exposures, to capture chemical plants carcinogenic discharges, to curb toxic sulfates and nitrate particles from coal combustion, has come only after protracted political and legal struggles.

J.C. Turner, president of the International Union of Operating Engineers, saw the same corporate attitude toward workers. In 1979 Turner charged that the Business Roundtable and other business groups did not simply want to stop labor's momentum. Their goal, he claimed, was to bust American unionism:[23]

> It has become apparent to me . . . that a systematic and well-planned campaign is being conducted to totally destroy the building trades. Following extensive research and analysis of the groups which are orchestrating this assault, I have concluded that the current

attack is the result of a decade of planning and
groundwork by the Business Roundtable acting in
concert with regional and local construction user
associations, the contractor association, the U.S.
Chamber of Commerce, pro-business academic institutions and their allies in government.

1974 RECESSION: THE CAMPAIGN BUILDS

The deep recession which followed the fourfold increase in OPEC oil prices after the 1973 Arab-Israeli War
marked an important turning point in the business offensive. By the late 1960s the economy began to falter.
Foreign competition was increasing, and the relatively low
unemployment rate during the Vietnam War—3.5 percent in 1969—gave workers the confidence to demand
higher wages to keep pace with inflation. American firms
found it increasingly difficult to continue raising both
wages and profits, as they had done fairly steadily since
World War II.[24]

It was not until the 1974–75 recession, however, that
the American public was jolted into realizing the economy was in serious trouble. President Nixon added to the
growing inflationary pressures, which had been triggered
by $30 billion a year of Vietnam War spending, by selling
too much wheat to Russia in 1972 and by precipitously
lifting wage-and-price controls after his re-election. Following the OPEC price hike, Nixon chose to fight inflation
by purposely creating a recession. The Federal Reserve
Board decreased the money supply and forced higher
interest rates. By mid-1975 unemployment reached 9
percent and nearly one-third of the nation's productive
capacity lay idle. Inflation dropped to 5.5 percent, but not
before the nation was in its worst recession since World
War II.[25]

The recession was both economically disruptive and
personally unsettling to many American workers. Several

million lost their jobs. People received a harsh reminder that their jobs and income were still far from secure, despite the long period of postwar economic prosperity. In the face of decreasing profits, resource shortages, foreign competition, and public demands for wage increases and regulatory protections, the business community accelerated its offensive against both worker *and* environmental protections. The strategy was an old one: hammering away on jobs. Dick Armstrong of the Public Affairs Council, a group which advises public relations directors and lobbyists of major American corporations, told his clients:[26]

> Politicians neither care about nor have much interest in words like 'profit' or 'capital formation.' But they sure understand JOBS and plant closings.

Armco Steel's chairman William Verity zeroed in on jobs when he opposed the 1977 amendments to the Clean Air Act. Verity claimed, "Most of the major urban centers in the U.S. will face stagnation in all industrial construction" —and, of course, job opportunities—if the amendments passed. That same year Elmer Fike, owner of the Fike Chemical Company in Nitro, West Virginia, complained to the National Association of Manufacturers (NAM) that the proposed Toxic Substances Control Act (TSCA) would drive his company out of business. With help from NAM, Fike sent letters to hundreds of small manufacturers warning that this legislation regulating the use, production, and disposal of hazardous substances would force them all to shut down.*

Even J. Robert Fluor, chairman of the vehemently anti-union Fluor Corporation, joined the chorus. When asked in 1978 why he and other members of the business

---

*The law passed in 1976. Fike Chemical is still in business: "We haven't had any layoffs, and we don't expect any problems from TSCA," Fike said in 1981.[27]

community had helped develop a network of tax-exempt, "public interest" legal foundations to counter environmental laws, he replied:[28]

> We felt somebody had to be there in court to give the other side; a lot of times, *in the case of jobs, for instance,* we felt the public interest wasn't really being represented by the public interest law firms. (emphasis added)

THE ATTACK ON WORKER PROTECTIONS

While corporate leaders like Fluor declared publicly their real concern was jobs, they intensified their opposition to occupational health and safety protections, the minimum wage, the right to a job at decent wages, and even the right to organize. Nowhere was this more apparent than in their steadfast opposition to legislation committing the nation to full-employment.

After World War II, organized labor and other constituencies pushed for full-employment legislation. But the effort met with stiff resistance from business groups such as the Committee for Economic Development, the Chamber of Commerce, and the National Association of Manufacturers. John F. Finnelly, executive director of the Committee for Economic Development, warned that full employment would eliminate business' cheap, mobile reserve of workers: "Full employment would be incompatible with the free enterprise system which carries with it the right to a normal float of unemployed."[29] Industry opposition was successful. The Full Employment Act of 1946 only directed the government to use fiscal and monetary policies to spur private sector growth.

Thirty years later, in 1976, Senator Hubert Humphrey (D-MN) and Representative Augustus Hawkins (D-CA) cosponsored the Equal Opportunity and Full Employment Act with support from a broad coalition of labor, church, and civil rights groups. An early draft of the legislation stated that "all adult Americans able and willing to work have the right to equal opportunities for useful paid employment at fair rates of compensation," and that the federal government should be responsible for developing "such policies and programs as may be needed to attain and maintain genuine full employment."

The coalition working for passage of the legislation crumbled under industry pressure and accepted successively weaker rewrites, abandoning the principle that every able and willing adult should have the right to a job. The federal government was limited to being the "employer of last resort." There was no consideration of the kinds of jobs to be created. Conventional fiscal and monetary policies were again to be used to generate full employment by stimulating the creation of sufficient private sector jobs.

But even these concessions did not satisfy business lobbyists, who made sure that the 1976 version was killed in committee before it ever reached the floor of Congress. Industry did not want government-created jobs: it feared competition from the federal government on wage rates, safety, and other working conditions, competition which would probably force improvements in private sector wages and conditions, and strengthen the bargaining position of workers.

The Full Employment and Balanced Growth Act passed in 1978 was weak indeed. There was no mention of the right to a job, nor of the federal government as the employer of the last resort. The Act was little more than a symbolic gesture of respect for the recently-deceased Senator Humphrey.

The defeat of enforceable full-employment legislation was only one example of business opposition to proworker initiatives in the late 1970s. When the minimum wage came before Congress in 1977, the U.S. Chamber of Commerce once again resorted to job blackmail to lobby against raising the minimum wage to a level that would lift 10 million *working* Americans above the poverty line.

Chamber lobbyists claimed that 2 million jobs would be lost if the minimum wage were increased to $2.65: "It's inflationary . . . it hurts small business . . . it costs jobs," declared J. W. Marriott, Jr.[30] The Chamber's statistical methods were shown to be so sloppy that the Chamber later publicly retracted its estimate. Three years later, however, the Chamber returned, predicting that without a subminimum wage for youth, hundreds of thousands of disadvantaged, unskilled black teenagers would remain unable to find work. Although Congress did not pass a youth subminimum wage, the Chamber's arguments received wide publicity.*

In 1978 common-situs picketing and labor law reform were victims of aggressive corporate assaults. Common situs, long a goal of the AFL-CIO construction unions, would improve the negotiating position of unions on construction sites by allowing workers to picket the entire worksite. This is a right which industrial workers won many years ago. The bill was resoundingly defeated in the Democratic-controlled House.

The battle over labor law reform followed soon after. Organized labor wanted several changes in the National Labor Relations Act, the 1935 law which recognized the right of workers to form unions free from employer interference. Unions wanted to amend the law (which had been severely limited by the Taft-Hartley Act of 1947 and the Landrum-Griffin Act of 1959) to prevent companies from stalling for months before holding a representation election for their workers; to speed up the

---

*President Reagan still supports the idea, and the Reagan administration may well make a serious effort to enact a subminimum wage bill for youth—using "jobs" as justification for a 2-tiered minimum wage.

processing of unfair labor practice complaints; and to empower the National Labor Relations Board to impose stiffer penalties for unjust firings of workers, lack of good-faith bargaining, and other employer violations. With support from the Carter administration, the bill passed easily in the House of Representatives. However, when the bill came to the Senate early in 1978, the Chamber of Commerce, the National Association of Manufacturers, the National Right-to-Work Committee, and their allies launched an elaborate campaign against it. The media effort was particularly effective, with job blackmail as its centerpiece. Articles opposing the legislation were sent—unsolicited—to hundreds of newspapers across the country, from the *Honolulu Star-Bulletin* to the *Hartselle* (Alabama) *Enquirer*. The articles warned of increased power for "union bosses," and coercion of workers into unions; but the major theme was unemployment. On 11 January 1978 the *Birmingham News* and other newspapers carried this report:

> Robert Thompson, chairman of the U.S. Chamber of Commerce's labor relations committee, also told a Washington press conference that [labor law reform], if enacted into law, could backfire by throwing innocent workers out of jobs.

Four days later the *Greensburg* (Pennsylvania) *Tribune Review* warned:

> The bite against business is coming. The legislative ledger tells the tale: The Labor Law Reform Act; the Humphrey-Hawkins Employment Bill; pregnancy disability drive; taxes grab; continuation of the Wage and Price Council; increased safety and environmental regulations, etc.; the outlook for protecting jobs, created by business profits, is poor in a Democrat dominated Congress.

Some papers printed this propaganda word-for-word as their editorials. Copies of all these articles were compiled in *The Press Against Labor Law Reform,* a volume three inches thick presented to every member of Congress.

The campaign worked. Senator Orrin Hatch (R-UT) (now chairman of the Senate Labor and Human Resources Committee) led a filibuster to kill the legislation without a vote. Supporters of the bill, including the President, were one vote shy of breaking this filibuster. Labor law reform died, victim of what Auto Workers' president Douglas Fraser called a "dishonest and ugly multi-million dollar campaign." Fraser promptly resigned from the President's semi-official Labor-Management Group, charging it had become a useless "facade" for "confrontation [rather] than cooperation." Upon resigning he issued a stern rebuke of the country's corporate leaders:[31]

> I believe leaders of the business community, with few exceptions, have chosen to wage a one-sided class war in this country—a war against working people, the unemployed, the poor, the minorities, the very young and the very old, and even many in the middle class of our society.

Lane Kirkland, then secretary-treasurer of the AFL-CIO, was equally upset. Kirkland told a group of business leaders that "close beneath that veneer of civility which your firms find expedient," American business is determined to maintain the "master-servant relationship" in dealing with workers.[32]

The campaign to weaken the labor unions and to defeat labor protections has not been limited to legislation. In recent years many employers have intensified their opposition to unionization itself. Some have turned to anti-union "management consultants" who design sophisticated campaigns to defeat union drives. Nearly 1,000 such firms are currently in business and have participated in as many as two-thirds of the efforts to defeat union organizing drives in recent years.[33] Basing their campaigns on fear and intimidation of workers, the consultants have been quite successful. Modern Management, Inc., the best known of these firms, boasts a 90 percent success rate.

According to the Industrial Union Department (IUD) of the AFL-CIO, union-busting is spreading to firms which have long been unionized. In June 1981, after three months of a bitter strike, management of the Sterling Radiator Plant in Westfield, Massachusetts, hired a non-union workforce in an effort to defeat a local of the United Auto Workers which had represented the plant's workers for nearly 30 years. After a number of employers in the southwest were able to decertify existing unions, the IUD Executive Council charged in July 1981 that corporations with long-standing union relationships were making "blatant efforts to destroy established collective bargaining relationships."[34] This trend "represents a menacing new direction taken by American industry, a threat not only to many individual unions, but to the basic role of free trade unionism in our democratic system."[35]

THE ATTACK ON HEALTH AND ENVIRONMENTAL PROTECTIONS

As the attack on unions intensified, business and government leaders refined strategies to weaken environmental and workplace health and safety regulations and to dampen public enthusiasm for such protections. Regulation not only led to layoffs, they said; it also contributed to inflation, lower productivity, slumping innovation, and slower growth—all of which undermined the job prospects for American workers. These new arguments, which have become increasingly elaborate, have provided the public justification for President Reagan's "regulatory relief" program.

Spurred by the economic and psychological impact of the 1974–75 recession, business and government made

frequent claims during Gerald Ford's presidency that
regulatory activity of the early 1970s had gone too far.
One Bethlehem Steel advertisement stated it was time to
end the "headlong rush" into pollution controls. In
November 1974 the President ordered all federal agencies
to prepare Inflationary Impact Statements for major new
rules and regulations. Ford's executive order gave the
Office of Management and Budget greater control over
the ostensibly independent federal regulatory agencies, a
strategy which Richard Nixon pioneered and which
Ronald Reagan institutionalized. The order also emphasized the administration's contention that regulation was
contributing significantly to the nation's high inflation
rate.

As Congressional debate on the 1977 Clean Air Act
amendments drew near, the Ford Motor Company released a study estimating that compliance with the proposed auto exhaust emissions standard would result in layoffs for 75,000 Ford workers.[36] This claim was indicative
of the tactical shift that was taking place among opponents of regulation. Ford was not blaming the emissions
standard for forcing a specific plant to close or for
endangering the survival of the entire automobile industry. The company did not argue that developing the
required technology was impossible. Rather, Ford announced the pollution control standard was going to raise
prices and slow sales, resulting in fewer jobs. It was a
claim difficult to prove either true or false. If prices
increased, how much of the increase could actually be
attributed to pollution controls? If sales dropped, how
much of the slump would be the result of the higher
prices? If Ford laid off 75,000 workers, would this be the
direct result of slumping sales? Perhaps Ford was ready to
cut back its workforce in favor of labor-saving machinery,
and was just waiting for the appropriate time. It was
impossible to know.

With inflation and unemployment high, productivity growth slowing, industrial innovation in eclipse, and prospects for an economic turnaround dim, it was easy for political and corporate leaders to point the finger at "government encroachment on private businesses."[37] While some were properly concerned with increasing the efficiency of regulation, others capitalized on the public's growing economic insecurity to counter the threat to corporate profits and power posed by environmental and health regulation.

By 1978 critics of overregulation found support in well-publicized economic studies. Murray L. Weidenbaum and Robert DeFina, colleagues at the Center for the Study of American Business at Washington University, claimed the cost of regulation had topped $100 billion (a figure which has been widely quoted, but which is wildly inflated, as will be shown in chapter 9). Edward F. Denison of the Brookings Institution published an influential study which identified pollution-control expenditures as a significant factor in the declining rate of productivity growth. In the summer of 1977 the American Enterprise Institute published the first issue of its bimonthly journal *Regulation*. The magazine became a forum for criticism of environmental, safety, and health protections. The drive to get the government off the back of business spread beyond the high echelons of industry, government, and academia to the mass media and to the public.

In 1979 the Business Roundtable released a study of regulatory compliance costs for 48 of the nation's largest companies, concluding that "much of the [cost was] considered by the companies to be wasteful and nonproductive."[38] But the business community and its supporters were not content to issue studies and press releases. In January 1979 representatives of the nation's most powerful (and heavily polluting) industries—the

American Petroleum Institute, the American Paper Institute, the American Iron and Steel Institute, the American Mining Congress, the Motor Vehicles Manufacturers Association, the Construction Industry Advancement Fund, and the National Forest Products Association—met in San Francisco specifically to launch a public and legislative campaign to gut the Clean Air Act.[39]

Later that year Senator Richard Schweiker (R-PA) introduced a controversial bill to "improve" OSHA. Schweiker's bill would have eliminated most safety inspections in 90 percent of America's workplaces. It would have made it easier for employers to avoid penalties and continue noncompliance, while making it more difficult for workers to monitor safety violations themselves. The bill died when union members, with the support of other constituencies (including environmentalists), mobilized and declared their strong opposition. However, the corporate counteroffensive was still building by the 1980 presidential election.

THE REAGAN ADMINISTRATION

The Schweiker bill was introduced before Ronald Reagan's victory. But its antiworker, anti-environmentalist thrust was in line with Reagan's own views. On the campaign trail Reagan often played on workers' job insecurities to drive home his attack on health and environmental protections: "We must realize," he told audiences in several states, "that many regulations impair the ability of industries to compete, reduce workers' real income and destroy jobs."[40] To a Youngstown, Ohio, audience of largely unemployed steelworkers and their families, candidate Reagan declared, "These 1970 [Clean Air] rules have helped force factories to shut down and cost workers their jobs."[41]

The new administration moved quickly to bring leading champions of "regulatory relief" into the government. James Watt became Secretary of the Interior, vowing to change "forty, fifty years of bad government."[42] Watt instructed his senior staff to avoid contact with representatives of national environmental organizations, because their only interest was "politics."[43] Anne Gorsuch, administrator of the Environmental Protection Agency, showed her bias in August 1981, when she urged industry to "light up the switchboard" at Congress in favor of weakening the Clean Air Act.[44] In one key position after another—at EPA, the Department of the Interior, the Forest Service, the Department of Energy, and the Office of Surface Mining—the administration appointed representatives of mining, oil and gas, timber, and other industries which stand to benefit directly from weak and inadequately enforced regulations. According to White House personnel director E. Pendleton James, "The common thread [of our appointments] is one of less regulation of business enterprises."[45]

Another thread is hostility to organized labor. The nomination of Raymond Donovan as Secretary of Labor was welcomed by the antilabor National Right-to-Work Committee, whose president Reed Larson explained, "We look forward to seeing the Department of Labor taken out of the hands of union professionals."[46] John Van De Water, Reagan's initial appointee for chairman of the National Labor Relations Board, had previously been an anti-union management consultant. And President Reagan's own decision to break the Professional Air Traffic Controllers Organization (PATCO) strike—and the union—was a clear signal to the nation where the administration stood on the principle of worker rights.

The Reagan program has been consistent with the appointments. James C. Miller, III, an associate of Murray Weidenbaum and one of the American Enterprise

Institute's most active critics of government regulation, initially joined David Stockman at the Office of Management and Budget. In his first press conference, Miller outlined the Administration's regulatory strategy: "The President will focus more on social regulations at the beginning," shifting from the Carter administration's concern with economic regulation because, he claimed, social regulations are "more burdensome and outlandish." Environmental rules would be under particularly close scrutiny, for that is "where the big bucks are . . . where the big payoff will come."[47]

In the administration's first nine months, Vice President Bush's Regulatory Relief Task Force slated nearly 60 major existing environmental, health, safety, and other regulations for "reconsideration," and blocked or terminated dozens of other proposed regulations. These ranged from controls on automobile pollution and safety to the testing of food and drugs, handling of hazardous wastes, noise reduction on the job, and health standards for asbestos, chromium, and cadmium.

The Reagan administration has intentionally crippled the governmental machinery for protecting health, environment, and worker rights. This has been done by cutting personnel and research budgets, firing experienced staff members, and slowing enforcement efforts. The Interior Department reorganization of the Office of Surface Mining eliminated five of its regional offices and nearly 400 jobs, including 57 percent of the enforcement staff.[48] The Council on Environmental Quality has lost more than half its staff and budget. At EPA budget cuts proposed for fiscal year 1983 will decrease the agency's staff by at least 27 percent, at a time when the workload should double to implement toxic substances statutes.[49] Cuts in all health and environmental programs have been so severe that, according to Anthony Robbins, former director of the National Institute for Occupational Safety and Health:[50]

> The Reagan people at the top seem to have a mission to destroy toxic and environmental research. There will be dozens of programs in the health and environmental area that just won't function—and that's exactly what these people want.

EPA enforcement efforts have all but stopped: "We are currently receiving no policy direction from the [top]," enforcement officer Steven E. Hoover told the *Washington Post* in November 1981. "Nor is our expertise being called on for decisionmaking. Were it not for the newspapers we would not even know what was occuring in the agency."[51]

Department-wide budget cuts have also meant layoffs of experienced staff and cutbacks in enforcement capabilities at OSHA, the Mine Safety and Health Administration, and the Employment Standards Administration. In the Reagan administration's first year, OSHA workplace inspections declined 17 percent and monthly follow-up inspections dropped 68 percent. Citations for "serious" health and safety violations declined 27 percent.[52] All but a small percentage of manufacturing firms have been exempted from routine inspections, achieving the intent of the Schweiker bill without new legislation. John Leslie was public relations director of the Labor Department for 22 years before resigning six months after Reagan's inauguration:[53]

> I sat for six months and watched a department in which I had worked most of my adult life systematically dismantled. I watched programs to serve and protect working people . . . slowly strangled or gutted.

The Office of Management and Budget has been responsible for coordinating the antiregulatory onslaught. In one of his first acts in office, President Reagan issued an executive order which gave OMB effective veto power over federal regulations. By mid-October 1981 OMB had rejected or delayed more than 55 proposed rules without any public explanation. "We don't know why OMB rejected the regulations and who OMB people met and what information they relied on," said Charles Ludlam of the Alliance for Justice, a coalition of poverty, law, and public interest groups.[54] Operating in secrecy, OMB has become the arbiter of national health, safety, and environmental policy, severely limiting the participation of workers in Labor Department policies and of environmental organizations at EPA and Interior.

The attack on health, environmental, and labor protections has not been motivated solely by concern about the financial burden of regulation. Employers and their government supporters have also been trying to curb protections which increase the democratization and accountability of business and government. OSHA decided not to issue regulations requiring "walkaround pay" for workers accompanying OSHA officials on plant inspection tours. The agency also withdrew proposed regulations on labeling hazardous materials to which workers are exposed. Both decisions were intended to weaken the ability of workers to take a more active role in improving workplace health and safety conditions. The Attorney General and the intelligence agencies have launched an attack on the Freedom of Information Act and the public's access to governmental records, forcing EPA, OSHA, and all other agencies to reduce their publication and distribution of information to the public. According to John Leslie:[55]

> I claim, without qualification, that the efforts today throughout the government to cut public information and public affairs activities are based not on a desire to save money, but are a cynical attempt by this administration to cover up efforts to destroy programs and services people want and need.

The business community's offensive against both worker and environmental protections is a response to the economic squeeze. Before-tax profits, which averaged 13 to 14 percent during the 1960s, dropped to 9 percent in the late 1970s.[56] It is also a reaction to successful efforts by workers and environmentally-concerned citizens to force the government to alleviate pressing social problems, and to do so in ways which increase political and economic democracy. Consequently, corporate antilabor and anti-environment activities of the past decade have had two central goals: to change government policy in ways which improve profitability; and to undo the progress made by workers and other citizens in demanding, winning, and exercising their rights to increased participation in business and government. Profits and prerogative: the same basic concerns which have traditionally motivated business leaders still guide their actions today.

The Reagan administration's policies have made it easier for business to achieve its goals. But the latest drive to weaken labor and environmental protections originated with the leadership of American industry a decade before Reagan's election. This assault is not restricted to changing government policies. Some of the fiercest attacks on labor rights and protections are taking place at the bargaining table.

Since the mid-1970s employers have been demanding contract concessions on wages, benefits, and work rules. Unions in the automobile, steel, rubber, newspaper, meat packing, mining, trucking, smelting, railroad, and airline industries have all agreed to significant concessions. As a long-time employee of Firestone Rubber said, "I've worked here for 30 years, and they want me to give up what we've won in the last 20."[57] For the first time in the postwar period, unions are not asking for more: they are primarily trying to protect what they have.

The corporate campaign against labor law reform made it clear to trade unionists that the postwar period of labor-management accommodation had ended. In contract negotiations since then employers have driven home the point, threatening plant closings and industrial collapse, in order to realign the labor-management balance of power in their favor. As MIT labor specialist Harley Shaiken said in early 1982, the corporate goal is "to ratchet down gains that workers and unions had won through years of collective bargaining."[58]

In certain industries labor concessions—along with major changes in investment and management practices —may be needed to help prevent a firm or a plant from closing down. But demands for "give-backs" have spread across industries and firms which are not in financial trouble, but simply want to capitalize on the antilabor momentum. For example, Kahn and Company, a subsidiary of Consolidated Foods Corporation, told its workers in late 1981 that without substantial wage, benefit, and seniority concessions, the company would shut down and move. Kahn and Company, which had been located in Cincinnati for 99 years, demanded that workers forgo all scheduled wage and cost-of-living increases for five years, give up four holidays and two weeks vacation, agree to cuts in seniority rights, and accept a change in the wage scale which would start new employees at $2.67 less per hour. Neither Kahn nor its parent company claimed these concessions were needed because the plant was losing money. Consolidated had a 1980 net income of $150 million and the company indicated that Kahn was a profitable member of its corporate family. Knowing this, members of Local 7 of the United Food and Commercial Workers voted overwhelmingly to reject the company's demands. In this instance, workers knew the company was financially secure. William Winpisinger, president of the Machinists, is concerned that some unions may be giving in too easily: "People are walking into these things without doing the tough, methodical work it takes to find out whether an employer is as bad off as he says."[59]

In this period of defensive battles against what Douglas Fraser called "one-sided class war," environmental and occupational health protections are extremely fragile.

Employers and their allies claim that "regulatory relief" can help save the nation from economic decline. They charge—as they have done regularly throughout the past decade—that environmental regulations must bear significant blame for the inflation, productivity, innovation, and growth problems which plague the economy, and which they claim are keeping people jobless. Workers who feel their power slipping, who see union membership shrinking, and their clout at the bargaining table disappearing, may feel they have no choice but to agree. And when workers view environmental protection as an obstacle to their jobs, the likelihood increases that, on their employers' behalf, they will attack environmentalists for standing in the way of economic recovery.

The next five chapters examine the evidence employers use to substantiate their claims that regulation harms the economy. The evidence is often weak, sometimes nonexistent. But the myths persist. That the evidence does not hold up must become common knowledge. Otherwise, as jobs, health, and the environment come under increased attack, the use of job blackmail and its economic variations will divide workers and environmentalists further —to the benefit of neither and to the detriment of the nation.

6
Inflation and Environmental
_____ Regulation

The United States entered the 1980s with a persistent
inflation rate of about 10 percent. Inflation—the annual
rate of increase in prices—rose steadily from 2.2 percent
in 1965 to 5.9 percent in early 1971.[1] The price jolts of
1972–73, primarily caused by oil price hikes and crop
failures, drove the rate of increase in the Consumer Price
Index (CPI) above 10 percent in 1974 for the first time
since 1947.[2] When national industrial activity collapsed
during the 1975 recession, the inflation rate dropped to
5.5 percent for three years. But sharp increases in food,
housing, and energy prices in 1978 sparked a new surge.
For a short time in early 1980, the Consumer Price Index
was rising at an annual rate of 18 percent.[3]

With each big jump in inflation during the 1970s,
government and business leaders tried to cast regulation
as the villain. President Ford publicly identified regulation
as inflationary when he ordered federal agencies to prepare Inflation Impact Statements (IIS) for all major
regulations. According to James C. Miller, III, who was

assistant director of Ford's Council on Wage and Price Stability and who had major responsibility for administration of the program, "Worry over inflation—and over regulation as a factor contributing to it—was the major reason the [IIS] program was established."[4]

When inflation began to climb again in 1978, the Democratic administration of Jimmy Carter also pointed a finger at regulatory costs. Robert Strauss, President Carter's special counselor on inflation, asserted:[5]

> Both simple logic and complex economic analysis suggest that the vast federal, state and local government regulatory apparatus that has grown over the last decade adds significantly to our rate of inflation.

The Reagan administration followed suit. Vowing to "gain control" of the "inflationary monster," President Reagan postponed more than 100 pending federal regulations during his first month in office.[6]

Although the connection between rapidly rising inflation and increased regulation of health and environmental quality in the 1970s appeared obvious to these policymakers, the economic evidence does not substantiate their claims. Environmental protection requirements have been at most a minor factor in the past decade's inflation. The same Data Resources, Inc., (DRI) analysis which evaluated the employment impact of federal air and water pollution legislation also examined the inflationary effects of these laws. The study concluded that between 1970 and 1980, federal environmental legislation added an annual average of 0.3 percentage points to the Consumer Price Index. In 1980 when the CPI rose to a steep 13.4 percent, only 3 percent of the total increase was attributable to pollution control legislation.[7]

There is no reason for environmental and occupational health regulations to have large direct effects on inflation or on other indicators of national economic performance.

Environmental control expenditures by industry and government account for a small fraction of GNP—less than 1.6 percent in 1979.[8] According to former Council on Environmental Quality economist Paul Portney, although annual spending on pollution control—before the Reagan administration's shift in environmental policies—had been growing faster than the economy as a whole, federally-induced environmental spending is still likely to constitute less than 2.5 percent of GNP by 1988.[9] Expenditures which constitute such a small percentage of national economic activity cannot play a significant role in either spurring or—when cut back—slowing inflation.

Moreover, the small inflationary impact of environmental regulations is only a short-term problem. Inflation reflects price increases from one year to the next. If a firm invests in new pollution control equipment one year, that expenditure is considered inflationary by economists. But once the equipment is installed and paid for, there is no further inflationary effect from its purchase. As American companies complete their transition to improved pollution control as legislated by the Clean Air Act, Clean Water Act, Toxic Substances Control Act, OSHA, and other existing laws, the one-time inflationary impact of pollution control spending will disappear.

It is impossible to justify cutting environmental and health regulations on the grounds that "regulatory relief" will reduce inflation. According to Gus Speth, former chairman of the Council on Environmental Quality, "If the inflationary impact of these [environmental] requirements could be reduced by 20 percent, a substantial relaxation, the CPI's increase would be restrained 0.1 percent."[10] James Miller, III, conceded this in the premiere issue of *Regulation,* published in July 1977:[11]

These officials [who were responsible for President Ford's Inflation Impact Statement program] were under no illusion that the program would *solve* the inflation problem or even make a substantial contribution for that matter. In contrast with fiscal and monetary policy, regulation has a very small effect on the rate of inflation.

REGULATION CAN BE ANTI-INFLATIONARY

Just as Gross National Product is a loaded measure, so is inflation as traditionally defined. Strictly speaking, an annual price increase is inflationary only if it is not accompanied by a corresponding increase in value to consumers and society. If changes in the way a good or service is produced increase its value as much as its cost, then the price hike is not inflationary. In fact, if the added value is greater than the added cost, the price increase is *deflationary*. But, as with other economic analyses, "nonmarketable" goods such as health, aesthetics, and the quality of community and worklife are not factored into these calculations.*

When a copper smelter is retrofitted to reduce the emission of arsenic and other pollutants, the company generally passes along to consumers the cost of installing, operating, and maintaining the new equipment. The rising prices are accompanied by increased value: the value to workers and local residents of cleaner air, safer drinking water, reduced exposure to hazardous wastes, lower cleaning bills, less illness, and lost work time. But these benefits go unmeasured. What is really a different and larger basket of goods, one which includes the

*The accepted definition of which price increases are inflationary and which are not depends on who does the defining. For example, when a major corporation builds fancy new headquarters, this is rarely considered inflationary, even though cost will be transferred to consumers in higher prices. Similarly, when Esso and Humble spent $100 million to change their name and logo to Exxon, the *Wall Street Journal* did not complain that the expenditure was "nonproductive" and "inflationary."[12]

protection of health and environment, is treated by economists as if no value had been added.

The authors of the DRI study acknowledge that their analysis "does not include the value of improvements in the quality of life which are not priced by the market system."[13] This study and others like it assess the impact of health, safety, and environmental regulation on the economy without considering the increased benefits—less disease, fewer accidents, and the preservation of the natural environment for the sustenance and enjoyment of future generations. In other words, these economic analyses of environmental legislation do not take into account the very improvements that the laws were designed to bring about.

This is a serious failing, and it produces erroneous conclusions. Imagine an "economic analysis" of our democratic process which did not place a value on "nonmarketable" democratic freedoms. Billions of dollars are spent so people can vote, be represented, stay informed of governmental activity, participate in public hearings, exercise and defend their constitutional rights. Democracy adds significantly to the cost of doing business—without increasing the market value of goods and services. Is democracy inflationary? A study which considered nonmarket values irrelevant would probably conclude that democracy is indeed inflationary and that it places America at a competitive disadvantage with countries which do not spend billions on the democratic process.

Neglect of health and environment by business and government can actually *add* to inflation: the costs of *not* regulating can be enormous. Hooker Chemical Company chose not to spend approximately two million dollars in 1952 to properly dispose of toxic wastes it was storing in upstate New York. Instead, Hooker simply covered the waste site with earth. Twenty-five years later, 82 different compounds, 11 of them known to be carcinogenic, began seeping through the soil into the backyards and basements of the 100 homes and the public school that had been built over Love Canal. Over $87 million in local and federal funds have already been spent on cleaning up.[14] Personal injury lawsuits, medical bills, and additional cleanup will cost many more millions of dollars in years to come.

Proper disposal could have been achieved at a much lower cost had it been mandated by law. As Dr. Samuel S. Epstein has explained, "The true costs of *failure* to regulate are excessive and inflationary."[15]

THE ROOTS OF INFLATION IN THE 1970s

In looking for explanations of the last decade's rising inflation rate, three factors deserve far more attention than environmental and health protections. One is the skyrocketing cost of energy since 1973. The price of a barrel of oil jumped from $1.77 to over $34 in seven years. Americans must spend much more than they did in 1973 to buy the exact same product. As MIT economist Lester Thurow wrote in 1979:[16]

> The impact of energy prices on inflation is enormous. With 10 percent of our consumption going toward the direct and indirect purchase of energy, a 100 percent increase in the price of energy generates a 10 percent rate of inflation all by itself.

A second inflationary pressure has been the ability of giant firms to set prices at will: "The abuse of market power in concentrated industries," economists John Blair and Gardiner Means call it.[17] In industries dominated by a few large corporations—including some of the most heavily polluting industries such as steel and automobiles, and industries most heavily dependent upon government contracts such as aerospace and defense—managers tend to raise prices not in direct relation to supply and demand but rather in response to profit targets they themselves set. The crucial determinant of price is not cost or demand, but how high profits can go before another firm will be able to enter the industry and compete.[18] In periods of economic slowdown, when prices would normally drop, the power of major corporations to dictate prices is highly inflationary.

Military spending has been a third important factor in the inflationary spiral of the past 15 years. In competitive industries firms strive to maximize profits by minimizing production costs. In the military economy, however, different rules apply. There is only one buyer—the Pentagon. And usually there is only one selected supplier with which the Pentagon negotiates. Cost-plus contracts eliminate the risk of loss: consequently, military suppliers have no incentive to be efficient. In fact they have an incentive to *maximize* their production costs.[19] This spurs inflation by forcing up the cost of materials, parts, engineers, and skilled mechanics in the civilian and defense sectors of the economy.

Between 1965 and 1973 spending for the Vietnam War was the principal cause of steadily rising inflation. The Reagan administration's planned peacetime military buildup of $1.6 trillion over 5 years can only be more inflationary. As Robert Muehlenkamp, executive vice-president of the National Union of Hospital and Health Care Employees, District 1199, told a labor gathering in 1981:[20]

> Increased military spending cannot be other than inflationary. Let's say you pay workers to build a bomb. When they go to the store, they can't bring it home for lunch. It's inherently inflationary.

In 1976 the Congressional Joint Economic Committee concluded that environmental, health, and safety regulation had little impact on inflation. The JEC report listed four reasons why there should be no general relaxation of regulatory standards for the sake of reducing inflation:[21]

    (1) the benefits of this investment clearly exceed the costs;

    (2) their contribution to inflation has been and will continue to be minimal;

    (3) delays will only increase the ultimate costs of environmental cleanup; and

    (4) the stimulative effects of these expenditures on employment in the near future will be beneficial to the economy.

What was true in 1976 is still true today. Health, safety, and environmental regulations have protected and benefited society without contributing significantly to inflation. Blaming regulation for inflation—like linking regulatory protections to increased unemployment—is a scare tactic without foundation. It, too, is blackmail designed to weaken support for government protection of public health and safety.

7
Productivity and Environmental _____Regulation

"It is clear why productivity has caught on as a slogan," wrote management consultant and Yale sociologist Rosabeth Moss Kanter in the *New York Times*. "It appears more neutral as a goal than 'profit'; 'raising productivity' sounds as if it benefits all of us, whereas 'making money' does not."[1]

Productivity has indeed caught on. This measure of how efficiently firms use labor, natural resources, capital, and energy has become a symbol of American economic decline and a preoccupation of those looking for the road to recovery. According to Kanter, productivity "has become an economic rallying cry, without enough agreement on what it means, how to measure it, what to do about it—or whether it is, in fact, the central issue in economic recovery."[2]

There is agreement that the average rate of productivity growth in the U.S. has slowed significantly since 1965. Between 1948 and 1965 productivity in the private sector grew an average of 3.2 percent each year. From 1965 to 1972 the annual rate dropped to 2.3 percent and between 1972 and 1978, it slowed further to 1.2 percent. Since then productivity has been fairly level.[3]

There is also agreement on why productivity is important. When output per work hour rises, there is more wealth to be divided among workers and owners as wages and profits. Without rising productivity, somebody must lose. For owners to increase their profits, workers must give back some wages or benefits. For workers to win higher wages, the company has to take money from stockholders. Owners and managers prefer that these distributional questions not arise. Continually-increasing productivity reduces conflict over the distribution of wealth.

There is little agreement, however, about what has contributed to declining productivity growth, what the drop means for the economy and for American workers, and what should be done about it. Warnings of a "productivity crisis" first surfaced in the early 1970s when foreign competition combined with Vietnam War inflation to squeeze profits.[4] At the time, employers focused the blame on workers, particularly on the influx of young, untrained, and undisciplined workers into the industrial workforce. More recently employers and government leaders have blamed environmental, health, and safety regulations for much of the decline in productivity growth. Vice President George Bush, in announcing the Reagan administration's first regulatory "hit list," spoke of the "regulatory relief our economy needs—to reduce costs, to reduce inflation, to increase productivity and to provide more jobs."[5] Whatever the "productivity crisis" may be about, business and the Reagan administration are clearly using it as one more excuse for rolling back regulations and attacking organized constituencies which challenge their autonomy.

THE IMPACT OF REGULATION

Although productivity is a measure of how efficiently the various factors of production are used, it is almost exclusively measured in terms of labor productivity: the amount of goods and services produced per hour of human effort. Productivity in the manufacture of cardboard boxes, for instance, is measured by dividing the total number of boxes produced in a year by total hours worked. Rising productivity means that it takes fewer labor hours this year to produce the same number of boxes as last year.*

Regulation can definitely cause a drop in productivity, as it is traditionally defined. Installing pollution control equipment may not increase production, but it often requires more employees to operate and maintain the equipment. Since more work hours produce the same level of output, productivity declines. Extracting resources in safe and environmentally-sound ways may require that the pace of production be slowed. This also results in a drop of measured productivity. Management does not welcome this change: lower measured productivity means higher labor costs.

In 1978 Edward Denison, a senior economist at the Brookings Institution, concluded that pollution abatement and occupational health and safety costs contributed significantly to declining productivity growth. He estimated that without the environmental, health, and safety legislation passed after 1967, productivity would have been 1.4 percent higher in 1975. Because his was the first detailed study on the impact of regulation on productivity —and probably because the study concluded the impact

*Calculating labor productivity is far from an exact science. Adjusting for inflation and for changes in the mix of products being made, measuring productivity in construction and service industries, and even determining the number of hours worked by employees, require creative and imaginative methods. There is much room for error.

was significant—Denison's work received wide publicity. Articles in the *Washington Post,* the *National Journal,* and *Forbes* lauded both Denison and his findings.[6]

However, Denison's study has been criticized by many economists. He assumed that a firm's pollution control expenditures would replace other capital investments dollar-for-dollar (that is, a million dollars more for air pollution control would mean a million dollars less in new production equipment which could raise productivity). But a Data Resources, Inc. (DRI) study found this is rarely the case. In the early 1970s pollution-control spending replaced only 33 to 40 percent of plant and equipment expenditures. Adjusting Denison's calculations to account for this finding alters his conclusions dramatically. His estimate of the productivity-growth slowdown attributable to environmental and worker health and safety regulation may have been 2 to 3 times higher than the data warranted. In its own study DRI concluded that cumulative productivity loss due to environmental regulation was about half Denison's estimate.[7]

In a follow-up study Denison himself noted a drop in the impact of regulation on productivity growth for the years 1975 through 1978. He estimated that because of reduced industry spending in those years (compared to 1973–75) for air, water, and solid waste pollution abatement, environmental regulations were responsible for an annual decline in productivity growth of only 0.08 percentage points.[8] Given the continued and even worsened general slowdown in the nation's productivity growth in those years, Denison's findings suggest that other, more significant factors were at work. By mid-1980 Denison acknowledged the productivity problem was more complex than he had originally assumed. He told a gathering of financial analysts, "Perhaps we have been experiencing a situation where everything went wrong at once."[9]

Robert Crandall, also a senior economist at the Brookings Institution, compared the performance of key "pollution control-impacted industries"—including paper, chemicals, petroleum refining, steel, copper, cement, grain milling, aluminum, and electric and gas utilities —before and after 1973. In his initial study Crandall found that after 1973, when the economic effects of required pollution-control spending became noticeable, productivity growth in these industries dropped precipitously.[10] However, when Crandall updated this study, including changes in energy use and in capital investment as possible explanatory factors, he found that in none of the 36 industries he studied was pollution control a statistically significant variable. Crandall decided it was difficult to make "definitive conclusions" from his analysis.[11]

In 1979, at the request of the Congressional Joint Economic Committee, University of Wisconsin economist Robert Havemen and two colleagues distilled and summarized the results of several dozen studies on regulation and productivity:[12]

> It seems clear that environmental and health/safety regulations bear some responsibility for poor productivity performance, but little evidence exists to suggest that as much as 15 percent of the slowdown can be attributed to them. A reasonable estimate would attribute from 8 to 12 percent of the slowdown to environmental regulation.

This summary raises more questions than it answers. What does an 8 to 12 percent slowdown mean? Is it undesirable? How does it affect workers? How does it affect management and stockholders? And would deregulation have any significant impact on productivity growth?

WHAT DO THESE FINDINGS MEAN?

When productivity statistics are broken down by specific sectors and industries, the trends are easier to explain. Between a third and a half of the total productivity slowdown has occurred in only three industries—mining, construction, and utilities.

Utility productivity growth dropped from 6.3 percent between 1948 and 1965 to only 1.0 percent for 1972–77. The reason is clear: Productivity in the utility industry depends primarily on the growth of electricity and gas use. No matter how much electricity is being produced, the power grid and all its switching stations, generators, and other costly equipment must be maintained. The number of workers required to maintain the system varies little with demand. When demand falls, productivity falls. The rate of electricity growth has dropped from around 7 percent a year before 1973 to 3 percent since 1973. Projections are for even further declines. The result will be less pollution, reduced natural resource waste, lower capital and operating costs—but also lower productivity.

The decline in construction industry productivity growth is, in large part, a measurement problem. Statistics indicate that in 1980 construction workers produced 20 percent less in an hour than they did in 1967. But few observers accept this: a February 1980 *Business Week* article on the construction industry was titled, "A Productivity Drop that Nobody Believes."[13] More likely the decline reflects a shift from large-scale standardized construction like massive highways, power plants, and water projects to more varied, custom-built office buildings and single-family homes. Declining productivity in construction is due, in large part, to changes in what is being built. Ironically, lower measured productivity in construction may also reflect more efficient use of materials, since construction productivity is usually determined by calculating the amount of materials used per worker.[14]

Mining productivity rose rapidly until 1968, but then

fell sharply and has been consistently negative since 1971. According to economist Lester Thurow, 80 percent of the decline in mining productivity is attributable to oil and gas well drilling—an activity which most people do not even consider mining. Energy price increases have encouraged the drilling of wells which yield less oil per well and which must be drilled deeper. Productivity declines because it takes more work hours to produce a barrel of oil.[15]

Mine safety and environmental regulations, according to Thurow, are responsible for some of the slowdown in mine productivity—as much as 20 percent. Installing mine roof bolts and better ventilation systems slows the pace of underground production. Restoring stripmined lands takes more work hours per ton of ore than leaving open pits and slag heaps.

But is this bad? Close to 100,000 workers have been killed in coal mines in this century, and there have been 1.7 million lost-time injuries since 1930.[16] More than 4,000 coal miners die of black lung disease each year. Yet the mines were noticeably safer in 1981 than before passage of the federal Coal Mine Health and Safety Act in 1969. Annual mining deaths had been cut in half. Increased mine inspections (which are being reduced by the Reagan administration) resulted in a noticeable drop in injuries and deaths. More than 300 miners died to produce 500,000 tons of coal in 1968; in 1981, 153 miners were killed while production had risen to 802,000 tons.[17] The slowdown in mine productivity is a slowdown in death and injury in the mines. It is an indication that the legislative effort to halt over a century of unsafe and unhealthy speed-up has been fairly successful. Although U.S. mines are *still* more dangerous than mines in most industrialized nations, they are much safer now than 20 years ago. For miners and their families that is a great improvement—and one that was worth fighting for.

THE PROBLEM WITH PRODUCTIVITY STATISTICS

Like so many other standard measures of economic performance, productivity statistics have a critical shortcoming, as the discussion of mining shows. Productivity measures *quantity* only. No distinctions are made between a steel beam produced in a plant that does not pollute the air and the same beam made in a highly polluting factory. An improvement in design which lowers operating costs to consumers, such as the development of more fuel-efficient car engines, is irrelevant to productivity statisticians. American Productivity Center chairman C. Jackson Grayson, Jr., has conceded that "while [expanded health services, industrial safety, environmental protection, and economic security] are socially desirable, they have not contributed to productivity as conventionally measured."[18]

Increasing the number of steelworkers on coke oven crews reduces cancer-causing emissions. It also contributes to lower productivity in the steel industry, since more people are doing "nonproductive" work. But many workers challenge the limited values implicit in the prevailing definition of productivity. According to Joe Frantz of Steelworkers Local 1010:[19]

> Clean air and clean water are products just like steel. The company does not view them as products. But people working to create clean air and clean water view themselves as productive.

Productivity statistics, like GNP and the CPI, are neither neutral nor objective concepts. Rosabeth Moss Kanter concludes, "Inevitably, there is a political aspect to it: Who controls the definition of acceptable output?"[20] In our society, Joe Frantz and other workers have little control over that definition.

PRODUCTIVITY AND JOBS

A 1981 *Wall Street Journal* survey of top managers at 221 firms found that 80 percent see "poor management" as the key reason for lackluster productivity growth.[21] Short-term planning calculated to increase next quarter's profits and productivity often preclude investment strategies that can spur more long-term productivity gains. Speed-ups which push workers faster and layoffs which force fewer workers to do the same amount of work can raise productivity temporarily. But pushing workers to the limit usually backfires: people get exhausted and begin to resist; absenteeism and accidents increase; quality control declines; added layers of hierarchy are required to police the worksite.

One way to increase productivity which employers have historically resisted is to move toward full employment. Lester Thurow has estimated that about 30 percent of the decline in productivity growth can be attributed to federal anti-inflation policies which have held the demand for jobs and services below what the economy could produce, leaving idle productive capacity—and high unemployment.[23] Movement toward full employment would decrease idle capacity, increase productivity, and create jobs. This would certainly be more constructive than rolling back health, safety, and environmental regulations.

Regulation is only one small factor in declining productivity growth. And in those industries where regulation has had a noticeable impact on productivity, the result has been better health, safer workplaces, cleaner environments, and improvements in the quality of life. Moreover, inadequate pollution controls and safety laws can, in the long run, lead to lower productivity. Over 1.7 million lost-time injuries in the coal mines since 1930 mean a lot of lost productivity. In 1977, according to EPA, air pollution was responsible for 7 million worker sick days.[24] An agricultural industry which is losing valuable topsoil is also sacrificing productivity. A fishing industry which harvests in polluted oceans, bays, and streams has the same problem. Decreasing basic environmental and health protections in the name of productivity is a mistake. As EPA's first administrator William Ruckelshaus said in relation to the Clean Water Act:

> It seems reasonable to me to spend less than one percent of the federal budget and two-tenths of one percent of the Gross National Product over the next several years to assure future generations of the very survival of the Gross National Product.

Those who blame productivity problems on environmentalists are primarily interested in manipulating public opinion to protect their particular interests. Productivity measures what employers value most: how much output they are getting from their investments. It does not take into account environmental quality, workplace safety, and job security. Weakening regulatory protections will not raise productivity, will not reduce inflation and will not put people back to work. The United Electrical Workers came to this conclusion in 1977, when the union resolved to "reject the productivity hoax and vigorously fight to protect jobs, rates and earnings, and the health and safety of members, which are increasingly being threatened by speed-up."[25]

8
Innovation and Environmental
_____Regulation

Are environmental, health, and safety protections sapping the innovative vitality of American industry? "There is now evidence that [U.S.] product innovation has either leveled off or declined in many industries," concluded a 1977 Office of Management and Budget report.[1] A National Science Foundation study warned that "the rate of growth of patentable ideas of international merit seems to be expanding at a greater rate in other countries than in the United States."[2] Many corporate critics see a direct correlation between declining industrial innovation and increased government "interference." As Gould, Inc., contended in a 1978 newspaper ad, "Since regulations tend to be so complex, comprehensive and contradictory, meaningful technological development isn't likely to happen."[3]

SOME REGULATIONS ARE MEANT TO SLOW INNOVATION

There is no doubt that regulation can impede and even prevent the introduction of new industrial products and processes. That is often the purpose of regulation: to force improvements and the consideration of alternatives, and to prevent some dangerous products from reaching the market. The 1976 Toxic Substances Control Act (TSCA) authorized EPA to test existing and new chemicals that may present an "unreasonable risk" of injury to public health and the environment. The Consumer Product Safety Commission (CPSC) was established to make sure new products did not present too great a danger to consumers. These laws were enacted in response to clear public demand for protective governmental action. By placing public health and safety above management's desire to introduce new substances and products at will, Congress affirmed the public's right to such protections.

Restrictions on industry mandated by TSCA and other legislation may make some innovation more complicated and costly. A firm entering the pharmaceutical industry must be prepared to pay for toxicological testing, premarket testing, and increased paperwork. This may discourage competition and reduce the pressure on existing firms to generate new products. Regulatory requirements can also slow innovation by forcing management to spend more time meeting standards and less time with long-range planning. Such added responsibility may be an obstacle to the development of new products or processes, especially in small firms.

A Denver Research Institute study of 200 innovative ideas which failed to make it into general use found that government regulations played a significant role in 12 percent of the failures.[4] The most common complaints about regulation focused on stringent standards, long or costly testing, and uncertainty about whether and how the regulatory requirements might change. However, the vast majority of attempts at innovation failed for reasons unrelated to regulatory rules: the public would not buy the product; the technology was inferior to competitors' or just did not work; the cost of developing the product or reaching markets was prohibitive; management made serious mistakes.[5]

The choice that Congress and the public have made is not, as some would claim, between innovation or no innovation. Thousands of new chemicals are still introduced each year. There is no shortage of new foods or drugs, new pesticides or new toys. Rather, the choice is between safe innovation and dangerous new products and processes. Some products—such as thalidomide or Kepone or PCBs—should never reach the market. Others should be carefully restricted in their availability and use. This is not capricious interference, but responsible public policy.

REGULATIONS CAN SPUR TECHNOLOGICAL ADVANCES

While critics try to blame government regulation for stifling industrial creativity, they often fail to acknowledge that health, safety, and environmental protections have spurred dramatic—and profitable—product and process innovation. Ruth Ruttenberg, senior economist for OSHA during the Carter administration, surveyed the 1980 annual stockholder reports of some of the nation's largest industrial firms. She found many of the companies were doing quite well in one of the fastest growing sectors of the economy—the pollution control industry. Not surprisingly they seemed far more eager to tell stockholders about their new successes than they were to admit to the general public that regulation was boosting their profits. Ruttenberg concluded:[6]

> In short, health, safety and environmental regulation has produced new lines of profitable products, by-products, substitutes and even windfall profits for manufacturers. The internal corporate literature singing the praises of new products and processes developed in response to regulation contrasts ironically with the op-ed advertising bemoaning the burdens of the same regulation.

Regulatory requirements shake up a firm. New personnel are hired to solve managerial and engineering problems. Their efforts to streamline and rework production processes can lead to important, and sometimes unexpected, improvements. Regulation can stimulate an entire industry by creating new markets and opportunities. Before EPA banned highly toxic PCBs, there was only one manufacturer, and there were no substitutes for major uses. Since the ban, competing firms have developed alternatives to PCBs. And a number of companies have invented processes for decontaminating PCB-laced electrical oils.

Health, safety, and environmental regulations have pushed many companies into profitable and efficient new ventures. For example, when petroleum refiners were forced to reduce the lead content of gasoline, they developed improved catalysts and a more efficient, less costly, refining process. Searching for ways to reduce sulfur emissions in the steel industry, American Cyanamid perfected a new carbide-based desulfurizing agent. The company took advantage of sharply increased demand and doubled its manufacturing capacity for calcium carbide.[7] These are only two examples. According to a 1978 National Science Foundation-funded study, one-third of all companies surveyed indicated improvements resulting from regulatory changes.[8]

Many European firms have worked hard to find ways to reduce waste, protect the environment, and cut the costs of energy and materials. Michael G. Royston noted the following examples in the *Harvard Business Review*:[9]

- Ciba-Geigy, a Swiss chemical company, has been able to reduce pollution emissions by as much as 50 percent by changing its manufacturing process and recycling water and solvents. The company saves an estimated $400,000 a year.

- The Sacilor steel works in Gandrange, France, now recovers its iron dust residues and saves $200,000 a year.

- North British Distilleries, near Edinburgh, has turned its highly-polluting still-bottom wastes into a nutritious animal food. Annual return on investment has been over 100 percent.

The United States has its own share of environmental improvement innovations:

- Hercules Power spent $750,000 to reduce its discharge of solids into the Mississippi River and has saved $200,000 a year.

- Dow Corning has found that recovering chlorine and hydrogen, previously lost to the atmosphere in refining silicon, can reduce operating costs by $900,000 a year. Dow invested $2.7 million in equipment and is producing a 33 percent annual return-on-investment.

- The Chairman of the Hanes Dye and Finishing Company has testified that "cleaning up our stacks and neutralizing our liquids was expensive, but in the balance we have actually made money on our pollution control effort. EPA has helped our bottom line."[10]

- The best known example of industrial innovation spurred by environmental regulation is the Minnesota Mining and Manufacturing Company's "Pollution Prevention Pays" program. Since 1976 3M has pursued an aggressive program of pollution control at its facilities in 15 different countries. Production has expanded by 40 percent since 1976, while the annual pollution load has dropped significantly. Each year 3M has eliminated an average of 112 million tons of air pollutants, 2,800 tons of water pollutants, 870 million gallons of wastewater, and 4,500 tons of sludge and solid waste. The company has saved nearly $100 million since 1975 in lower energy and operating costs, reduced pollution control equipment purchases, and retained sales of products which might have been forced off the market because they were being produced in an environmentally unacceptable manner.[11]

Clearly government environmental, health, and safety protections can both encourage and inhibit innovation. Ultimately, however, a firm's level of innovation depends on management's ability to adapt to changing economic and social conditions. Most companies have made the commitment to adjust to new health and environmental laws. Some have turned the new business conditions to their advantage. Those which have resisted change have suffered for their lack of foresight. In the summer of 1978 Ford Motor Company's chief economist John Deaver told a Senate committee that fuel economy standards should be eased so that cars would not have to be downsized. Congress disagreed and retained existing standards, leaving the industry no choice but to build smaller cars. It was a good thing it did: by late 1979 Americans were buying cars with fuel efficiency at or above the standards mandated by law. Had the standards been relaxed as Ford wanted, few of the new cars Americans were buying would have been Fords—or GMs or Chryslers. As Douglas Fraser, president of the United Auto Workers, explained, "If it hadn't been for the regulation, there'd be no X-car, no Omnis and Horizons"—the small cars whose sales kept Detroit from total collapse in the late 1970s.[12]

The more creative a firm's management, the more likely it will be to develop new products, processes, and markets. American management, however, seems to shy away from such creativity—and then blame government for its own failings. As Professors Robert Hayes and William Abernathy of the Harvard Business School have explained, "Conditioned by a market-driven strategy and held closely to account by a 'returns now' return-on-investment oriented control system, American managers have increasingly refused to take the chance on innovative product/market development."[13] Xerox President David T. Kearns agreed in a May 1980 guest editorial in *Newsweek:*[14]

> Lay the blame on management . . . for providing workers with old and outmoded production equipment that might have served their grandfathers well, but can't do the job today. American industry no longer seems willing to risk its resources on capital investments for the future. . . . Indeed, America's dismal economic record during the last decade reflects, more than anything else, an astonishing decline in research and development, innovation and productive risk-taking.

Kearns concluded, "American businessmen, in fact, are hiding behind government regulations."[15]

9
Is Environmental
Protection Worth
_____the Cost?

Less than one month after his inauguration, President Reagan issued an executive order requiring analysis of both the costs and the benefits of all major new proposed regulations (except those related to military and foreign affairs). In late March 1981 OSHA announced that it was reviewing its 1978 cotton dust regulations to determine whether the costs to industry of limiting worker exposure were greater than the benefits to workers and society. The Supreme Court upheld the cotton dust standard a few months later, noting specifically that Congress had not required cost-benefit analysis as justification for worker health standards.* But OSHA administrator Thorne

---

*Writing for the 5-3 majority, Justice William J. Brennan, Jr., said that, in creating OSHA in 1970, Congress "chose to place pre-eminent value on assuring employees a safe and healthful working environment. Congress itself defined the basic relationship between costs and benefits by placing the 'benefit' of worker health above all other considerations save those making attainment of this 'benefit' unachievable."[1]

Auchter was undaunted: the Reagan administration, he explained, might still choose to subject both new and existing regulations to such analysis.

At first glance it seems perfectly reasonable to calculate the costs and benefits of a proposed government regulation. Such analysis, it seems, can only improve government policymaking. But as the Reagan administration was well aware when it rushed to require expanded use of cost-benefit calculations, cost-benefit is not simply a neutral, mathematical tool. As currently conducted, cost-benefit analysis is a biased exercise —and its bias is decidedly antiregulation. After three years as EPA administrator under President Carter, Douglas Costle acknowledged, "I became uncomfortably aware that antiregulation players in this cost-benefit game were using a loaded deck: both economic history and economic method stacked the cards in their favor."[2]

The deck is loaded because regulatory costs to industry are routinely exaggerated while the benefits to society are just as routinely underestimated. Cost-benefit analysis is more a politically sensitive procedure than a scientifically rigorous one. A Congressional subcommittee investigating the strengths and limitations of cost-benefit analysis suggested "the most significant factor in evaluating a cost-benefit study is the name of the sponsor."[3] Dr. Baruch Fischoff told the subcommittee that researchers can—and do—manipulate their methodologies and data to produce the results they want. He told of one researcher in a Washington-based consulting firm who freely admitted revising the study on which he was working:[4]

> The analysis didn't come out the way my client wanted it. However, there's quite a bit of wiggle room in almost all of the cost, benefit and probability assessments. I'm just going to alter each a little bit until I get

the right conclusion. No one will notice and my client will be happy with this justification for what he was going to do anyway.

EXAGGERATED COST ESTIMATES

Most estimates of regulatory compliance costs are based on data provided by the very firms which stand to lose or gain from regulatory action. The temptation is great for these firms to protect their interests by padding cost estimates. Many have succumbed. According to Dr. Samuel S. Epstein:[5]

> Detailed analyses of the track record of industry, with reference to a wide range of case studies in the workplace, consumer products, and the general environment, provide ample documentation for the overall thesis that information provided by industry, or by individuals and institutions with direct or indirect industry connections, should be suspect until proven otherwise.

When OSHA was considering its vinyl chloride standard, for example, an industry-sponsored study estimated compliance costs at between $65 billion and $90 billion. When the standard went into effect, the industry complied at a total cost of well under a billion dollars. Surprised members of Congress asked vinyl chloride producers for the raw data on which the estimate was based. They were told that all the data had been destroyed.[6]

Such "advocacy estimating" by industry sources is common:

- In 1978 Energy Secretary James Schlesinger used industry's figures on the cost of reducing carcinogenic beryllium dust and fumes to warn that beryllium producers would have to close if forced to clean up their plants. National security would be threatened if that happened, stressed Schlesinger, since beryllium is used in making nuclear weapons. The estimate given Schlesinger was $150 million. The actual cost was between $3.7 and $4.6 million.

- In 1974 the Swedish automaker Volvo wrote to the U.S. General Accounting Office pointing out that most data released by U.S. auto companies on regulatory compliance costs were "aimed purely at resisting regulation."[7] And why not? The companies could not lose by inflating their cost estimates. If they successfully resisted the regulation, their goal was achieved. If not, the companies could pass the inflated costs to the consumer, publicly blaming the government while pocketing the difference. For example, the auto industry attributed a $25 increase in 1968 car prices to the government-mandated installation of shoulder harnesses. An investigation conducted by Senators Walter Mondale (D-MN) and Warren Magnuson (D-WA) revealed that the actual cost of harnesses was under $5 per car. The auto industry made an extra $100 million in profits that year—and blamed the price hike on government regulation.[8]

- The Securities and Exchange Commission found that U.S. Steel kept two sets of books on EPA compliance costs. The lower set of figures was for investors, the higher was for the media and the public. B.F. Goodrich and several other rubber companies used a similar strategy when they warned the public and the courts that the OSHA benzene standard "would bring the tire manufacturing industry to a standstill," while assuring stockholders that "if presently proposed standards are adopted, it is expected that such standards will have no material adverse effect on operations."[9]

There is another reason why industry's estimates of compliance costs are unreliable and inflated. Businesses usually calculate their "regulatory burden" by figuring the cost of meeting regulatory requirements with currently available technologies. But every industrial engineer knows there is a "learning curve" to industrial innovation and over the years more efficient and less expensive ways of producing goods, or, in this case, abating pollution, are usually discovered. Former OSHA senior economist Ruth Ruttenberg has explained:[10]

> Industry makes the assumption of current technology being used forever for cost estimates. The fact is, many OSHA and EPA standards are technology-forcing, in that they make industry come up with newer and cheaper means of compliance.

These cheaper innovations are rarely factored into industry estimates of regulatory costs.

In 1978 Murray Weidenbaum and Robert DeFina, colleagues at the Center for the Study of American Business, projected that federal regulations would cost the nation $102.7 billion in 1979. And they claimed that "the great bulk of the regulatory budgets (approximately four-fifths) is devoted to newer areas of social regulation, such as job safety, energy and the environment, and consumer safety and health."[11]

Weidenbaum and DeFina were wrong on both counts. But their exaggerated figures are regarded as gospel in the business community, among government officials, and even among many members of the media. The cost estimate, which one critique has labeled "ideological arithmetic," is cited by opponents of regulation as proof the nation is paying too much for what it is getting. It is important to understand what is wrong with this inflated figure—and why Weidenbaum and DeFina's work has been called a "questionable procedure" by the Congressional Research Service.[12]

The $102.7 billion estimate was derived by taking the federal administrative budget for regulatory agencies ranging from EPA and OSHA to the Coast Guard, the Customs Service, and the Library of Congress Copyright Office, and then estimating the compliance cost to industry of meeting federal guidelines. Weidenbaum and De-

Fina calculated 1976 federal regulatory costs at $3.1 billion and industry compliance costs at $62.9 billion, 20 times the administrative costs. To arrive at the $102.7 billion projection for 1979, they applied the same multiplier of 20 to the $4.8 billion federal regulatory budget for that year. Because of inconsistent rounding-off of figures, Weidenbaum and DeFina arrived at a projection of $97.9 billion compliance costs which, when added to the $4.8 billion administrative costs, totals $102.7 billion.

The errors in this exercise are numerous, leading to a figure which Queens College economist William K. Tabb charges is "grossly exaggerated."[13] He questioned whether some agencies included in the study, such as the Army Corps of Engineers and the Customs Service, should be considered regulatory agencies at all. And he also concluded that many of the regulatory agencies which Weidenbaum and DeFina claimed were in the "newer areas of social regulation," such as the Federal Energy Regulatory Commission and the Drug Enforcement Administration, did not belong in that category. Tabb calculated the 1979 federal administrative cost for social regulatory functions (EPA, OSHA, the Consumer Product Safety Commission, and other health, safety, and environmental regulatory agencies) to be only $1.778 billion —less than half Weidenbaum and DeFina's estimate.

Weidenbaum and DeFina generalized from their 1976 figures that for every dollar a federal regulatory agency spends, business must spend $20 to comply. They chose this multiplier of 20 even though they admitted readily that "there is no assurance that larger budgets for federal regulatory agencies generate a constant multiplier effect on the private sector."[14] William Tabb calculated the EPA multiplier to be 12:1 rather than 20:1. Weidenbaum and DeFina's choice of the higher figure results in an inflated estimate of business compliance with social regulation.

Weidenbaum and DeFina made another inaccurate generalization. Over one-third of their estimate of busi-

ness costs came from a calculation of regulatory paperwork requirements. They incorrectly assumed that the
paperwork required by different agencies is roughly the
same. They failed to acknowledge that *over half* the
federally-required paperwork in 1979 consisted of daily
program logs and operational and maintenance logs required of radio and television by the Federal Communications Commission—neither of which has anything to do
with social regulatory functions of protecting environment, safety, and health. In contrast to Weidenbaum and
DeFina, William Tabb has estimated that EPA, OSHA,
the Consumer Product Safety Commission, and the National Highway Traffic Safety Administration account for
only a little more than *1 percent* of all federally-required
paperwork.[15]

Criticism of his work has not changed Murray Weiden-
baum's cavalier approach to cost-benefit research. In
November 1981 Weidenbaum and other members of the
Reagan administration confidently announced that their
"regulatory reform" work had already saved the public $6
billion. Weidenbaum said he got the figure from Vice
President Bush's Task Force on Regulatory Relief, but a
Task Force staffer told the *Washington Post:*[16]

> The estimates . . . are not precise. We cannot be sure
> they have been derived in a consistent manner. For
> example, in some instances, there is double counting.
> . . . The actual savings could be lower.

IGNORING AND UNDERESTIMATING BENEFITS

The Vice President's Task Force was quick to exaggerate the costs of regulation to industry. But neither the
Task Force nor anyone else in the administration even
tried to estimate the costs to society of injuries, illnesses,
and deteriorating quality of life resulting from regulations

rescinded or postponed. They were not interested in calculating the benefits of regulation. It may seem like common sense to say that costs of regulation are only one-half of any cost-benefit equation. Yet the two most widely-quoted studies of the burden of environmental, safety, and health regulations *ignore benefits entirely.* Such an omission led one Congressional subcommittee to conclude that Weidenbaum and DeFina's study "by itself is meaningless."[17] The authors of the 1979 Business Roundtable survey of health, safety, and environmental spending of 48 *Fortune 500* corporations tried to justify omitting benefit estimates, explaining that by focusing only on regulatory costs, "The Business Roundtable hopes to stimulate additional efforts to identify the benefits to society obtained by high cost regulations."[18]

Basing regulatory policy on one-sided analyses which calculate costs but ignore benefits is like "measuring the pain of a hypodermic needle without considering the value of the injected penicillin."[19] Or as Mark Green has suggested, it is like General Motors telling stockholders how much it costs to make cars without letting them know how much revenue resulted from sales.

In fact, the public benefits of environmental regulation have been significant. The major environmental protection laws of the 1970s sparked the reversal of over a century of industrial, municipal, and public pollution. Today, as a result of the national effort and expenditures on pollution control, fewer people die or become ill due to unhealthy air and water. Fish and animals have returned to areas once too polluted to sustain life. The tide of environmental degradation has been reversed.

According to the 1980 annual report of the Council on Environmental Quality, air quality improved steadily in the 1970s. National annual average concentrations of carbon monoxide, sulfur dioxide, and total suspended particulates (smoke and dust) all decreased between 1973 and 1978.[20] An examination of 23 urban areas between 1974 and 1978 found the number of days in violation of National Ambient Air Quality Standards dropped 18 percent.[21] From 1972 to 1978 ambient levels of particulates were reduced 10 percent, sulfur dioxide 17 percent, carbon monoxide 35 percent, and lead 26 percent.[22] This progress occurred during a period when industrial production and automobile mileage increased. According to Douglas Costle, "Simply staying even would have amounted to a considerable achievement."[23] This view was confirmed by the National Commission on Air Quality's 1981 report:[24]

> While it is impossible to state precisely what pollution levels would be if the [Clean Air Act] had not been passed, it is clear that for a number of pollutants, the level of emissions would now be several times as great in many areas.

National indicators of water quality have not improved as markedly in the past five years as those for air quality. But as the 1980 CEQ annual report concluded, "The fact that the nation's surface water has not deteriorated despite a growing population and an increased gross national product is an accomplishment for control efforts."[25] Despite limited national water quality gains, there are numerous examples of significant improvements in the quality of particular rivers and streams. In 1967 the Izaak Walton League described Oregon's lower Willamette River as a "stinking, slimy mess, a menace to the public, aesthetically offensive and a biological cesspool."[26] The Buffalo River in 1968 was[27]

> so polluted by steel, chemical, petrochemical, and coke plants around Buffalo that its ink-black, oil-fouled surface broke into flames on four separate occasions. It was poisoned by oil spills, phenols, iron and unoxidized steel wastes, and by nutrients from municipal wastes.

Today every "unsafe for swimming" sign on the Willamette River is gone and fish are back in increasing numbers. The river looks and smells cleaner. In 1972 a fish was caught in the Buffalo River—the first in 30 years. Slowly the river has been changing in color and oxygen levels and has been attracting new aquatic life.

Wastes dumped from pulp and paper, nylon, acrilonitrile, and PVC production facilities in the Escambia Bay off the Florida coast became so concentrated in the 1960s that fish kills "had to be measured in miles."[28] Commercial harvests of shrimp dropped from 902,000 pounds in 1968 to 236,000 in 1969 and 52,000 in 1970.[29] Since 1970, however, spurred in some cases by citations from the Florida Department of Pollution Control, most industries have drastically reduced their waste discharges. Today, according to EPA, "the waters are getting cleaner, the fish kills are smaller in size and less frequent, and shrimp and oysters are gradually beginning to come back."[30]

Worker health and safety protections have also saved lives and limbs—despite both industry and government attempts to undermine OSHA. In the 1960s the workplace accident rate climbed steadily. Between 1972 and 1978, however, total injuries and illnesses in American workplaces dropped from 10.9 to 9.4 per 100 workers—a decrease of about 14 percent.[31] During the same period, reported deaths due to on-the-job accidents dropped about 20 percent, with even greater declines in high hazard industries, such as construction and metal manufacturing, where OSHA had targeted its efforts.[32] In 1980 the total injury and illness rate fell to 8.7 per 100 workers. The total workdays lost per 100 full-time workers dropped from 67.7 in 1979 to 65.2.[33] A study of illness and injury in the chemical industry, conducted by the New York-based Council on Economic Priorities (CEP), is consistent with the Bureau of Labor Statistics' national figures. In the first eight years of OSHA standards, according to CEP, the recorded rate of injuries and illnesses among chemical workers dropped 23 percent—and at an annual cost of only $140 dollars a worker.[34]

Environmental and occupational health regulations have improved human health, saved lives, and added to the quality of life for most Americans. These improvements have saved the nation billions of dollars over the past decade. In late 1979 the Council on Environmental Quality published a thorough evaluation of the benefits of both air and water pollution control, prepared by economist A. Myrick Freeman, III, of Bowdoin College. After reviewing the existing benefits studies, Freeman prepared his own summary conclusions:

- Total national benefits from reductions in air pollution since 1970 range between $5 billion and $51 billion. The most reasonable estimate for 1978 is $21.4 billion.

- These $21.4 billion in benefits from reduced air pollution include: $17 billion from reduced pollution-related death and injury; $2 billion in reduced soiling and cleaning costs; $700 million in increased agricultural production; $800 million in increased property values; and $900 million in prevented corrosion.

- Total national benefits from water pollution control projected for 1985 (assuming strict enforcement of the Clean Water Act) range from $6.5 billion a year to about $25 billion a year. The most reasonable estimate, according to Freeman, is $12.3 billion a year. Half that is attributable to cleaner water for recreation uses. Much of the remainder is attributable to benefits such as improved property values, enhanced beauty, and reduced damage to ecological systems.[35]

Freeman emphasized that his estimates were conservative: he did not consider the benefits to other countries, specifically Canada and Mexico, from reduced U.S. air pollution. Nor did he try to estimate benefits from the prevention of air quality degradation that would have occurred if the 1970 Clean Air Act had not been passed. In estimating water pollution control benefits, Freeman also excluded the benefits from lowered levels of toxic substances in our nation's waterways and drinking water, an omission which he admitted "might understate considerably the true water pollution control benefits to be enjoyed in 1985."[*][36]

But even with these qualifications and omissions, Freeman's study shows pollution-control spending has been a wise national investment. When compared to CEQ's estimate of \$16.6 billion in air-pollution control costs for 1978, Freeman's mid-range estimate of air-quality improvements worth \$21.4 billion for 1978 indicates a net savings of \$4.8 billion. Although the projected mid-range benefits of water-pollution control in 1985 are lower than CEQ's cost projections for the same year, it must be remembered that this estimate does not include the undoubtedly considerable health and agricultural benefits of eliminating chemical contaminants from water supplies.[37]

A major 3-year study commissioned by EPA and conducted by environmental economists at the universities of Wyoming, Southern California, and New Mexico also concluded that existing air-pollution controls have clearly benefited the nation and the economy. The Wyoming study found pollution-related illness and discomfort led to a much higher rate of sick days and lost work hours than was previously thought.[38] In 1977, for example, air pollution caused an estimated 13,000 deaths, seven million sick

---

*The few economists who have analyzed the benefits of water pollution regulation have adopted an extremely narrow definition of benefits. They calculate recreation, property value and drinking water benefits, but ignore benefits from cleaner water for commercial fishing and agriculture and, as Freeman noted, benefits from preventing or reducing the levels of toxics in the nation's water.

days, and 13 million days of restricted activity, affecting 40 million people (or roughly 1 of every 5 Americans).[39] The authors of the study concluded that if pollution levels across the country were reduced by 60 percent, the annual benefit to the nation in reduced death and illness would be about $40 billion. Since pollution levels dropped an average of 12 percent between 1970 and 1977, EPA officials estimated that benefits of air-pollution control during those seven years averaged $8 billion a year. CEQ estimated that controlling pollutants from stationary sources in 1977 cost $6.7 billion. So EPA officials concluded that the benefits of controlling air pollution outweighed the costs on an annual basis by more than a billion dollars.*[40]

Mark Green and Norman Waitzman, in their 1981 study *Business War on the Law,* calculated that the regulations of five government agencies vigorously criticized by Murray Weidenbaum—OSHA, EPA, the National Highway Traffic Safety Administration, the Food and Drug Administration, and the Consumer Product Safety Commission—provided greater economic benefits to society than they cost. Green and Waitzman calculated that regulations issued by these agencies cost government, industry, and the public $31.4 billion in 1978 but generated benefits worth $37.1 billion—a savings to the economy of $5.7 billion.[41]

---

*EPA is the only government agency which devoted much effort to calculating the benefits of regulation. Yet even during the Carter years, EPA took little initiative, despite Douglas Costle's public pronouncements that such studies were critically important. One year into the Reagan administration, several benefit studies commissioned under Costle remain unpublished and their findings unissued. It is unlikely that Reagan's EPA will initiate new efforts to improve benefit-study methodologies and estimates. Since major benefits studies require several years of data collection and analysis, there is little prospect that significant new work will be available in the next few years to counter the inflated cost studies being churned out by business and the Reagan administration.

ECONOMICS AND VALUES

It is not easy to quantify the benefits of regulation. Economists undertaking each of the studies summarized had difficulty placing dollar values on all the benefits of environmental, safety, and health protections. How does one measure the benefit of an accident which does not occur or a vista which remains unspoiled? How can an accurate estimate be made of cancers prevented?* What is the extent of society's loss when a species is wiped out? What is the value of a human life? It is difficult to calculate the dollar value of lives saved, injuries and diseases prevented, pain and suffering avoided, jobs preserved and created, joy and pleasure made possible. The summarized benefits studies attempted to develop methodologies and data; but so many aesthetic and health benefits cannot be accurately priced that even these estimates should be considered incomplete, and, therefore, too low.

The costs of regulation are large because environmental and health damage has been so extensive; but, as has been shown, the benefits are also impressive. The claim that health and environmental regulations have been burdensome to the nation is not justified by the available evidence. This does not mean that specific regulatory actions or policies might not prove inappropriate or that regulators might not be able to do their jobs more efficiently. It would be surprising if a complex regulatory framework, in place for only a few years and under constant political and legal assault, could not be made more efficient and cost-effective. But people who quote

---

*For most toxic substances, the health danger at different levels of exposure is unknown. This leads to wildly fluctuating estimates of risk. In a National Academy of Sciences study of cancer risk from drinking one can of diet soda a day, estimates varied from an increase of 1/10,000 of a case of cancer each year to 364 additional cases a year. The highest estimate was 5 million times greater than the lowest—not a very firm basis for policymaking.[42]

only industry-supplied cost figures, who tally unreliable figures and glibly tell the public that regulation costs over $100 billion a year, while failing to acknowledge the significant social and economic benefits from these regulations, are misleading the public for political purposes. They are using cost-benefit analysis not as a policy tool but as a political weapon.

Cost-benefit analysis as currently practiced helps industry reduce policy questions to a comparison of two columns of figures. This simplistic preoccupation with numbers enables opponents of regulation to obscure a central issue: who benefits from regulation and who pays? Environmental, safety, and health regulation involves a redistribution of rights. It also shifts costs from workers and the public to firms responsible for causing the damage. Redistributing costs, benefits, and rights is the reason regulatory protections were initially enacted. Because of this, Steven Kelman, a Harvard professor and former Federal Trade Commission official, has concluded that " . . . since the costs of injury are borne by its victims and the benefits are reaped by its perpetrators, simple cost/benefit calculations may be less important than more abstract conceptions of justice, fairness and human dignity."[43]

Business leaders and their advocates who argue for expanded use of cost-benefit analysis rarely want to discuss justice, fairness, and the rights of individual workers and citizens. In fact may critics of regulation do not care whether benefits actually do outweigh costs. They are concerned about *industry's* costs and *industry's* benefits. From their perspective the less the public—and its policymakers—know about regulatory benefits to society and the more they know about regulatory costs to industry, the better. In 1979 when David Stockman was still a Michigan Congressman, he argued vigorously against the development of more and better benefit studies. Stockman urged the National Commission on Air

Quality, of which he was a member, "to narrow the range of estimates on damages prevented and benefits gained by air pollution control." While he seemed to be comfortable with the cost estimates of Murray Weidenbaum, Stockman was clearly troubled by efforts to calculate the positive results of regulatory policies—and by the impressive findings of such studies. "I suggest we establish a more modest agenda for benefit analysis," he argued, "and discourage the quest for an absolute number to be used by a congressional committee or subcommittee."[44]

This "more modest agenda" has been achieved. In the coming years the public will be bombarded by studies of the cost of regulation to industry but will hear nothing about the cost to society of not regulating. The Reagan administration's insistence on cost-benefit analysis has little to do with concern for efficient regulatory policy. It has everything to do with creating a seemingly scientific and economically sound rationalization for attacking worker and environmental protections.

10
The Mythology
_____ of Growth

Herbert Meyer, an associate editor of *Fortune* magazine, wrote in 1979:[1]

> Today, the environmental movement is little more than a weapons system in the war against progress. Nearly all of the . . . groups that comprise this movement are now working to prevent even the smallest amount of growth from taking place anywhere in this country.

Meyer concluded, "To the environmentalists and their allies . . . , people are apparently less important than caribou, grizzly bears, walruses and sea lions."[2]

Meyer may have been purposely overstating his case, but he is not alone in charging that environmentalists oppose the expansion of economic activity, and by extension, the creation of new jobs and better lives for poor and working Americans. The charge that environmentalists are antigrowth and antiprogress has often been made by business and government leaders. Many of the past decade's heated confrontations between environmentalists, labor, and minority organizations have focused on this alleged conflict between "growth" and "no-growth."

At a 1976 meeting of labor and environmental activists held at the United Auto Workers' educational center, Thomas Donahue (who was then assistant to AFL-CIO president George Meany, and is now AFL-CIO secretary-treasurer) explained that the labor federation's support for all kinds of energy development, including nuclear power, was "essentially a question between growth and no-growth."[3] That same year, civil rights and labor activist Bayard Rustin, director of the A. Philip Randolph Institute, wrote in the *New York Times*:[4]

> Many of those who profess concern about unemployment and poverty also actively support the concept of limiting economic growth in order to protect the environment. That notion, if translated into conscious policy, would measurably worsen the nation's—and the world's—economic plight. And its promoters would bear the responsibility for having shattered the hopes of those who have never had a normal role in the world economy, among whom the darker-skinned people of the world rank most prominently.

Business and government officials have exploited these fears that environmental protection is an obstacle to economic progress. Energy Secretary James Schlesinger told members of the AFL-CIO at their 1977 national convention:[5]

> We can have nothing to do with that kind of unrestrained attitude which is anti-growth. Restraining growth means restraining the growth of jobs. It means unemployment. It means the failure to provide the best part of the American way of life to a growing number of our citizens.

This strategy has often worked. Posing stagnation and economic collapse as the inevitable consequence of environmental protection, employers and their supporters have been able to isolate the environmental movement from the civil rights and labor movements. Some labor and minority leaders have even actively mobilized their constituents against environmental laws, goals, and organizations. But the charge that environmentalists are against progress and broader economic opportunity is untrue. In their efforts to equate growth with jobs and slower growth with higher unemployment, proponents of this charge make several false generalizations: (1) opposition to one kind of growth is the same as opposition to all growth; (2) growth inevitably creates jobs; and (3) growth automatically generates jobs for those who need them.

WHAT IS "GROWTH"?

"Growth" is a word so vague and imprecise as to be almost meaningless. And the contention that one can only be *for* growth or *against* growth is absurd. Yet opponents of strict environmental protection laws frequently attack environmentalists for being "antigrowth" and congratulate themselves for being "progrowth."

James Schlesinger and Herbert Meyer know very well there are many different ways for an economy to provide the jobs, services, and goods which people want and need (and which are, after all, the goals of economic activity and growth). Schlesinger, a seasoned cabinet official, understands how federal tax, grant, and procurement policies can be used to spur an industry's growth or block its development: he himself helped shape national policy which encouraged the development of nuclear power over solar energy and conservation. Encouraging one kind of development over another is not "antigrowth": rather, it is a statement of priorities and goals. Different growth patterns reflect different values. Some investment strategies create more jobs than others. Some create better jobs. Some produce more pollutants, disease, and environmental destruction. Some development and growth is of primary benefit to wage-earners; some yields the greatest benefit to stockholders and investors. What mix of industries and business enterprises is preferable? Who should decide? These are important questions for any society to consider. And they are questions answered daily, intentionally or not, in the choices made by government and business planners. They are also questions which corporate leaders prefer not to open to public debate.

Worker and citizen participation in decisions on national industrial policy and development priorities increases the likelihood that business leaders may have to reveal their clear preference not for "growth," but for a particular kind of growth: development which enables existing firms to pursue the highest profits with the least interference from government or the public. Corporate planners would rather not acknowledge that the public might have values and criteria different from their own. They would rather not publicly discuss alternative patterns of development which might challenge their ways of doing business.

Consequently, advocates of continued corporate dominance use "growth"—just as they use inflation, productivity, cost benefit, GNP, and other concepts—to divert public attention from fundamental social choices about the use of resources, capital, and labor. They try to shape the public debate to their advantage. All growth benefits society, they argue. Growth is precisely what business provides. Therefore anyone who opposes or questions particular corporate production or investment decisions opposes growth—and, of course, jobs and expanded economic opportunity.

As workers and minorities watched environmentally unsound development projects being blocked and heard business and government officials blaming environmentalists for various economic problems, many began to believe environmental activism ran counter to their interests. Environmentalists walked right into the trap. They were quick to oppose what they considered unwise development, but somewhat slower to propose alternative ways of investing capital to meet people's needs and to put people to work. Despite the urging of some of its leaders, the environmental movement was slow to use its organizational strength in support of labor, civil rights, and other struggles for social and economic justice. Consequently labor and minority representatives sometimes accepted the growth/no-growth formulation uncritically. By so doing, however, they were not necessarily furthering their own priorities—more employment, higher incomes, and better quality of life for working people and the poor. All too often they were simply adopting corporate priorities which emphasized neither employment, equity, nor quality of life.

GROWTH AND JOBS

One of the most hotly-debated issues in the 1970s was the relation between energy and jobs. Until the latter part of the decade, oil and utility companies insisted there was a direct correlation between energy growth and economic growth. They claimed that if they were not permitted to expand energy production freely, the economy would falter and countless jobs would be lost. The Chase Manhattan Bank concluded in 1974 that "an analysis of the uses of energy reveals little scope for major reductions without harm to the nation's economy and its standard of living."[6] Former administrator of the Energy Research and Development Administration Robert Seamans frequently declared that each worker in the United States consumed a certain number of barrels of oil performing a day's work. He warned that for every decrease in oil imports without substitution of domestic energy supplies, people would be thrown out of work.[7]

Today it is clear that these warnings were unfounded. Given the huge amount of energy wasted daily in this country, increased economic activity is *not* contingent upon increased energy consumption. In 1979 GNP rose 3.2 percent. Energy consumption rose only 0.8 percent, down significantly from the 2 to 5 percent annual energy growth of previous years. John Lichtblau, executive director of the Petroleum Industry Research Foundation, told the *New York Times,* "People were saying this kind of thing [reduced energy consumption] would lead to a stagnation of the economy, but it hasn't."[8] The National Academy of Sciences' Committee on Nuclear and Alternative Energy Systems concluded in 1978 that a "major slowdown in [energy] demand growth can be achieved simultaneously with significant economic growth."[9] Increasing the efficiency of energy use through conservation and design improvements is not a strategy for *no-growth,* as was so often claimed, but rather for a *different kind* of growth—one which increases economic efficiency, creates jobs, improves public health and environmental quality, while reducing the need for energy.

Similarly the correlation which Americans have been led to believe exists between economic growth and jobs is neither so simple nor so sure. In the past 30 years manufacturing production and profits have certainly increased. But as AFL-CIO President Lane Kirkland acknowledges, "There has not been a net job added to manufacturing since the Korean War."[10] In many industries automation has resulted in dramatic increases in productivity-per-worker and total output—while reducing the number of production workers. In 1947 there were more than 600,000 people employed in the basic steel industry. In 1979 twice as much steel was being produced by fewer than 400,000 workers.[11] American manufacturing is following the same path as farming and mining, becoming a highly automated capital- and information-intensive industrial sector which will provide an inadequate number of new jobs.

The United States and other industrialized nations have entered a new period of rapid automation, based on the introduction of sophisticated small computer technologies in both factories and offices. *Business Week* has estimated that roughly 45 million jobs, almost half the jobs in the American economy, could be affected by microchip-based automation in the next few years.[12] For many the result will be unemployment. A study conducted at Carnegie-Mellon University concluded that computer-run robots could perform seven million existing factory jobs (45 percent of which are covered by union contracts).[13] The UAW estimated in 1980 that because of robots, programmable machine tools, and other new technologies, even if annual domestic car sales rose 1.8 percent through 1990, the union's membership would still drop by over 20 percent—a permanent loss of 200,000 jobs.[14]

The most rapid employment growth in the past 20 years has been in finance, insurance, services, and government —industries which provided an incredible 92 percent of all new jobs between 1966 and 1973.[15] Microchip computer technologies are likely to cause extensive job loss in these industries. Several European studies have predicted massive job losses in this decade because of office automation. One report to the President of France warned that 30 percent of the jobs in the French banking and insurance industries could be eliminated by computers during the 1980s. An unpublished study by Siemens Corporation has suggested that 30 percent of West German office jobs could soon be automated.[16]

New growth industries and jobs will be created because of the boom in microchip computer technologies. However, as Colin Norman of the Worldwatch Institute has emphasized, there will also be employment reductions in segments of the electronics industry. A micro-electronic circuit can replace hundreds of moving parts in cash registers, telephones, and other equipment. One West German company which manufactures Telex machines replaced 936 separate parts with one microprocessor. It now takes the firm's workers 18 hours instead of 75 hours to produce each Telex. The result? Increased productivity and fewer jobs.[17] A report published by a committee of the International Organization for Economic Cooperation and Development concluded:[18]

> Electronics has dramatic growth prospects ahead in the next decade. If this industry expects to achieve such growth with little or no increase in employment, then the question may be asked: where in the manufacturing sector is . . . growth in employment to come?

The United States and other industrial nations may be facing a future where productivity is once again rising, sales and profits are increasing, but employment in many industries is either steady or dropping. Growth without jobs, already the case in agriculture and many industries, may spread rapidly across the entire economy.

Some people believe enough new industries and jobs will be created in the coming decades to offset technology-related job loss. Even these observers, however, realize the kinds of jobs which will be available in 1990 will be very different from today's. Trained, skilled, manufacturing jobs—generally high-wage jobs in unionized shops —will continue to disappear. Technical and professional positions will increase, although the work is likely to become more routine and employers' control of professional staff more extensive as a result of computer-set work pacing. The need for low-skill, low-pay workers in service jobs which cannot be automated will increase. So will the disparity between the shrinking number of "good" jobs and the growing number of "poor" jobs with low wages, inadequate benefits, and little job security. Both skilled and unskilled unemployed will face increasingly bleak job prospects—unless a concerted effort is made to retrain and reemploy them. But providing jobs for all who need them requires national planning for jobs *and* growth, as well as democratic participation in that planning. Business leaders and their supporters, therefore, do what they can to direct worker frustration toward visible "obstructions to progress" like environmentalists. They do so even though creating new jobs and improving the mismatch between available jobs and workers' skills will benefit poor and working Americans far more than will any weakening of environmental, safety, and health protections.

GROWTH AND PROFITS

By maintaining the fiction that all economic growth leads automatically to more jobs and a richer society, corporate leaders justify pursuit of their private goals in the name of the public good. They use "growth" as yet another variation of job blackmail. Steel companies assert environmental regulations are slowing growth and causing job loss, even though jobs in steel production were disappearing due to automation before the 1970 Clean Air Act. Oil and utility companies claim energy growth is needed to improve minority employment. Yet their own record in hiring minorities is weak: in 1978 minorities accounted for only 10 percent of total employment and less than 3 percent of managerial staff in oil and gas extraction and in the electric power industries.[19]

Despite its claims, corporate America's chief interest in growth has little to do with jobs or distributional equity.

Growth is important because it means more profits and more power—and because it means the reduced likelihood that large segments of the American public will risk challenging corporate dominance. At a 1975 federal policy summit on inflation, Marina von Naumann Whitman, a member of President Nixon's Council of Economic Advisors, emphasized that the best way to solve economic problems was to keep the economy growing. According to Carl Pope, then executive director of the League of Conservation Voters:[20]

> The beauty of the traditional focus on growth, she said, was that it avoided the question of who got how much of the benefits. No one, in her words, knew "exactly whose ox was going to be gored."

Constant expansion of the GNP obscures this country's unequal distribution of wealth and benefits by enabling most people to have more. When the economic pie is growing people are more hopeful about their prospects and less concerned that relatively few people still get the lion's share. Continued growth, like continued gains in productivity, makes it easier to satisfy workers' wage demands and owners' demands for higher profits. Slower growth means increased pressure from both workers and owners and a greater likelihood of public interest in determining what is growth and who gets what.

GROWTH, JOBS, AND ENVIRONMENTAL PROTECTION

In 1972 British economist H.V. Hodson wrote, "Growth is no panacea for the familiar ills of the economic body, like unemployment or business fluctuations."[21] He added that "with less growth there could be more employment, for instance through a switch of national resources from advancement of industry to creation of jobs."[22] The advancement of industry does not guarantee the creation of sufficient jobs. If Americans want a full employment economy, one which provides jobs for all who want to work, the goal cannot be left to private industry. Full employment requires public involvement in national planning for jobs and government responsibility for creating worthwhile jobs for the unemployed. Without these a private sector eager to keep its labor costs low will continue to generate insufficient jobs at inadequate wages.

If Americans want both full employment *and* protection of workers' health and environmental quality, then growth strategies incorporating those goals must be developed democratically. Gus Speth, former chairman of the Council on Environmental Quality, has suggested a long list of projects which would create jobs while also protecting and improving environmental quality:[23]

> A pro-environment policy could direct federal jobs programs and other economic measures toward environmentally-beneficial activities, such as rebuilding the railroads, recycling programs, the improvement of solar energy measures, the rehabilitation of old but sound buildings and so forth, and away from interstate highways, interceptor sewers, massive water resources projects and energy developments—all environmentally risky and capital-intensive activities that stress limited natural resources and require large amounts of equipment . . . and only a few relatively highly paid workers.

The problem is not finding worthwhile things to do. As MIT economist Lester Thurow concluded in his book, *The Zero-Sum Society:*[24]

> Anyone with even a little imagination can think of many things that could be done to make this society a better one. If the option is between idleness and work, the choice is simple. As long as any useful output is

produced, a work project takes precedence over involuntary unemployment.

The difficulty is turning good ideas into reality in the face of intense opposition from a business community which is unwilling to share its power, prerogative and wealth. The first and critical step in this process is overcoming job blackmail in all its variations so people are not afraid to challenge business and government and to demand investments which meet their needs.

It has been done. Throughout American industrial history people have resisted job blackmail and forced both business and government to abandon their threats and false choices. Persistence has required taking risks and believing that more is won by fighting than by giving in. But people have been successful in banding together to expand democratic rights and protections—on the job and in their communities.

Understanding why certain claims of job loss are merely threats is only part of the battle. People must also challenge those threats and force change. The previous five chapters have shown the weakness of current anti-regulatory arguments and how they amount to different forms of job blackmail. The next section examines the long history of struggle against job blackmail and for protection of workers, public health, and the environment—struggles which have overcome false choices like "growth/no-growth" and "jobs versus the environment."

PART III

Learning from History

INTRODUCTION:
Two Movements, Shared Goals

Economist Richard Edwards has referred to the workplace as "contested terrain," where workers and employers each try to shift the balance of power in their favor. Labor-management relations have always been adversarial. Workers have fought for rights and protections which increase their control over their work and share of the profits. Employers have insisted on controlling the workplace—and the worker—as much as possible.

The workplace, however, is not the only "contested terrain." The environment is also a battlefield where the interests of producers and citizens collide. As was shown in Part I, employers resist environmental and public health protections much as they do labor protections, and for the same reasons: to maintain tight control and to protect their profits and their competitive position.

Struggles to defend both human and natural resources from unrestrained industrial production have had much in common. From the early years of rapid industrial growth following the Civil War, people have stood up to employers and fought to limit the exploitation of workers and the environment. Although these battles were usually fought

153

by different people, often from different social classes, the goals were the same: greater democratic participation in economic and political decisions, changes in national priorities and values, improvements in the standard of living and the quality of life.

Both the labor and environmental movements have organized broad popular support for their demands. They have mobilized time and again to force business to recognize, and the federal government to codify and enforce, the right to organize unions, the right to safe workplaces, the right to clean air, clean water, and the preservation of wilderness and wildlife.

Both movements have had to contend with determined opposition from employers who wanted to maintain business as usual, whatever the social costs. Invariably they were confronted with job blackmail. In 1976 Leonard Woodcock told a gathering of trade unionists and environmentalists that corporate blackmail on health and environmental issues was nothing new:[1]

> The idea that businesses will be driven to bankruptcy if strict environmental standards are adopted is the same tired line that has been brought up again and again since workers first organized to improve working conditions. It was brought up when child labor was eliminated, when the minimum wage was introduced, when Social Security and Unemployment Insurance were developed.

But despite the effectiveness of this "same tired line" and other corporate tactics, the labor and environmental movements have learned through experience that popular activism can achieve great gains, even against corporate giants backed by the government. Both have also learned there are no final victories, only constant struggles to defend and expand previously-won rights and protections.

The histories of labor and environmental struggles— and the similarities between them—are inadequately appreciated today. Although efforts of various disenfranchised and powerless groups to win and maintain new rights and increased shares of the nation's bounty are central to American history, much of this legacy remains unincorporated into the national awareness. This is not accidental: history is generally written from the perspective of the powerful. Americans have been taught that history is a progression of ever-expanding benefits and rights for all. Those whose struggles or fates contradict this view are all too often written out of history, and the lessons of their successes and failures are lost to succeeding generations.

Given the interconnections between employment, health, environment, and equity, and the centrality of each to the well-being of all Americans, it is important for labor and environmental history to be rescued from what historian Herbert G. Gutman has called the "condescension of silence."[2] Labor and environmental activists can learn from the history of *both* movements, since they are part of the same broad, ongoing struggle for greater corporate accountability and democracy.

11
The Struggle for Workplace
_____Rights

Work in America has changed dramatically since the Civil War era when only 1.5 million of the nation's 31.5 million residents were wage-earners. Most people were farmers. Manufacturing was done largely by hand, in small shops or in the home. After the Civil War change came rapidly. Entrepreneurs, many of whom had become wealthy supplying the war effort, used their new riches to build industrial empires of unprecedented scale. Across the nation, machines and factories replaced hand-work and family businesses. People left farms and plantations to find factory work. Millions of immigrants from Europe and Asia joined the burgeoning industrial workforce.

By 1880 only one-third of the labor force consisted of independent property owners or professionals; two out of three workers had become wage earners, working for someone else. Today 90 percent of Americans are dependent upon others for work.

1860–1900: THE RISE OF INDUSTRIAL AMERICA

It is difficult for those who did not fight for the 8-hour day, the minimum wage, unemployment insurance, or the right to organize, to appreciate the intensity of these struggles and the importance of these victories. Yet it was not so long ago when people lacked very basic protections in the workplace. Not until 1935 did Congress formally recognize the rights of most workers to bargain collectively with employers. Strong national child-labor laws were not enacted until 1938. It was only in 1970 that the Occupational Safety and Health Act guaranteed all Americans the right to safe and healthy workplaces.

In the middle and late 1800s, workers had only those rights they demanded and won from their employers. Many workers organized and fought for higher wages, shorter hours, and better working conditions. But their efforts in the nineteenth century were largely frustrated by the awesome economic and political power of their employers. Employers used job blackmail to capitalize on the desperation of most workers who, whether they had a job or not, were never far from starvation. And employers backed up their threats with firings and violence.

Few rules governed the chaotic industrial growth. Entrepreneurs built vast empires by exploiting both natural resources and labor. Child labor was common in coal mines, textile mills, garment shops, shoe factories, and other industries. In southern textile mills, 6-year-old children worked 13-hour days with a 35-minute break for dinner. It was not unusual for 7- and 8-year-old children to work 72 or even 84 hours a week.[1]

In most industries long work hours and low pay were the rule. A typical day for adult textile workers in the 1850s lasted 14 to 16 hours. Brewers worked a 16-hour day, bakers from 14 to 18 hours a day.[2] Miners in the west worked 12 hours a day, seven days a week.[3] The wages received by millions of Americans for their long hours were often insufficient to keep their families from hunger and abject poverty. When workers were injured, they lost their jobs and incomes, usually without compensation. And when employers wanted to fire workers or cut wages, they did just that, leaving workers to bear the brunt of recurring economic downturns.

Workers fought as best they could, organizing strikes, boycotts, and education campaigns to counter employer attacks on their livelihoods and dignity. The first national strike-wave developed in 1877, four years into the nation's first major industrial depression, by a 10 percent wage cut ordered by the Baltimore and Ohio Railroad. Railroad workers in Martinsburg, West Virginia, refused to accept the cut and walked out. The strike spread quickly across Maryland, Pennsylvania, and New York, to St. Louis and Chicago and into the south. It was broken after several months with help from the police and the National Guard.

The exceedingly high unemployment of the mid-1870s helped the railroad companies regain control over their workers. More than three million people were unemployed, and only one-fifth of those who were working had steady jobs.[4] Under these conditions employers could easily find people who were eager to work for any wages. Then, as now, job blackmail was a handy and persuasive weapon. As New York machinist John Morrison told a Senate committee, "if [our employers] know that we open our mouths on the labor question, we are quietly told that 'business is slack' and we have got to go."[5]

In the mid-1880s the economy again collapsed, with predictable results. Hundreds of thousands of people were thrown out of work. With unemployment high, employers cut wages. Once again, desperate and angry workers mobilized.

In 1885 wealthy industrialist Jay Gould cut the wages of shop workers on his vast Southwest System railroad. The railroad men went on strike, threatening to shut down all 10,000 miles of Southwest track. Gould capitulated, agreeing (at least for the moment) to arbitrate all labor disputes and not to discriminate against members of the Knights of Labor, the nationwide labor organization with which many of his workers were affiliated. This was the first time a leading American business had recognized the legitimacy of a workers' organization. The effect was electric. As one historian put it:[6]

> All the pent-up feeling of bitterness and resentment which had accumulated during the two years of depression, in consequence of the repeated cuts in wages and the intensified domination by employers, now found vent in a rush to organize under the banner of the powerful Knights of Labor.

Membership in the Knights soared from 111,000 in July 1885 to 730,000 in July 1886. More than 500,000 people went on strike that year—not just over wages, but also over work organization, hiring and firing policies, the arbitrary power of supervisors, and long hours.[7]

In 1886 workers across the country joined to demand a shorter workday. The 8-hour day had become a key labor demand as early as the 1860s. Workers hoped a shorter work week would alleviate chronic high levels of unemployment by spreading work among more people. The 8-hour day, they reasoned, would improve the bargaining strength of *all* workers by reducing the number of people "waiting at the gate." In 1885 the Federation of Organized Trades and Labor Unions (which became the American Federation of Labor in 1886), frustrated with the failure to win the 8-hour day in state and local legislatures, passed a resolution calling for a general strike:[8]

> It would be in vain to expect the introduction of the eight-hour rule through legislative measures . . .

whose execution depends upon the good will of aspiring politicians or sycophantic department officials.

By the middle of May more than 190,000 workers had walked off their jobs and another 150,000 had marched in cities from Boston to Milwaukee.[9] As a result nearly 200,000 workers won shorter hours (many also won higher wages) in industries such as beermaking, bricklaying, baking, cabinetmaking, cigarmaking, and horseshoeing. One labor correspondent wrote jubilantly of the strike in Chicago:[10]

> It is an eight-hour boom and we are scoring victory after victory. Today the packing houses of the Union Stock Yards all yielded. . . . [People] are wild with joy at the grand victory they have gained.

The euphoria, however, did not last long. A bomb thrown at the conclusion of an 8-hour-day rally in Chicago's Haymarket Square in May 1886 killed one policeman and wounded seventy, prompting a fierce wave of antilabor reaction and government repression. This reaction, combined with persistent high unemployment, undermined the workers' ability to maintain their gains. Of the 200,000 workers who won the 8-hour day in 1886, only 15,000 were still working 8 hours one year later. Given the choice of longer hours or no jobs, workers accepted the longer hours.

Employers and workers began to understand that unions could make an enormous difference in workers' lives. Organized workers were better able to resist threatened and actual layoffs, wage cuts, and other "takebacks." They could also win greater workplace control and a greater share of business profits. Employers responded to the momentum for unionization—as they would in later periods—by trying to break the backbone of the young labor movement.

In 1892 Andrew Carnegie and his manager, Henry C.

Frick, decided to test whether the Carnegie steel empire was strong enough to bust the powerful union of skilled steel workers at its Homestead, Pennsylvania, mill. Carnegie and Frick saw the Amalgamated Association of Iron and Steel Workers as an obstacle to increased production and higher profits. As Frick put it, "The mills have never been able to turn out the product they should owing to being held back by the Amalgamated men."[11] Instead of renewing the union's contract, set to expire in July, they announced an 18 percent wage cut for the 750 Amalgamated members. In July Frick hired several hundred Pinkerton National Detective Agency guards to lock out the union members, whom he knew would not accept the cut. Amalgamated members called a plant-wide strike. On 5 July the Pinkertons arrived. They were met by 10,000 angry workers and local residents. Fighting broke out, forty strikers were shot and nine killed, but the Pinkertons were defeated: they surrendered and left Homestead.

Carnegie kept up the pressure, bringing in trainload after trainload of unemployed strike-breakers. Strike leaders were arrested and tried for treason and murder. As winter approached, the strikers' effort collapsed. Many returned to work, but not as union members. The Amalgamated, which had been among the strongest unions of its time, had been crushed.

Workers paid dearly for the union's defeat. Disorganized and fragmented, they were unable to retain their former bargaining power. Between 1892 and 1907 the daily earnings of highly skilled workers at Homestead *dropped* by 20 percent, while their hours *increased* from 8 to 12.[12]

Two years later another powerful union was crushed, this time with the help of government troops. During March and April of 1894 a majority of the workers at Pullman Palace Car Company outside Chicago joined a new labor organization, the American Railway Union (ARU), led by Eugene Debs. Unlike existing railway brotherhoods, the ARU accepted anyone who worked for any railroad company, not just workers in particular crafts. In early 1894 the ARU struck against James J. Hill's Great Northern Railroad and quickly won a cancellation of threatened wage cuts.

The emboldened Pullman workers presented a long list of grievances to management. The company responded by firing three leaders. Workers walked out. In sympathy, over 250,000 railroad workers struck against all Pullman cars on every railroad line in the country. By late June, according to Debs, "the combined corporations were paralyzed and helpless."[13]

Pullman turned to the United States government for help. Army troops arrived in Chicago on 4 July, ostensibly to keep the mail moving. Two days later the state militia ousted strikers from their positions at the Pullman Works. Debs was arrested on 10 July and the ARU office was wrecked by federal marshalls while troops guarded the trains rolling from Chicago. Striking Pullman workers were replaced by unemployed nonunion workers. George Pullman had successfully defended what he called "the principle that a man should have the right to manage his own property."[14]

1900–1930: CONCENTRATION AND CONFLICT

Employer efforts to extend control over their workforce and the production process itself accelerated in the late 1800s and early 1900s as industrial firms grew from small family-run concerns into huge national corporations. By 1890 large manufacturers like Carnegie, Pullman, the Pabst Brewing Company, and the McCormick Harvesting Machine Company, had taken advantage of mechanization and standardized product design to expand production and employment dramatically. Between 1890 and 1920 American business and financial leaders consolidated their empires. Financier J. P. Morgan turned 165 competing companies into U. S. Steel, which controlled over 60 percent of the national steel market. By 1900 only General Electric and Westinghouse survived in the electrical industry. By 1917 International Harvester, Standard Oil, American Telephone and Telegraph, Alcoa, General Motors, International Paper, and United Fruit had also been created from multiple mergers.[15]

The formation of these giant corporations permanently altered the American economy. Competition was reduced and profits skyrocketed. The centrality of the large corporation in economic and political life was firmly established. Large employers used their size to great advantage —and to the distinct disadvantage of their workers. Employers could outlast strikes by moving production to facilities in other parts of the country (as they can today by moving to facilities in other countries). They had the resources to bring in waves of strikebreakers and to outlast worker resistance. They had the political clout to enlist the aid of government. Employers also used their size and new wealth to introduce more and more machines. These not only speeded production, but also built employee discipline into the manufacturing process, undermining traditional shopfloor knowledge and taking power from workers.

In earlier eras, industrial workers often exercised broad discretion over their own work. Many felt it was *their* responsibility, not their employers', to determine just how a job was to be done. Consider, for example, the reaction of a Massachusetts' machinist who found regulations posted in his shop one day in 1867 requiring all employees to be at their benches in work clothes at the first daily bell and to remain there until the last. He recalled, "Not having been brought up under such a system of slavery, I took my things and went out, followed in a few hours by the rest of the men."[16]

In many industries skilled workers, not management, decided who would use which tools, who would perform what tasks, and even how much would be produced in a day. As enterprises expanded, employers looked for ways to minimize this worker control and to transfer worker responsibility for planning production to management. Frederick Winslow Taylor, who in the early 1900s became chief theorist of what he called the "scientific management" of work, explained:[17]

> [The] foreman and superintendents [who comprise the management] know, better than anyone else, that their own knowledge and personal skill fall far short of the combined knowledge and dexterity of all the workmen under them. . . . They recognize the task before them as that of inducing each workman to use his best endeavors, his hardest work, all his traditional knowledge, his skill, his ingenuity, and his goodwill —in a word, his "initiative," so as to yield the largest possible return for his employers.

By simplifying work tasks management increased its domination over production and, therefore, its ability to generate profits. Workers were left with fewer responsibilities and skills, and a sense they were less essential to production than they had been. Individual workers became largely interchangeable, making it more difficult for employees to disrupt production in order to win workplace demands. Mechanization at Homestead, for example, made it easier for Andrew Carnegie to break the 1892 strike: he replaced skilled workers on strike with inexperienced workers who could be trained relatively quickly to perform simplified production tasks.

Another critical factor in changing employer-employee relations in the late 1800s and early 1900s was the growing fragmentation of the American workforce along racial, ethnic, sexual, and occupational-status divisions. Employers took advantage of the influx of new immigrants, the legacy of slavery, and the tensions between skilled and unskilled workers to keep workers fighting each other. Some employers would bargain only with skilled workers, isolating them from unskilled workers during strikes. Different racial and ethnic groups received different pay and treatment, one group being used to undercut the others. One early historian described an employment office he visited in 1904:[18]

> I saw, seated on benches around the office, a sturdy group of blond-haired Nordics. I asked the employment agent, "How comes it you are employing only Swedes?" He answered, "Well, you see, it is only for this week. Last week we employed Slovaks. We change about among different nationalities and languages. It prevents them from getting together. We have the thing systematized."

As production grew rapidly and employers consolidated their power, work conditions remained oppressive and, in many cases, even deteriorated. In 1910 over 2 million children still worked to supplement family income. Almost one-half of all boys whose hours were reported to the government in 1910 worked 10 hours a day. For many the wages of work were death at an early age. A 1916 study of cotton mill workers in Fall River, Massachusetts, revealed tuberculosis deaths among 15- to 19-year-old male mill workers to be nearly double those of boys the same age who were spared work in the mills.[19]

Long hours were still the norm of industrial employment. In 1908, when nonfarm unemployment reached a peak of 16.4 percent, 92 percent of those people who had jobs worked regular schedules of 48 or more hours a week. Nearly 70 percent of all workers spent more than 54 hours a week on the job.[20]

By the first years of the 1900s occupational accidents and illness had become so common and damaging that the demand for reform spread across all segments of society. The federal government calculated in 1908 that between 15,000 and 17,000 workers were killed annually. One journalist writing in the same year estimated that 35,000 workers were killed and 536,000 injured every year, in a workforce of only 30 million.[21] Thousands of other workers died or became disabled as a result of job-related diseases: stone cutters died of lung disease; cigar and tobacco makers suffered from heart and respiratory ailments; hat makers contracted nerve disorders when they inhaled the mercury used to treat furs and felts; women who ingested radium while painting numbers onto clock faces died of radiation poisoning. Journalists began focusing on the plight of American workers, describing in vivid detail the pain and suffering with which they were paying for America's growth and prosperity. Public outrage was further fueled by spectacular industrial tragedies, such as two mine explosions in December 1906 which killed 595 men, and the Triangle Shirtwaist Company fire in New York City, which took the lives of 145 people, mostly young immigrant women. In August 1910 the *Cleveland Citizen* editorialized that the United States had become an "industrial slaughterhouse."[22]

Intolerable conditions and the growing threat of worker rebellion in the years between 1900 and 1918 (usually called the Progressive Era), led to a clamor for greater government intervention in the economy. Pressure from workers, labor leaders, and journalists led to some new legislative protections for workers—and also to business-initiated proposals for reforms which would not threaten their power and prerogative. Social workers from urban settlement houses actively sought laws limiting child labor. By 1913 most states had mandated minimum wages and maximum hours for working children. The Women's Trade Union League, which included both working women and middle-class allies, pushed for minimum-wage and maximum-hour laws for women factory workers. These legislative initiatives were of only limited effectiveness. Business prevailed in many states to force legislatures to exempt industries which employed large numbers of children and to exempt children from poor families. Enforcement by state officials was usually lax.[23]

Organized labor stayed away from the legislative arena, leaving the reform work to concerned citizens with more leisure time and greater wealth. There was a general belief among labor leaders that the legislatures and the courts were so dominated by businessmen and their friends that no effective legislation would ever be passed. Yet a number of state legislatures did pass a very effective reform intended to provide better protection to workers on the job—employer liability laws. Throughout the 1800s and into the early 1900s, employers had been able to avoid financial responsibility for industrial accidents. If workers were injured on the job, they could win compensation only if they could prove in court that the employer, rather than another worker, had been negligent. This could rarely be done. Between 1906 and 1912 U.S. Steel lost only six verdicts to employees.[24] Since employers rarely paid the cost of the injury or death, and since there were always plenty of unemployed workers to take the place of the dead and disabled, employers had little incentive to reduce occupational dangers.

In the first decade of the 1900s, however, reformers in 26 states passed employer liability laws, making it easier for workers to win in court against their employers. These laws, which labor unions did support, increased employer liability for accidents and improved workers' chances of winning compensation for their injuries. Although most of these laws applied only to railroad workers, business leaders were concerned. Fearful of generous proworker decisions by juries, they acted quickly to prevent a rush of court battles and costly compensation settlements.[25] They decided to shape legislation to create a new system of workers compensation, one which recognized employer liability for injury but which severely limited the amount employers would have to pay injured workers.

Business leaders developed workers compensation to preempt public outcry for more drastic changes in the way business conducted itself (much like the railroad industry's efforts to create the ICC a few decades earlier). The campaign was led by the National Civic Federation (NCF), the Progressive Era's leading organization of politically astute corporate leaders, similar in composition and outlook to today's Business Roundtable. Some labor and socialist leaders were suspicious of the NCF's enthusiasm for workers compensation. Socialist Party official Morris Hillquit objected that the NCF plan took "nothing from capital," gave "nothing to labor," and did it with "such an appearance of boundless generosity" that "some of the more guileless diplomats in the labor movement are actually overwhelmed by it."[26] Indeed, after initial opposition, AFL President Samuel Gompers and other trade unionists gave their support. With business leaders convincing labor leaders to go along with them, workers compensation laws were passed in one state after another. By 1920 all but six southern states had some type of workers compensation law.

For the American worker, workers compensation was a partial victory. The public outcry over business' treatment of workers forced the business community to accept greater liability for dangerous working conditions and more of the cost of worker accidents. State governments codified the new employer responsibilities into law. But once forced to act, business leaders and state governments created a system which served employers well: safety and accident costs became more predictable; further liberalization of employer liability laws and possible full compensation for accidents were avoided; public outrage was calmed without business being forced to make workplaces much safer, or to give any control over working conditions to the workers themselves.

After the enactment of workers compensation laws, the cost to employers of occupational accidents and disease stabilized for many decades at an average of only one percent of payroll. By the 1920s corporate executives were no longer worried that safety efforts might cut into profits. The president of one large corporation even told his "safety man:"[27]

> You know, I am very busy and have little time to give to safety, but keep me in touch with your work. It is a non-controversial subject. I can make train conversation of it."*

When workers went on strike over specific health and safety demands, employers were not so blasé. At Standard Oil's Bayonne, New Jersey, refinery, still cleaners were forced to enter the stills before they cooled. They were exposed to temperatures as high as 250°F and to deadly coke dust. In July 1915 all 1,500 of the plant employees went on strike over this and other grievances. The company responded with court orders, strikebreakers, and police. Nine workers were killed and at least 50 injured.

---

*Today, workers compensation payments still cost companies so little—and force workers to absorb so much of the cost of their accidents and illnesses themselves—that the system encourages employers to pay for the limited treatment of accident victims rather than for the prevention of accidents. This 1973 description shows how the low level of compensation payments paid by Chrysler actually works to the detriment of employees' safety and health:

> Every year, the compensation representatives at the various plants were instructed to compute and estimate the Workmen's Compensation costs for that plant for the coming year and we had to turn those estimates in to the accountants for the corporation. The safety personnel at the plants did the same. They computed their costs . . . then it was just a question of the corporation deciding which was cheaper, to take some injuries, take some deaths, pay some Workmen's Compensation or spend a lot of money and make it safe.[28]

Workers went back to their jobs, having gained nothing.*[30]

Two years later, in June 1917, 10,000 copper miners walked off the job after 164 miners were burned to death in an explosion at the North Butte Speculator copper mine in Montana. The strike was led by members of the Industrial Workers of the World (IWW), who were joined by AFL electrical and other craft workers. IWW miners in Arizona walked out in solidarity, and to settle their own grievances over unsafe blasting practices.[31] The Phelps-Dodge company responded first in Arizona: 1,164 workers were arrested and shipped by cattle car to a detention camp in Columbus, New Mexico. The Arizona strike collapsed. On 11 August federal troops were brought to patrol the streets of Butte. On 5 September federal authorities raided IWW offices and halls across the country and seized five tons of records. A week later the AFL unions went back to work. Isolated, the Butte miners gave up their strike—and their new union.[32]

When World War I began in Europe, unemployment in the United States was about 15 percent. Except for a dip to 8 percent in 1913, unemployment had been above 10 percent since 1908. Major strikes were rare: high unemployment made those who had jobs more afraid of losing them and not finding others. But war production revived the slumping economy and, by 1918, unemployment dropped to 1.4 percent.[33] With this low unemployment came increased worker militance for higher wages, shorter hours, and better working conditions. Strike fever spread: more workers walked out during each year of American involvement in World War I than had ever been

---

*Chemical-tank cleaning remains a dangerous job. On 6 August 1980 day laborer Linwood Bryant, working at a Conoco Plant in Baltimore, died two hours after he began cleaning a tank that was partially filled with benzene. Bryant was given the job a day after four other men became dizzy doing the same work. The Maryland Occupational Safety and Health Agency proposed fines of $1,800 each on Conoco and the two subcontractors, Chesapeake Environmental and Peakload Labor.[29]

on strike before.[34] Union membership soared. The International Association of Machinists, which had only 54,000 members in 1910, claimed 331,000 in 1919. The revived railroad unions claimed 1.8 million members by the end of the war.[35]

Virtual full employment reversed the traditional situation of too few jobs for too many workers. This gave workers great leverage over their employers. They could pick and choose among job offers. According to Yale historian David Montgomery, workers might accept 6 to 8 jobs in a single day of searching and then show up at the one most to their liking.[36] Collectively, workers were also able to make great gains. In the battle for the 8-hour day, which had begun in the 1860s, the second decade of the twentieth century was decisive. By 1915 the editors of *Iron Age* magazine were warning employers against capitulating on the 8-hour day just because the American war industry was beginning to boom:[37]

> The unparalleled situation which has made victory in Europe turn not only upon sheer tonnage in steel projectiles, but upon the metal-cutting capacity of American machine tools, must not be allowed to settle for years to come so important an issue as the 8-hour machine shop day.

But by the end of that year, 25 state legislatures had passed laws limiting the length of the workday. In 1916 Congress passed the Adamson Act which provided for an 8-hour day and time-and-a-half for overtime for interstate railway workers—a precursor to the broad maximum hour protections finally legislated by Congress in 1938. As unemployment fell the number of hours worked by most people dropped significantly. Between 1915 and 1917 over a million workers achieved the 8-hour day. By 1919 nearly half of all American workers worked 48 hours a week or less, up from only 8 percent in a period of 10 years.[38]

Between 1914 and 1919 consumer prices doubled while

many workers' real wages dropped. Buoyed by the realization that they had been indispensable to the nation during the war years, workers took the offensive to protect their standard of living. Only four days after the armistice, 60,000 clothing workers went on strike for a 44-hour week and a 15 percent pay raise. The IWW, together with the AFL Metal Trades Council in Seattle, led 110 locals in a general strike in solidarity with striking shipworkers. In the fall of 1919, 350,000 steel workers and then 400,000 miners struck for higher wages.[39] Over 4 million workers—one-seventh of the workforce—were involved in thousands of strikes and lockouts. It was the largest strike wave in American history.

Already nervous about the Bolshevik revolution in Russia and revolutionary activity throughout Europe, employers responded swiftly to labor activism. They used the same tactics that had worked so well in other eras: harassing and intimidating activists; crushing the most powerful unions; and giving in on demands that did not significantly weaken employer control.

The prime target of the federal government's campaign against labor radicals was the openly revolutionary IWW, which had not agreed to the AFL's no-strike pledge during the war. Federal marshalls raided IWW offices, seized documents, and arrested members. The government tried, convicted, and imprisoned key IWW leaders, effectively breaking the union. On 2 January 1920 over 10,000 "socialists," "anarchists," and other "radicals" were arrested in raids across the nation orchestrated by Attorney General A. Mitchell Palmer. Many foreign-born activists were deported.

The 10-week steel strike in 1919 was smashed by strikebreakers, violence, court injunctions, the denial of free-speech rights, and the companies' ability to outlast the strikers, who received no strike benefits. Striking coal miners fought for four years against their employers and government troops before withdrawing in defeat. When 5 million more people lost their jobs during the severe recession of 1921–22, employers took advantage of the downturn, and the antiforeign and anticommunist hysteria they had fanned, to step up their offensive. The president of the National Association of Manufacturers (NAM) joined other business leaders in charging that unionism itself was "an un-American, illegal and infamous conspiracy." Individual corporations and employer associations like NAM launched massive campaigns to abolish union shops. In San Francisco and Chicago, where the Building Trades Council had been strong, the union shop in construction was defeated. By the end of 1922 unions in meat packing, steel, lumber, and the maritime industry were virtually nonexistent. Over the remainder of the decade, unions in coal, textile, building, printing, and railroads were greatly weakened. By 1929 the United Mine Workers had lost 5 of every 6 members it had only 10 years earlier.

Employers added the carrot to the stick in the 1920s. Widespread automation made possible the mass production of low-cost consumer goods. The high profits that resulted enabled employers to grant some wage increases and new fringe benefits to workers and still keep the lion's share of the new wealth. Higher wages for many workers, extensive advertising, and the introduction of consumer credit made the 1920s the first decade of consumerism. But, in 1929, the bubble burst. The stock market collapsed. Production virtually ceased.

THE 1930s: LABOR'S BREAKTHROUGH

When the economy collapsed union membership was at a low point, and the power of organized labor was minimal. Industrial workers, who were experiencing unparalleled suffering and disruption of their lives, had no place to turn and no protection from disaster. In cities like

Toledo, Ohio, which were dependent on steel, automobile, and other heavy industries, unemployment climbed as high as 80 percent. By 1932, 15 million workers were jobless—25 percent of adult workers. People roamed the country looking for jobs. Many had to fight for or steal food, coal, and bare essentials.

Employers exploited the desperation of the vast army of unemployed workers and the weakened state of their unions. Layoffs and wage cuts, speed-ups, long hours, and a total disregard for worker health and safety were the realities of depression worklife. It was once again a "buyers' market" for labor. As one midwestern gypsum worker explained:[40]

> You would come to work in the morning [during the 1930s] and the plant manager told you your wages were cut to 25 cents an hour. This stuff sticks in your craw; you don't forget that easily. The men were working then at 30 to 45 cents an hour for a 33 hour week. The plant manager put it down to 25 cents and said, "If you want to work, you can; if you don't, I can get plenty of men at that price."

Management knew that workers would accept intolerable conditions just to have a job, including work conditions which could kill. At the 1936 United Auto Workers convention, Dr. I. Ruskin reported there had been 13,000 cases of lead poisoning in auto factories since 1929—4,000 in 1934–35 alone. John W. Anderson, who worked at the Dodge plant in 1932, described the conditions:[41]

> [There] was no attempt to ventilate the work areas or to take the pollutants out of the air. . . . It was an accepted fact that thousands of metal finishers in the auto industry suffered from lead poisoning.

Many workers paid with their lives. In 1930–31 near Gauley Bridge, West Virginia, a subsidiary of Union Carbide cut a tunnel through a mountain to divert water from the New and Kanawha rivers for a new hydroelectric power plant. Most of the workers recruited for the work were black and unskilled. Pay was low and the contractor cut wages further as the depression deepened. Workers faced murderous conditions: carbon monoxide poisoning from gas-powered trains in the tunnel, and dust so thick visibility was usually under 10 feet. Although state law required a 30-minute break before workers could enter a tunnel after blasting, foremen physically forced workers into the tunnel immediately after each blast. Men exposed to dust that was 90–95 percent silica were never told prolonged exposure to even 30 percent silica dust could cause silicosis and death. Workers were dying less than a year after brief exposure to the dust. By the time the tunnel was completed, 476 workers had died and 1,500 were left permanently disabled. In a 1936 article in *The New Republic,* Representative Vito Marcantonio of New York City reported the paymaster of the job was overheard telling the superintendent, "I knew they was going to kill those niggers within five years, but I didn't know they was going to kill them so quick."[42] During Congressional hearings held to investigate the company's treatment of its workers, Senator Rush Drew Holt of West Virginia said, "That company well knew what it was going to do to these men. The company openly said that if they killed off those men, there were plenty of other men to be had."[43]

As the ranks of the unemployed swelled in the early 1930s, a powerful change in attitudes emerged among both the working and the unemployed. The widespread suffering helped people see they were not at fault for their unemployment and poverty. Workers realized business and government policies were largely to blame—and that the business community had no solution to the crisis it had caused. The result was a burst of protest and organization which forced the establishment of basic worker protections. Workers translated their fears into anger and then into action. Employed and unemployed workers alike knew their survival depended upon their ability to join together to fight for and win economic protections.

The first signs of new activism came from unemployed workers in major cities who joined Unemployed Councils (usually led by Communist organizers). These Councils used sit-ins and other tactics to block evictions and demand government relief. In Ohio 187 locals claimed 100,000 members.[44] The agitation had a significant impact. Upon taking office President Franklin D. Roosevelt promised direct-relief payments to the poor and unemployed. By early 1934, 20 million people were "on the dole"—one of every six Americans, and nearly one-third of the nation's black population.[45]

Industrial workers received their greatest boost when their activism forced the federal government to moderate its long and violent antilabor stance. Although every twentieth-century president had endorsed collective bargaining in principle, the federal government had regularly interceded against labor.[46] Congress took a tentative first step in reversing this history with the 1926 Railway Labor Act, which recognized the right of railway brotherhoods to bargain with their employers, but which lacked adequate enforcement provisions.[47]

Faced with uncontrollable worker militance and the renewed spread of political radicalism, the Roosevelt administration formally accepted and supported the principle that workers should be able to form unions without interference from their employers. Section 7(a) of the National Industrial Recovery Act, passed in June 1933, recognized the right of workers to "organize unions of their own choosing" and to bargain collectively with their employers. The Act stipulated that if employers would conform to codes establishing minimum wages, maximum hours, child labor prohibitions, and the right to unionize in each major industry, they would be exempted from antitrust laws and would be allowed to fix prices to achieve some stability and rebuild their industries.

The United Mine Workers of America, under the aggressive leadership of President John L. Lewis, took immediate advantage of the new legislation. One hundred organizers went into the coal fields, declaring from sound trucks the somewhat exaggerated claim that "The President wants *you* to join the union." Inspired by the hope that federal opposition to unionization would finally cease, thousands of miners joined or rejoined the UMW. Membership climbed from 60,000 to 300,000 within two months. Wildcat strikes and rank-and-file pressure forced major concessions from the coal operators. The bituminous coal code established under the NRA provided for a $4.40 per day minimum wage, a 40-hour week, an 8-hour day, dues check-off for the union, an end to company-town exploitation, and the prohibition of coal sorting by young "breaker boys."

The UMW, as it had often done in the past, played the role of the shock troops of labor. Workers in textiles, steel, rubber, auto, and other mass-production industries followed the UMW's lead, joining existing unions or creating new ones.

Industry resisted. Section 7(a) may have given workers the right to unionize, but it did not guarantee them protection from employer retaliation. Employers regularly fired union members and kept blacklists of union activists and sympathizers. They formed company unions and were spending $80 million a year by 1936 for armies of union spies.[48]

This time the old anti-union tactics could not deter worker militance. In Toledo in May 1934, 10,000 people fought the Ohio National Guard and won union recognition at the Electric Auto-Lite Company. In Minneapolis Teamsters Local 574 closed the trucking industry and brought the city to a standstill until employers recognized the union. On the west coast longshoremen closed the port of San Francisco and, after a violent confrontation with police and National Guard, led the city's workers in a general strike which won limited reforms of waterfront hiring practices. In September 375,000 textile workers struck. As industry considered its response, the trade journal *Fibre and Fabric* suggested that "a few hundred funerals would have a quieting influence."[49]

In 1935 Section 7(a) and the NRA were declared unconstitutional. But Congress, well aware of the anger and defiance of the nation's workforce, passed the National Labor Relations Act (NLRA), also known as the Wagner Act, in its place. The NLRA recognized workers' right to organize and also provided a mechanism for enforcement. It established the National Labor Relations Board (NLRB) to oversee union elections, to prevent employers from restraining or coercing employees, and to require employers to negotiate with legally-elected unions. Although the law was immediately challenged by employers and tied up in court for several years, workers took its passage as a signal of government support for unionization. In the three years that followed labor activism again surged. More than half of all strikes between 1935 and 1937 were prompted by employer refusal to recognize a union of their employees.[50]

In 1935 John L. Lewis decided to capitalize on the momentum which he saw among industrial workers. Along with David Dubinsky of the International Ladies Garment Workers Union (ILGWU) and Sidney Hillman of the Amalgamated Clothing Workers, Lewis formed the Committee for Industrial Organization (CIO) within the AFL to organize unions in the major mass-production industries.* The CIO unions—the Auto Workers, the

---

*The CIO broke with the AFL in 1938, forming an independent federation, the Congress of Industrial Organizations, after the AFL began expelling CIO unions. The two groups merged in 1955.

Mine Workers, the Steelworkers, the Rubber Workers, and others—benefited from the government's support of unionization and the right to collective bargaining. The rapid growth of these unions would have been more difficult without it. But the CIO's greatest victories came not because of government policy decisions but because of the determination of industrial workers in their factories, mines, and mills to take risks and challenge employers. These workers adopted a powerful and successful tactic—the sit-down strike.

Although John L. Lewis and the CIO leadership did not approve of sit-downs, it was the use of this tactic which broke industry's resistance in the late 1930s. The sit-down enabled workers to stop production without having to endure employer-provoked violence on the picket line. Mingling inside the plants in safety (since employers were reluctant to take any action which might damage their machinery), workers spent time together, compared grievances, and developed the trust necessary to withstand the hardships of the fight and threats of employers. The sit-down strike was most effective in highly automated plants. When the assembly line was stopped, all production ceased and all workers became part of the strike. The sit-down tactic gave workers the opportunity to shift the balance of power in the workplace to their advantage.

Sit-downs began in the rubber factories of Akron, Ohio, in 1933—primarily in opposition to exhausting production speedups. On 29 January 1936 Firestone workers on the night shift sat down, demanding union recognition. When Goodrich and Goodyear workers followed suit, the companies were forced to accept the United Rubber Workers as the bargaining agent for its employees. Sit-down strikes spread from rubber to the the auto industry. In late December 1936, 7,000 workers in Cleveland's Chevrolet body plant stopped work. Two days later

GM workers in Flint, Michigan, sat down. "By the end of the first week of the new year," as labor historian Irving Bernstein put it, "the great General Motors automotive system had been brought to its knees."[51] The company tried to break the strike in Flint, but when it realized that workers were standing firm, and that the community, led by the Women's Emergency Brigade and other support groups, was overwhelmingly prolabor, GM recognized the fledgling United Auto Workers.

People across the country began sitting down—nearly 400,000 workers in 1937 alone.[52] The momentum and excitement spread from industrial workers to hospital workers, garbage collectors, saleswomen, and countless others. As one AFL business agent explained:[53]

> You'd be sitting in the office any March day of 1937, and the phone would ring and the voice at the other end would say, "My name is Mary Jones; I'm a soda clerk at Liggett's; we've thrown the manager out and we've got the keys. What do we do now?"

Workers across the nation felt *entitled* to challenge both management and government. Business leadership had failed and workers knew it. The legitimacy of business dominance, which can seem so strong in periods when the economy is expanding and opportunities improving, was called into question. In such a climate job blackmail had little hold over the industrial workforce. When the Steel Workers Organizing Committee (SWOC) signed 100,000 members during six months of 1936, the industry tried to use both physical force and job blackmail threats to scare steel workers into opposing unionization. The American Iron and Steel Institute responded to the organizing drive with a public statement:[54]

> The steel industry is recovering from six years of depression and huge losses and the employees are now beginning to receive the benefits of increased operations. Any interruption of the forward movement will

seriously injure the employees and their families and all businesses dependent upon the industry, and will endanger the welfare of the country.

The workers were not swayed. Several weeks after General Motors capitulated to the UAW, U.S. Steel backed off and agreed to recognize SWOC.

In April 1937 the U.S. Supreme Court finally upheld the constitutionality of the Wagner Act, reaffirming the right to organize. By 1937 the CIO numbered 32 different unions, representing 3,817,000 members. Total union membership had jumped to 7 million.

Workers continued to pressure Roosevelt and Congress. In January 1938 Congress passed the Fair Labor Standards Act, which established a minimum wage and provided for time-and-a-half pay for any hours worked in excess of 44 hours a week. In 1937 and 1938 Congress passed legislation initiating the federal public housing program, expanding the work relief rolls, and speeding the introduction of social security payments. By the end of the 1930s, American workers had secured their own bill of rights. Through collective action they had challenged corporate power and prerogative, altered the balance of economic control, won improved wages and working conditions, and forced both government and employers to recognize certain basic worker rights.

The determined activism of the mid-1930s also helped workers regain some control in the workplace. Union contracts secured workers against arbitrary dismissals and stipulated that companies would have to deal with delegates elected by the workers. With the threat of more sit-down strikes, workers forced lower production quotas, and the dismissal of unpopular foremen. It was an extraordinary period in the history of American democracy. As historian David Montgomery has emphasized:[55]

Lifting the suffocating burden of absolute managerial control from the working lives of Americans . . . was one of the greatest chapters in the historic struggle for human liberties in this country.

WORLD WAR II AND AFTER: BUSINESS REACTS

Many in business and government were eager to stem the tide of worker militance that had developed by 1937. Employers continued to resist worker attempts to unionize. In June 1937 SWOC failed to win recognition from the remaining major steel companies, which held firm during a bitter strike. Business leaders and their government allies also attacked labor gains in the political arena. In 1938 the House Un-American Activities Committee opened hearings on Communist influence in the CIO —the opening salvo in a virulent new red-baiting campaign. Business leaders and many members of Congress sought to undercut the Wagner Act: thirty antilabor bills were introduced in Congress in 1941 alone.[56] The NLRB was reconstituted with fewer prolabor members. In 1939 the Supreme Court ruled that sit-down strikes, the most successful weapon in labor's arsenal, were illegal. By 1940 four southern states passed anti-union laws outlawing secondary boycotts and jurisdictional strikes, restricting picketing, and imposing other limits on union activities. By the end of 1941, 16 states in the south and southwest had such laws.[57]

Despite this coordinated counterattack, labor militance surged again before the United States entered the Second World War. During 1941 the CIO unions made impressive gains against some of the largest and most anti-union employers. The Steel Workers won recognition from Bethlehem Steel after a long, violent strike. The UAW closed Ford's mammoth River Rouge complex in Detroit until its right to bargain collectively with management was recognized.* The UMW forced U.S. Steel to recognize its right to represent the company's mine workers.

As war production expanded rapidly and millions of Americans left the mines and factories to become soldiers, a decade of intolerably high unemployment was reversed almost overnight. As in World War I full employment gave workers a sense of their own power. Against the wishes of the AFL and CIO leadership, both of which had pledged not to initiate strikes during the war, workers staged thousands of strikes in hundreds of factories and mines, usually over safety and working conditions in the new defense plants. In 1943 nearly 2 million war workers engaged in over 3,500 separate strikes.[58]

But the war changed everything for America's workers. Although the number of local strikes increased, labor's clout was steadily declining. One factor was the mounting tension between union leaders and their membership. Having agreed to a no-strike pledge and to participation on the War Mobilization Board, leaders found themselves disciplining their own members to keep production moving (something which business and government leaders were eager to force on unions). If workers went on wildcat strikes, it was the union's responsibility to get them back

*In both these strikes, efforts to organize both whites and blacks were critical. Most unions, especially the older craft unions of the AFL, had traditionally excluded blacks from their ranks. Before the 1930s blacks—and women—rarely shared the successes of the union movement. Until the Steel Workers and the UAW began to recruit blacks, the largest contingent of black workers protected by a union was the 10,000-member Brotherhood of Sleeping Car Porters led by A. Philip Randolph. The show of strength against Bethlehem and Ford began the slow reversal of union opposition to minority membership. It also encouraged Randolph and other militant black leaders to plan an all-black march for jobs to be held in Washington in July 1941. Afraid of vocal and visible black militance in America, Roosevelt issued an executive order prohibiting racial discrimination in the government and in war industries in exchange for cancellation of the march. Blacks saw that the threat of mass action could move the federal government to take action which it would rather not take—a lesson not lost on the civil rights movement.

to work and to discipline the instigators. Some union leaders, like the CIO's Philip Murray, saw this growing conflict
between members and leaders as a serious threat to continued labor gains. Others, however, were eager to con-
tain rank-and-file militance, fearing that unpredictable
worker activism might destroy public confidence in unions
and encourage a government crackdown.

Other factors contributed to a weakening of labor's political power during the war years. While union membership increased by over 4 million, to 14.5 million people
(about 28 percent of the workforce), organized labor had
difficulty winning electoral victories. Even in Detroit, where
union membership was quite high, labor candidates for
local office failed in both the 1943 and 1945 elections. At
the same time the intense involvement of local leaders and
rank-and-file activists that had existed in the 1930s was
rapidly diminishing. Veteran labor activists joined the armed
forces. The activist cores of many unions, people who had
fought together in the formative battles of the 1930s, were
severely disrupted by this and by the shifting of weapons
production to new plants. Labor's political influence in
Congress and the executive branch declined, along with
its ability to sustain pressure at the local level.

When the war ended, the impact of these changes became painfully obvious. Unemployment rose and real wages
fell as war production dropped. Prices skyrocketed. Workers went on strike in greater numbers than at any time in
history. But the bitter strikes resulted in few labor successes. In the 1945-46 strike wave, workers won wage
increases, but most settlements did not enable them to
keep pace with the rising cost of living. After a 113-day
strike the Auto Workers settled for a little less than half
the wage increase they demanded. Other contracts followed the same pattern.

Strikes over speedup and safety, which had been so
common during the war, declined significantly after the

war. This pleased employers—and also suited union leaders who, sensing the changing political climate, avoided direct challenges to management on workplace control questions. Many workers were eager to devote their attention to family and community life. Union, business, and government officials encouraged this shift to a home-centered, consumption-oriented lifestyle—and away from intense labor-management confrontation. Business leaders assumed there would be adequate profits from pent-up domestic demand and from international trade to satisfy wage and benefit demands. They felt this would be a small price to pay for industrial peace. In March of 1945, even before the war was over, the AFL and the CIO worked out an agreement with the U.S. Chamber of Commerce calling for a "new Charter for Labor and Management" for the postwar period. One of the seven points read:[59]

> The inherent right and responsibility of management to direct the operations of an enterprise shall be recognized and preserved. So that enterprise may develop and expand and earn a reasonable profit, management must be free as well from unnecessary governmental interference and burdensome restrictions.

Business and government moved quickly to make this agreement stick and to thwart renewed worker militance. The government reentered labor disputes on management's side. When miners struck in 1946 the government seized the mines and fined the unions $3.5 million for contempt. President Truman proposed drafting striking workers and he continued to use his wartime powers to seize, and then reopen, "nationalized" factories, railroads, and mines closed by strikes.

Employers undertook a major campaign to weaken public support for unions and to undermine the ability of unions to win large wage increases. Union wage demands,

they claimed, were the chief cause of price inflation. If the
unions did not moderate their demands, they would only
add to the inflation which was eating into workers'
paychecks. Like the current crop of claims about government regulation, this argument had no basis in fact. But it
justified the employers' harder line against union demands: employers could say they were acting in the public
interest.

In 1947 Congress dealt a serious blow to the labor
movement, destroying many worker gains of the previous
decades by passing the Taft-Hartley Act. This act greatly
restricted the right to strike and the ability to organize
new workers. It outlawed secondary boycotts and strikes
by federal employees, and made union officials subject to
fines and jail terms if they refused to oppose wildcat
strikes. Taft-Hartley enabled states to outlaw the union
shop and empowered the President to impose a 90-day
"cooling off" period before certain national strikes could
take place. It stipulated that unions could be sued for
striking while a current contract was still in effect. The
Act also restricted workers' civil rights, prohibiting unions
from contributing to candidates for federal office, requiring unions to file a variety of annual financial reports with
the government, and most importantly, barring individuals with Communist Party affiliation from holding elected
union office.

The "takebacks" enacted in Taft-Hartley shaped labor-
management relations in the postwar period. Organizing
became much more difficult. Unions became increasingly
bureaucratic in response to the law's requirements that
they take responsibility for workers' actions and for
reporting to the government. The prohibition on
Communist-affiliated leadership exacerbated political in-
fighting which quickly tore the unions apart. In 1949 the
CIO expelled 11 of its member unions, including its third
largest affiliate, the United Electrical Workers. Most of
these leftist-led unions died quickly: employers broke

their contracts and other AFL and CIO unions raided their memberships. By 1950 CIO membership had dropped from a wartime peak of 5.2 million to only 3.7 million.[60]

In 1950 the UAW and GM signed what is often referred to as "The Treaty of Detroit," a 5-year contract which set the precedent for union contracts through the postwar period. Union leadership promised five years without a strike in exchange for a cost-of-living escalator, pension improvements, welfare and insurance plans, and bonuses for increased productivity.[61] Workers won higher wages and benefits; employers gained worker discipline, predictable labor costs, and preservation of their prerogative. In this, as in all postwar contracts, the union signed away its right to challenge most management production and investment decisions.

Union leaders had chosen to act on the belief that employers would provide for their workers. They began to view the stability of their organizations as more dependent on the well-being of their industries than on the informed activism of their members. Automatic dues checkoff gave the unions a flow of funds which did not depend on being in close contact with the membership. By the mid-1950s, the leadership of the labor movement, with few exceptions, abandoned the adversarial stance which had forced great changes in the 1930s.*

---

*It is important to acknowledge that American unionism is not monolithic. During the 1950s and 1960s, public employee unions grew rapidly, coincident with and emerging from the civil rights movement. The struggle to establish workplace rights for public employees was aggressive and showed daring which was rare in other unions in the same period. Under Walter Reuther the UAW took more imaginative and farsighted positions on social issues and worker rights than most unions. The industrial unions in general tended to retain more of their tradition of confrontation and "social unionism" than did the craft unions of the AFL. Within the merged AFL–CIO, however, the conservatism and "business unionism" of the building trades, epitomized by former plumber George Meany himself, tended to dominate. This is not to suggest that unions across the country, at local and district levels, did not engage in many fights and confrontations over both "business" and "social" issues, or that individuals and groups of union members did not agitate aggressively for change.

In 1956 George Meany, president of the merged AFL–CIO, boasted to the National Association of Manufacturers:[62]

> I never went on strike in my life, I never ordered anyone else to run a strike in my life, I never had anything to do with a picket line. . . . In the final analysis there is not a great deal of difference between the things I stand for and the things that the National Association of Manufacturers stands for.

This approach greatly influenced union priorities and activities in the first two postwar decades—with mixed results. Because the economy was expanding, unions could demand and win wages and benefits which significantly increased their membership's disposable income. But union leadership was slow in challenging management and government on a broad spectrum of social and control issues, including civil rights, health and safety, automation, full employment and the right to a job, military spending and the Viet Nam War, and, in many instances, environmental protection.

When the profits of major industries were squeezed by increased foreign competition and continued wage demands in the late 1960s, management abandoned the facade of employer-employee cooperation and intensified its attack on workers. In order to maintain profit levels, management in many industries speeded the pace of production and delayed investment in new equipment: the accident rate soared. Workers responded with protests, wildcat strikes, and even sabotage. By 1970 work time lost through strikes climbed to three times its 1963 level.[63] But union leadership neither encouraged nor supported this renewed militance. Still operating under assumptions of labor-management cooperation, union bureaucracies retreated from the intense confrontation triggered by management.*

As was shown in chapter 5, the business counteroffensive against labor has intensified. Yet, while labor leaders have delivered fiery speeches about "one-sided class war" being waged by business and about business efforts to "bust American unionism," unions have been slow to translate their rhetoric into action. They have been relatively ineffective mobilizing the membership and taking a strong stance in defense of rights and protections which are under attack. They remain reluctant to acknowledge that it is difficult to cooperate with management and government when neither is particularly interested in cooperating with organized labor. Through the years, it has been the determination of workers and their unions to challenge management power which has led to the most important labor and social gains. Machinists president William Winpisinger acknowledged this in a 1978 interview: "The adversarial relationship [between workers and employers] is needed for justice in our society and justice in the workplace—industrial democracy."[65] How organized labor—and also unorganized workers—respond to this challenge in the coming years will determine how well the public's interest in employment, health, and environmental protections will be represented.

---

*The Chevrolet Vega plant in Lordstown, Ohio, was the most publicized case of early 1970s labor-management conflict. In 1971 the plant was redesigned to produce about 100 cars an hour, 40 more than the one-a-minute average of most GM plants. The predominantly young workforce resisted. They let cars go through without repairs. Absenteeism was high and wildcat strikes frequent. In January 1972 the increased work pace was a key grievance in a 3-week strike. Although Lordstown received much publicity, it was not unique. Older, more experienced workers in GM's Norwood, Ohio, plant struck for 174 days in 1972, prompted by the speedup initiated by the company as part of its Assembly Division reorganization plan.[64]

12
The Fight for Environmental
_____Protections

When the United States was an agricultural and pioneering nation, there was no environmental movement. The dominant ethic was to "subdue" the land, to "conquer" nature. There was little concern with waste or resource exploitation: the land seemed vast and its riches limitless.

As early as 1827, however, when John James Audubon recorded his travels through the Ohio Valley, the shape of future problems and conflicts was emerging. Audubon wrote about the "destruction of the forest" and warned that "the greedy mills told the sad tale that in a century the noble forests . . . should exist no more."[1] By mid-century artists and writers were concerned the American wilderness might not survive the great American growth machine. In 1851 Henry David Thoreau articulated a belief shared today by millions of Americans: "In wildness is the preservation of the world."[2]

After the Civil War, as rapid industrialization reshaped the lives and surroundings of most Americans, environmental concern developed along two distinct paths: wilderness preservation and pollution control. The first focused on protecting the undeveloped environment and the second on rescuing the developing urban habitat.

In the nation's rapidly-growing cities, pollution problems mounted. Traditional sanitation practices could not handle the volume of sewage. Coal burned for home heating and industrial use generated a dark, heavy smoke which burned the eyes, made breathing difficult, and left a sooty residue everywhere. Industry operating within and around population centers made matters worse.

By 1868 industrial pollution posed such a serious threat in New York City that the newly created Metropolitan Board of Health campaigned to clean up the city's slaughterhouses, chemical and fertilizer plants, and fat-melting facilities. According to Board Director Edward Dalton, these industries "resulted in the corruption of the atmosphere, thus undermining the health and destroying the lives of those whom poverty debarred from escape." Dalton criticized employers who looked upon pollution as "a fancied right."[3]

The Board of Health recommended that 200 slaughterhouses in overcrowded tenement neighborhoods move to the outskirts of the city and reduce offensive odors. The Board instructed gas-light companies to change their purification process which was "poisoning the atmosphere" with foul sulfur gas.[4] Fat melters were told they, too, would have to find a way to reduce their intolerable stench.

Each industry refused to comply. Even then employers understood blackmail. The city's butcher shop owners declared the slaughterhouses "were the necessary and only means of supplying the citizens of New York with meat." Representatives of the illuminating-gas companies, sounding like electric utility companies in the 1970s, told the Board of Health that "The city must either be in darkness or pay this dreadful penalty for light." The fat melters said their smell simply had to be tolerated, for it was the unavoidable result of an essential industry and the price of progress.[5]

The Board of Health was not convinced and pressed the companies to comply. Once forced to do so, the offending industries adapted rather quickly—and without losing money. The construction of new slaughterhouses outside the city enabled butchers to make better use of hides, horns, hoofs, and blood. The gas companies changed purification processes and eliminated the offending odors. Fat melters substituted a closed tank for open burning, "permanently benefiting" the producers, according to the Board of Health.[6] No jobs were lost because of these changes.

As production expanded and the size of industrial facilities grew, coal smoke emerged as the major urban air pollution problem. In 1881 the Chicago City Council passed the first antipollution law in the United States, declaring the "emission of dark smoke from the smoke-stack of any boat or locomotive or from any chimney anywhere within the city shall be [considered] a public nuisance."[7] By the early 1900s many of the same reformers who had worked for child labor laws were lobbying for local antismoke ordinances similar to the Chicago statute. They saw a clear connection between the polluted air in the cities and the exploitation of workers: both were the result of business priorities and both required governmental action if they were to be corrected. In a 1915 novel entitled *Growth,* Booth Tarkington criticized the business community's single-minded pursuit of profit:[8]

> There is a midland city in the heart of fair, open
> country, a dirty and wonderful city nesting dingily in

the fog of its own smoke. The stranger must feel the dirt before he feels the wonder, for the dirt will be upon him instantly. It will be upon him and within him, since he must breathe it, and he may care for no further proof that wealth is here better loved than cleanliness.

Burr McCloskey grew up in Akron, Ohio, in the years following the First World War. McCloskey, who became a member of the United Rubber Workers in the 1930s, remembered industrial air pollution as part of life in Akron, a one-industry town dominated by Goodyear and Firestone:[9]

> I knew that my mother could never keep a table because Goodyear was burning its filth and blowing it out its smoke stacks right into our kitchen . . . I grew up in it, and I knew who did it and I knew what it was doing to me and my mother and our food.

By the late 1800s water pollution was endangering public health, affecting fishing, and even interfering with interstate commerce. Typhoid outbreaks reached epidemic proportions in Lawrence, Massachusetts, in the 1890s. A 1910 New York State Sewage Commission study concluded, "Practically all waters within fifteen miles of Manhattan Island are decidedly polluted."[10]

Industrial pollution of rivers and streams posed far more serious problems in many areas than pollution from municipal sewage dumping. Wastes from coal mines, paper mills, metal refineries, food processing plants, steel mills, oil refineries, and other heavy industries were simply dumped into the nearest waterways. Fishing enthusiasts were among the first to protest. Just after the turn of the century, a sportsmen's group in Maryland traced the decline of Potomac River bass to wood-pulp shavings dumped 60 miles upriver at Harper's Ferry. In 1926 the Izaak Walton League's 2,700 chapters of fishing and hunting enthusiasts analyzed the water quality of local streams: 85 percent of America's inland waters were noticeably polluted.[11]

States and municipalities had jurisdiction over both water and air pollution problems, but neither level of government restricted industry in any enforceable way. The New York Metropolitan Board of Health was the exception, not the rule. Because rivers and oceans were used for interstate transport and commerce, the federal government had the authority to enact pollution control laws if commerce were threatened. By the 1890s the widespread dumping of wastes into the nation's rivers interfered with river transport. In 1899 Congress passed the Refuse Act banning the dumping of solid materials which impeded waterway commerce.

Industry leaders lobbied hard against federal and state efforts to hold corporations responsible for water clean-up. Rivers and harbors were cheap dumps. In 1924, when Congress tried to stop ocean-going ships from polluting harbors with waste oil, intense pressure from steamship lines led to a weak, unenforceable law. Into the 1930s the American Petroleum Institute, the Manufacturing Chemists Association, and the American Iron and Steel Institute maintained that dumping industrial wastes into rivers and streams presented no environmental or public health hazard whatsoever. Attentive to these business groups, the Senate Natural Resources Committee declared that "streams are nature's sewers," giving industrial polluters the go-ahead to dump as they pleased.[12]

This policy did not go unopposed. Kenneth Reid, head of the Izaak Walton League, declared in 1936 that water pollution was the "result of Man's utterly selfish and shortsighted business economy."[13] He asked for support from the National Audubon Society and other conservation groups to get strong enforcement provisions for the Refuse Act. However, three separate efforts between

1936 and 1940 failed to obtain stronger federal water pollution control legislation.

The most intense environmental battles of the period before World War II were fought over the control and use of publicly-owned lands and their vast resources. In 1872, after a group of explorers visited what is now northwest Wyoming, Congress set aside two million acres of that remote wilderness as Yellowstone National Park. It was the first time this or any other nation had decided to preserve wilderness exactly as it was, to be, as the statute read, a "public park and pleasuring ground." In 1886 this principle was put to the test. A railroad company tried to secure a right-of-way across Yellowstone in order to reach a mine. The railroad's advocates were quite candid about their priorities: "I cannot understand the sentiment," said Representative Lewis Payson of Illinois, "which favors the retention of a few buffalos to the development of mining interests amounting to millions of dollars."[14] Congress voted against the railroad in Yellowstone; but this basic conflict between private economic benefit and long-term public "pleasure" has been a constant factor in environmental politics ever since.

The ethic which led to the establishment of national parks and wilderness is often called "preservationist." This is in contrast to the "conservationist" ethic which guided the growing ranks of professional engineers, technicians, and conservation experts in the late 1800s and early 1900s. The leading spokesman for the conservationists was Gifford Pinchot, first head of the U.S. Forest Service which was created in 1905. Pinchot felt government needed to step in to eliminate waste and to "rationalize" development. At the same time he believed firmly that "the first great fact about conservation is that it stands for development."[15] Conservationists believed the goal of conservation to be "national efficiency." As historian Samuel P. Hays explained:[16]

The conservation movement did not involve a reaction against large-scale corporate business but, in fact, shared its view in a mutual revulsion against unrestrained competition and undirected economic development.*

The preservationists in the late 1800s were led by naturalist John Muir, who helped found the Sierra Club to protect California's wilderness. Muir and others who shared his views feared that any for-profit use or development of certain wilderness areas would lead inevitably to their ruin and their loss to future generations.

The early preservationists were people of some wealth and influence. Although guided by their sense of the long-range public interest, their initial methods were not particularly democratic. Charles Sargent, director of Harvard's Arnold Arboretum, once told Muir, "We have got to act promptly and secretly in these matters or the politicians will overwhelm us."[17] But the rapid deforestation of many states, the wholesale slaughter of game and songbirds, and the unrestrained exploitation of the nation's resources moved more and more people to action. Local Audubon Societies were created in the 1880s, the Sierra Club in 1892. Many began to believe the greatest challenge was not promoting industrial efficiency, but rather protecting the national heritage.

Muir and his colleagues saw value in wilderness and in wildlife whether or not those resources were used for human consumption. In the late 1880s Muir and friends in California launched a campaign to make the awesomely beautiful Yosemite Valley into the nation's second nation-

---

*Both conservationists and preservationists opposed resource policies that catered to the crass self-interest of firms in resource-hungry extractive industries. But Pinchot and other conservationists shared many of the views of more sophisticated business leaders, particularly those who led the National Civic Federation in the early 1900s. Like them Pinchot advocated industrial cooperation, government assistance to business, the "scientific management" of resources, and national policy priorities favoring industrial efficiency over democratic participation.

al park. Robert Underwood Johnson, editor of *Century* magazine and a close friend of Muir's, worried that "the valley is going to destruction in the hands of a political commission owned by the Southern Pacific Railroad—as everything and everybody seems to be."[18] As a result of their efforts, Yosemite National Park was established by an act of Congress in 1890.

A few years later the city of San Francisco proposed that a dam be built in the Hetch Hetchy Valley in Yosemite's northwestern corner, and that the valley become the city's water reservoir. That proposal pitted Muir and the newly formed Sierra Club against the city government, the Pacific Gas and Electric Company, and other business interests. Muir's reaction was intense: "Dam Hetch Hetchy!" he wrote. "As well dam for water tanks the people's cathedrals and temples, for no holier temple has ever been consecrated by the heart of man."[19]

The fight continued for many years. City engineers and consultants kept pushing for the dam. Preservationists mounted a determined and increasingly public campaign, reaching out to civic clubs, outing and conservation groups, and scientific societies. Leaflets were sent to organizations, individuals, and newspapers. Environmental activism was reaching a larger segment of the population than ever before. One circular from 1908 proclaimed:[20]

> We do not believe that a great national property preserved for the enjoyment of the people of the entire nation should be thus unnecessarily sacrificed and diverted from its dedicated purpose for the mere pecuniary benefit of a local interest.

In 1912 the conflict came to a head. President Wilson appointed former San Francisco city attorney Franklin Lane as Secretary of the Interior. Muir and the Friends of Hetch Hetchy intensified their efforts. One senator estimated he received 5,000 letters against the bill, an impressive showing for that time. But it was to no avail: with Lane's encouragement, Congress authorized construction.

Environmentalists have never forgotten what happened at Hetch Hetchy. The dam was a disaster. It cost $100 million, more than twice the initial estimate. Water was not pumped to San Francisco until 1934. Years before that, San Francisco's sister city of Oakland found a cheaper source of water in the Sierra foothills. In the end the only beneficiary was the Pacific Gas and Electric Company, which profited handsomely from its access to electricity generated by the dam.

The Hetch Hetchy fight convinced preservationists they had to build broad popular support and encourage greater activism on wilderness and wildlife issues. As a result, the number of people who were active in organizations and campaigns to defend the natural environment increased. The Izaak Walton League was founded in Chicago in 1922 by 54 hunters and anglers, most of whom were business and professional men. Within three years the League had recruited over 100,000 gun enthusiasts as members, primarily in the midwestern states. The League became the largest conservation organization of the period. One of its major victories in the early 1920s was to stop a private developer from draining 300 miles of river bottom on the Upper Mississippi in Minnesota and Illinois. Congress decided instead to turn the whole area into a federal wildlife preserve—the largest in the nation.[21]

Through 1940 the environmental movement made little progress in stemming air and water pollution. But significant strides were made in saving wilderness lands and protecting wildlife by establishing national forests, parks, and wildlife refuges. In industrial as well as wilderness areas, however, the same basic question was being posed: does business have the right to impose its will upon the public whenever and however it chooses?

AFTER WORLD WAR II: THE CRISIS BUILDS

Just as the Second World War greatly altered relations among employers, workers, and their unions, it had an equally decisive impact on environmental quality and politics. The war pulled American industry from a decade of depression. Wartime demand, along with federal planning and financing, revived industry and spurred the rapid introduction of technologies and products. New materials were introduced into the workplace and the environment, with little or no calculation of potential health and safety problems. Chemicals and petroleum-based synthetic products began to replace natural products like wood, steel, soap, and cotton. Oil became the lifeblood of industry: its use as an energy source rose dramatically. Technological innovation had been delayed in many industries during the Depression. During and after the war the explosion of new products and processes was central to the strength of the American economy. But, as became increasingly clear during the 1950s and 1960s, these technological changes were also causing unprecedented degradation of the environment and public health.

The United States emerged from World War II as the dominant economic and political power in the world. The next 20 years were golden ones for U.S. industry. America did not need to rebuild its industrial facilities, as did other countries ravaged by the war. American companies even received a bonus: after the war the government handed over publicly-funded war plants to private companies.* Large corporations moved aggressively to secure their positions in world markets. The economy boomed.

There were no rivals overseas for the American busi-

---

*According to C. Wright Mills, "It had cost some $40 billion to build all the manufacturing facilities existing in the United States in 1939. By 1945, an additional $26 billion worth of high-quality new plant and equipment had been added—two-thirds of it paid directly from government funds."[22]

ness community—and no rivals at home. Neither the federal government nor organized labor resisted the elevation of business' private pursuit of maximum profit as the nation's primary goal.

During the war industrial production and policy had been determined by a few decision-making boards. While they included labor representation, they were dominated by officers of America's largest corporations. After the war the preeminent role of big business in national economic planning continued. In 1953, the Business and Defense Services Administration (BDSA) was established in the Commerce Department to assume the functions of the wartime National Production Authority. This new office, developed with the assistance of leading corporate managers, was staffed by executives recommended and donated by their industries. These executives received no government salaries, but served as advisors to the Secretary of Commerce. The result was institutionalized corporate control of national industrial policy. The House Anti-Trust Subcommittee called BSDA's structure and operation "a virtual abdication of administrative responsibility on the part of government officials in charge of the Department of Commerce."[23]

The Business Advisory Council, another group of executives from the largest corporations in the country, also had great influence over federal industrial policy. One business journalist called the Council "an exclusive and self-perpetuating club of top corporate executives that had enjoyed a private and special relationship with the government since 1933," and which "from Administration to Administration . . . had a continuous privilege to participate in government decisions with no public record or review."[24]

Labor resistance to corporate free rein in the postwar period was also limited. Organized labor entered into an unwritten agreement with management: the unions promised industrial peace and stability in return for steadily increasing real wages and improved working conditions. Although health and safety grievances were a major source of rank-and-file discontent and disruptive action during the war, workers made little progress toward winning on-the-job health and safety protections in the first two decades after the war. The labor movement itself did not pursue health and safety issues aggressively. When considered during collective bargaining, as one union health and safety director put it, all too often "health and safety came after coffee breaks" in priority.[25] Few unions, with the notable exception of the United Auto Workers, had full-time paid staff working on health and safety in the 1950s.*

In 1951 the Bureau of Labor Statistics surveyed 2,411 union contracts covering 2.25 million workers. Only 28 percent established any structure for worker participation in safety and health decisions, typically a joint safety committee with a management majority. In fewer than 6 percent was the joint safety committee allowed to recommend action to eliminate plant safety and health hazards. Language permitting regular inspections and reporting of hazardous conditions was written into only 3 percent of the contracts.[27] This situation changed little until the 1970s.

Because there was so little pressure for corporate accountability from labor or government, industry was free to pursue almost any production process it chose—

---

*Other exceptions should be noted: after their bitter strike in 1946, the United Mine Workers negotiated an agreement with anthracite coal operators (only a small segment of the coal industry, located primarily in the old Pennsylvania coal fields) to have black lung victims treated at Jefferson Hospital in Philadelphia. But the union made no demand that the companies protect workers *in advance* from coal dust exposure. The United Auto Workers had won the right to strike over local safety hazards in the 1930s. Unions in especially dangerous occupations, such as the International Brotherhood of Electrical Workers and the International Longshoremen's and Warehousemen's Union, had also won the right to refuse dangerous work.[26]

regardless of the pollution generated, the resources wasted, or the health dangers created. Postwar problems intensified as production expanded. In one notorious incident dense, poisonous smoke from a coal-fired steel mill and a zinc reduction plant killed at least 20 people and sickened half the townspeople of Donora, Pennsylvania, in 1948. In this case the United Steelworkers of America took an aggressive stance. The union demanded a Congressional investigation of the incident and when the Senate decided against releasing the report, a Steelworker local in Pennsylvania published it.

The fight for clean water began where it had stopped before the war, with reformers pushing Congress to pass tighter federal water pollution control laws and industry trying to maintain its "right" to pollute. In 1948 industry won another round. A Water Pollution Control Act was passed which actually lowered federal appropriations for sewer construction for the years 1950–55. Representative Charles Faddis (D-PA) was outraged:[28]

> This is a bill to once more lull the forces that are working against pollution into sleep, to get their minds off the subject of the real cause of pollution . . . pollution from industrial waste.

Wilderness and public land battles in the early 1950s were also reminiscent of earlier conflicts. President Eisenhower's Interior Secretary Douglas McKay opened almost all national wildlife refuges to oil and gas leasing. He was so responsive to private interests eager to capture the wealth on and under public lands that he was nicknamed "Giveaway" McKay.[29] The biggest wilderness fight of the period was an eerie throwback to Hetch Hetchy: during the Truman years the federal government decided to build a 575-foot dam for water and power on the upper Colorado River at Echo Park in Dinosaur National Park. Nearly all national conservation groups joined to fight the dam, which they considered unnecessary and inappropriately sited. Letters to Congress ran 80 to 1 against the project: "I am amazed," said one observer, "at the aroused spirit of conservationists and their greatly increased numbers."[30] In 1955 the government was forced to abandon the idea.

When conservation groups followed this victory with an attempt to pass federal legislation establishing wilderness protection as a right and priority, they met with stiff opposition within Congress and from industry. Industry turned to an argument which it had often used against its opposition: environmental advocates were anti-American, leading the nation toward economic disaster. Testifying against the Wilderness Bill, A.P. Morris of the Kennecott Copper Company warned:[31]

> Certainly the Soviet Union, the enemy of the free world, would be delighted with the passage of such legislation that would limit the development of the natural mineral reserves given us by a bountiful Providence.

As the country prospered, resource use and wilderness policy continued to create major conflict. But serious, new environmental problems began to demand public attention: between 1946 and 1970 the measured levels of all air pollutants and most water pollutants rose faster than would have been predicted from the increase of population and production during the same period. Energy use soared as industry shifted to inefficient and capital-intensive production and as suburban expansion required greater gasoline and electricity use. Natural resource exploitation increased. New and hazardous pollutants were introduced into the environment at a phenomenal rate.

By the early 1950s automobile smog emerged as a serious new problem. In Los Angeles, New York, and other major cities automobile emissions surpassed factory smoke and gases as the greatest contributor to air pollution. While more people were driving more miles, automobile manufacturers made the problem worse by building heavy, high-powered vehicles which consumed more gasoline per mile and required gasoline with higher lead content. The average 1968 passenger car, for example, emitted more than twice the nitrogen oxide exhaust as the average 1946 car. Because of the increase in engine power and compression, cars in 1971 polluted the environment with nearly twice as much lead for the same amount of actual use as they did in the immediate postwar years.[32]

Why did the companies make this environmentally damaging change? The low price of gasoline was one factor. Another was that government-subsidized suburbs and super-highways made bigger, roomier, more powerful cars attractive. The real reason, however, had less to do with consumer preferences than with corporate profits. While it cost GM $300 more to build a Cadillac Coupe DeVille than it did a Chevrolet Caprice in the late 1960s, consumers paid $3800 more for the Cadillac. General Motors pocketed the difference.[33]

The automobile industry avoided taking responsibility for air pollution. When Los Angeles County Supervisor Kenneth Hahn asked the president of Ford Motor Company in 1953 whether the company planned to reduce auto exhaust vapors, Ford denied there was a problem. It was not until 1961 that GM introduced pollution control devices on cars sold in California—and this device cut hydrocarbon emissions only 25 percent. In 1966, under Congressional pressure, the industry finally put exhaust control devices on all new cars sold in California. For the first time hydrocarbon emissions from cars in Los Angeles began to drop.[34]

On 10 January 1969 the Anti-Trust Division of the Justice Department filed a civil complaint against the four major automakers and the Automobile Manufacturers

Association for conspiring to delay the development of antipollution devices. The case was settled out of court. The companies pledged never to conspire to cause such delays in the future.[35]

The auto industry was not the only one where accelerated growth and technological change in the postwar years proved profitable to firms but unnecessarily harmful to public health and the environment. The chemical industry provides the most extreme example of such private success and public failure. Before World War II U.S. production of synthetic organic chemicals totaled fewer than one billion pounds a year. By 1976 production had soared to 162.9 billion pounds.[36] The number of commercially available compounds rose from 17,000 in 1958 to about 58,000 in 1971 and 70,000 today.[37]

The proliferation of chemical compounds and chemically-based products—such as polyesters and nylons, detergents, plastics, lubricants, insecticides, pesticides, and herbicides—made chemicals one of the major growth industries of the postwar period. A Commerce Department study of 22 major industrial groups for the period 1966–78 ranked chemicals as the top performer in terms of growth, profitability, hourly wages, and relative success in generating exports and resisting imports.[38] By 1976 chemical companies owned 14 percent of all manufacturing plants and equipment. Between 1975 and 1979 the chemical industry's profit rate averaged 38 percent higher than the average for all manufacturing industries. Its profits accounted for 11 percent of all manufacturing profits.[39]

Today the chemical industry also accounts for 60 percent of the nation's toxic wastes. As production of chemicals, plastics, and synthetics has increased, people have been exposed to a poisonous array of health hazards at work and in their communities. *Business Week* reported in 1974:[40]

> After three decades of unprecedented and virtually
> unregulated proliferation of new chemical products,
> American industry now confronts a frightening fact.
> . . . Long-term exposure to an unknown number of
> chemicals can produce irreparable damage to the
> organs of employees who work with them—and chem-
> icals are used in every nook and cranny of U.S.
> industry, not just the $70 billion, 1-million worker
> chemical industry.

Many of the health problems caused by excessive
exposure to chemical liquids, dusts, mists, fumes, and
vapors were identified long before the industry's postwar
boom: rashes, lesions, and other skin diseases; emphyse-
ma, bronchitis, and a variety of lung diseases; chronic
irritation of eyes, nose, and throat; anemia; liver damage;
kidney damage; circulatory disorders; urinary infections;
nervous system disorders. What distinguishes the postwar
period, however, is the dramatic increase in chemically-
caused cancers and genetic defects, both inside and
outside the workplace.

Acrilonitrile, a synthetic developed in the early 1950s
for use in clothing, carpeting, home furnishings, and other
products, and which was a $1.5 billion industry in 1978,
was found in 1977 to be related to a high rate of cancer of
the colon and lungs among workers in Du Pont's synthetic
textile plant in Camden, South Carolina.[41] Vinyl chloride,
a gas widely used in plastic products and as an aerosol
propellant, was confirmed in 1974 to be a cause of
angiosarcoma, a type of liver cancer which is usually fatal.

It is not known how many other chemicals in commercial use might cause cancer—alone, in combination, or
under particular conditions of use or exposure. But
according to Robert Hoover of the National Cancer
Institute, "Much descriptive evidence . . . suggests that a
substantial number of cancers may be due to exposures to
toxic chemicals."[42] Moreover, according to Hoover, cancers attributable to chemicals are likely to escalate:[43]

With marked increases in the production of potentially toxic chemicals over the last 30 years and the long latency periods that lapse between exposure and manifestation of the illness, there is reason to believe that the problem of chemically-induced cancers may become more severe as time passes.

The chemical revolution was just beginning in the 1950s. Thousands of new chemical compounds have been introduced since. According to Dr. Bruce Ames, "We haven't seen the effects in terms of carcinogenicity of the modern chemical world. That is going to hit us in the 1980s, because of the 20 to 25 year lag period."[44]

American steel companies, buoyed by the lack of foreign competition in the early postwar period, made good profits but failed to look ahead. Rather than sink significant capital into new or retrofitted coke ovens and other facilities, many companies chose to milk their plants for as long as they could. The result was high short-term profits through the mid-1960s at the cost of antiquated plants that could not compete with rebuilt—and less polluting—European and Japanese mills. These plants, which spewed forth noxious air pollutants, left coke oven workers with unusually high rates of lung and other cancers. The first conclusive epidemiological study, completed in 1966, showed lung cancer mortality for Allegheny County, Pennsylvania, coke oven workers to be more than double that predicted by the experience of other steel workers in the area.[*45]

In 1944 the paper industry produced 319 pounds of paper for every person in America. By 1969 production had climbed to 476 pounds per person. The industry dramatically increased production of disposable paper bags, plates, boxes, cups, and anything else people would

---

*Even though the 1966 study pointed conclusively to increased incidence of lung cancer among coke oven workers, the steel industry fought until 1980 to prevent OSHA from implementing a 1971 standard regulating coke oven emissions.

buy. In so doing the paper industry exacerbated the costly problem of waste disposal. In addition the paper industry was generating about one-fourth of the nation's industrial water pollution and significant air pollution by 1970. This need not have happened. As James Fallows noted in his 1971 study of industrial pollution in Savannah, Georgia, ". . . the paper industry is *potentially* one of the most environmentally safe in the country." Forests can be replanted, air and water pollution reduced, and paper waste minimized. But it did not pay companies to conserve in the 1950s and 1960s. As Fallows explained, "When natural resources appear on the balance sheet, then conservation becomes part of normal business practice. . . . But whenever resources are free . . . then the public pays."[46]

In one industry after another the pattern was the same: increased production and growth during the postwar heyday, accompanied by increasingly serious damage to the natural environment and health. American industrial leaders *could* have looked ahead and modernized their facilities in environmentally-sound ways. Had they done so, they would probably be more competitive internationally today—and less subject to strict federal regulation. But American industrial leaders pursued maximum short-term profits, used the postwar trade advantage and, in effect, cashed in their chips while they could. Business leaders created their own opposition. By the mid-1960s the demand for the government to step in and stop corporate America from exploiting the environment and assaulting public health was being pressed by a wide cross section of the American people.

THE MOVEMENT EVOLVES

The first organized postwar protest against environmentally-dangerous technologies focused on the radiation dangers of both military and civilian uses of nuclear power. A number of scientists who worked on the development of atomic power, and who understood the effects of radiation, led the call for strict controls on the spread and use of nuclear power. Barry Commoner, a biologist at Washington University in St. Louis, began investigating nuclear radiation after the 1953 showering of Troy, New York, with fallout from Nevada A-bomb tests. Commoner and other scientists founded the Committee for Nuclear Information in St. Louis in 1958. Local Committees of Concerned Scientists spread to a number of cities. These groups were instrumental in informing people of the dangers of nuclear fallout. They also organized a campaign to end atmospheric testing of nuclear weapons, collecting baby teeth from tens of thousands of children to dramatize the pervasiveness of strontium 90 contamination. The campaign succeeded when Congress approved the limited Nuclear Test Ban Treaty in 1963.

Opposition to the siting and construction of several nuclear power plants also began in the 1950s. Pacific Gas and Electric Company (PG&E), California's largest electric utility, announced in 1958 a plan to build the world's largest nuclear reactor, north of San Francisco on the coast at Bodega Head. The company claimed that the facility would provide two-thirds of San Francisco's electricity by 1965. One member of the Sonoma County Board of Supervisors, envisioning the boost in tax revenues which the plant would provide, felt that "A million dollars ought to affect anybody's thinking."[47] Not everyone in the area agreed. A small group of local residents, opposed to having a nuclear facility in their town and on the coast, formed the Committee to Preserve Bodega Head and fought the plant construction. In 1963 a seismologist who was consulting both for the U.S. Geological Survey and the citizens' group fighting the plant found the site sat on top of the San Andreas Fault. In November 1964 PG&E finally abandoned the project. It was the first time citizens concerned about the dangers of nuclear power were able to prevent construction of a nuclear plant.[48]

In Detroit, also in the late 1950s, the United Auto Workers tried to halt construction by Detroit Edison of an experimental fast-breeder reactor. The Atomic Energy Commission (AEC) had encouraged Detroit Edison to build the reactor and issued a construction permit in August 1956, despite warnings from its own safety committee. Walter Reuther, then president of the Auto Workers, which had over 500,000 members in the Detroit area, demanded a public hearing. The UAW was joined by the United Electrical Workers and the United Papermakers and Paperworkers of America, but their joint effort to halt construction failed. In the spring of 1961 the Supreme Court ruled the AEC was within its rights and the reactor could be built. It should never have been built: in October 1966, before the reactor passed its final tests and began full operations, a series of accidents caused a partial meltdown of the reactor core and came within seconds of causing a major calamity. The experimental breeder reactor never produced another kilowatt. It stands now, empty and fenced off, entombed for hundreds of years until in-plant radiation drops to safe levels.

Citizen opposition to the Bodega Head and Detroit nuclear plants reflected two distinct concerns of the environmental movement as it developed in the 1950s and 1960s: the threat to the local environment from building industrial facilities and other massive projects; and the public health threat posed by dangerous, toxic materials. As these two problems became more serious and better understood by the public, people joined together to prevent further deterioration of both health and environment.

Suburbanization and rising energy demand spurred a

variety of large-scale environmentally-unsound developments in the 1960s. Many of the key turning points in the evolution of the environmental movement involved citizen opposition to these developments, particularly those which threatened either wilderness or urban neighborhoods. There were battles over dams, such as the fight to prevent the Tennessee Valley Authority (TVA) from damming the wild Obed River and building the Tellico Dam on the Little Tennessee River, and the well-publicized campaign by David Brower and the Sierra Club to stop two large dams being considered for the Grand Canyon.* There were "freeway revolts," particularly in cities where interstate highways were slated for construction through predominantly black and poor neighborhoods. One of the most well-known was a 25-year campaign to stop highway construction through 300-acre Overton Park in Memphis, Tennessee, which finally ended successfully in 1981. In New York suburban residents and conservationists fought Consolidated Edison's plan to build a hydroelectric power plant at Storm King Mountain on the Hudson River, one of the few remaining stretches of unspoiled waterways in the northeast. In Florida citizens fought and defeated construction of the ill-conceived Cross Florida Barge Canal. Across the nation these conflicts became more and more common —and hotly contested.

The other main strand of environmental activism, opposition to the public health threat posed by pollution, received a big boost in 1962, when Rachel Carson published *Silent Spring*. The book confirmed what many Americans suspected: the environmental problems facing the nation were different from those of earlier

---

*The Sierra Club launched a national campaign to stop these dams, publishing newspaper and magazine ads which were inspired by John Muir and Hetch Hetchy: the ads featured a photograph of Michelangelo's "The Creation of Adam," suggesting that the dam builders might just as well flood the Sistine Chapel as the Grand Canyon.

decades. The book was a devastating attack on chemical pesticides, particularly DDT. Carson, a marine zoologist who had worked for the federal Fish and Wildlife Service, showed that, like radioactive wastes (which she called "the most dangerous materials that ever existed in all the earth's history"), toxic synthetic chemicals were working their way through the food chain and causing extensive damage.[49] The book's title referred to the death of songbirds caused by DDT poisoning: if pesticide use was not curbed, Carson warned, America might well emerge from one cold, grey winter into a deathly silent spring. The book stayed on the *New York Times* bestseller list for 31 weeks. The call to action reached a broad segment of the American public.

Environmental awareness and growing activism also reached into the workplace, where many hazardous new technologies and substances had their first and most damaging effects. In coal mines, for example, the introduction of continuous mining machines in the 1940s not only sharply reduced the number of miners needed to produce coal, but also increased the amount of coal dust miners were inhaling. The new machines actually increased the likelihood of coal miners developing black lung disease. The 250,000-member United Rubber Workers found, early in the 1960s, that new production processes could cause unexpected and serious health problems. In 1961 more than 312 of the 2,220 workers at Uniroyal's plant in Eau Claire, Wisconsin, developed a respiratory illness. The union traced the disease outbreak to a new vulcanizing process.*

---

*When the union pressed the company to acknowledge responsibility, Uniroyal contested all compensation claims. Local URW President John Basamian called a meeting of his members to discuss the possibility of a strike. While he was addressing the members, the company hand-delivered a note agreeing to pay the benefits. Yet, even with a commitment in hand, it was seven years before the compensation levels for permanently disabled workers were finalized.[50]

By the mid-1960s a growing body of scientific research made it clear to workers and their unions just how dangerous on-the-job exposure to certain substances could be. Dr. Irving J. Selikoff, a chest physician specializing in tuberculosis, founded a medical clinic in Paterson, New Jersey, in 1953. By chance, 17 of his early patients were employed by an asbestos plant nearby. Selikoff found that 15 men showed some signs of pulmonary defects resulting from the inhalation of asbestos.[51] Selikoff (now on the staff of the Mount Sinai School of Medicine in New York) made contact in 1962 with the New York and Newark locals of the International Association of Heat and Frost Insulators and Asbestos Workers and conducted an extended study of workers at the Paterson plant. The results were widely publicized in the mid-1960s: asbestos workers were contracting unusually high rates of asbestosis, lung cancer, and mesothelioma.

At the same time researchers were finding deadly occupational health problems in other industries. Dr. William Lloyd, now on the staff of OSHA, conducted studies of cancer deaths among residents of Allegheny County, Pennsylvania, the steelmaking area around Pittsburgh. He found very high rates of cancer among steelworkers exposed to coke oven emissions (compared both to other steelworkers and the public at large).[52] In the coalfields evidence gathered by Dr. I.E. Buff, Donald Rasmussen, and Harley A. Wells provided further proof of what coal miners already knew: black lung disease was killing bituminous coal miners. Throughout the 1960s invisible occupational killers were being made more visible. And, unlike many studies conducted by industry researchers in the 1930s and 1940s, the results were being publicized to affected workers and the American public.

Toward the end of the decade the various strands of the environmental and occupational health/safety crises catapulted into public consciousness almost simultaneously.

On 20 November 1968 a coal mine explosion at Consolidation Coal Company's No. 9 mine in Farmington, West Virginia, killed 78 miners. Two months later a Union Oil Company oil well blew out in the bay off Santa Barbara, California, covering 13 miles of beautiful and valuable ocean beach with millions of gallons of viscous, black oil. Both disasters received extensive network television coverage and became symbols of the unfulfilled promise of "the good life." For many Americans it was their first in-depth exposure to environmental disaster and to the pain and suffering of workplace accidents. These events touched the public nerve and added to the momentum for change.

In February 1969 10,000 coal miners in West Virginia walked out of the mines to demand the state legislature pass a bill authorizing workers' compensation payments for black lung victims. Hundreds marched to the state Capitol in Charleston, forcing passage of the compensation bill. Later in 1969 U.S. marshalls seized over 10 tons of frozen salmon in Wisconsin and Minnesota because of excessive DDT levels. Cleveland's industrial waste disposal, the Cuyahoga River, burst into flames. In August Los Angeles residents were warned that an air inversion was causing smog so poisonous that no one should engage in strenuous outdoor activity requiring deep breathing.[53] In large cities and small towns, in poor and wealthy neighborhoods across the nation, on the job and in the community, payment had come due for decades of uncontrolled business development.

As environmentally-concerned people tried to address the intensifying crises in their communities, in wilderness areas, and in their workplaces, they saw both business and government openly obstructing environmental activism. The experience of hundreds of thousands of people fighting their particular and varied battles was similar. And they drew a similar conclusion: in order to bring about change they needed to rely on themselves and on the strength of their numbers.

Between 1966 and 1970 paid membership in the National Wildlife Federation, the Sierra Club, National Audubon Society, Wilderness Society, and Izaak Walton League almost doubled from 439,400 to 842,100. The Sierra Club alone grew from 35,000 members in 1966 to 113,000 in 1970.[54] Thousands of new environmental organizations formed on the local, state, and national levels. Many were ad hoc groups created to protect one particular area or stop one specific polluter. Others, like Friends of the Earth, the Environmental Defense Fund, and Environmental Action, evolved (not unlike the CIO's evolution out of the AFL in the 1930s) from frustration with the moderate political stance and inertia of older conservation groups.

Environmental activists became increasingly sophisticated. They learned to organize. They formed groups, conducted grassroots educational activities, recruited members, and established information networks. Environmentalists learned how to do research for themselves, and to confront government officials, politicians, and corporations. Perhaps most importantly they became convinced that much pollution and environmental destruction was unnecessary, that there were alternatives, that business and government were inadequate to the task of environmental protection, and that people were *entitled* to be protected against environmentally-destructive and harmful activities. Given the abysmal record of most states and municipalities in controlling pollution, environmental groups turned to Congress, the national executive agencies, and the courts.

In response to widespread public pressure during an era of intense political turbulence and relative economic plenty, Congress passed a series of unprecedented environmental and occupational safety/health laws. Spurred by the Farmington disaster and fearful of a national coal miners' strike like the one in West Virginia, Congress passed the Federal Coal Mine Health and Safety Act in 1969. This was the first federal legislation to accept medical evidence connecting a disease to a specific occupation, and the first to mandate eradication of a major occupational disease. That same year Congress passed the National Environmental Protection Act (NEPA) which established environmental quality as a leading national priority. The Act opened federal agency decisionmaking processes to individuals, groups, and communities which might be affected by the outcome. NEPA also required federal agencies and private developers funded with federal money to prepare Environmental Impact Statements. This opened the door for litigation to ensure that federal programs were consistent with environmental protection and that alternate options had been considered.

Richard Nixon signed NEPA into law on 1 January 1970, ushering in what has since been labeled the Environmental Decade. Soon thereafter he created the Environmental Protection Agency (EPA) to coordinate and execute national environmental policy. On 22 April 1970 the environmental movement seized the public imagination with the coordinated activities and media events of Earth Day. With impetus from then-Senator Gaylord Nelson (D-WI), and four months of organizing spearheaded by college students working in the nation's capital, environmental rallies were held at some 1,500 colleges and 10,000 schools.

In 1970 Congress passed amendments to the Clean Air Act which established the first enforceable federal legislation mandating protection of the nation's air quality. The Act instructed EPA to set and enforce standards for pollution emissions from automobiles and from industrial facilities so specific national ambient air quality goals could be met. Later that year Congress passed the Occupational Safety and Health Act, which asserted the right of all Americans to clean and safe workplaces and established the Occupational Safety and Health Administration (OSHA). Together OSHA and the federal Coal Mine Health and Safety Act changed the legal framework for occupational rights. These laws established the rights of every worker to participate in setting workplace environmental standards; to be informed about workplace hazards; to request federal inspection of the workplace; to contest the federal determination on whether a hazard exists; to be protected against employer discrimination for taking an active role in shaping health and safety decisions; and to have access to personal health records kept by the company.

Throughout the 1970s public pressure remained strong. Ralph Nader sponsored in-depth journalistic reports on air pollution, water pollution, occupational health and safety, and other environmental problems. These studies set a high standard for investigative work and public information which has been met regularly by researchers and journalists covering (and uncovering) environmental problems. The frequency of major environmental disasters has also sustained public concern. Crises like the contamination of Virginia's James River with the toxic pesticide Kepone, the pouring of PCBs into the Hudson River, the discovery of toxic waste dumps like Love Canal and Kentucky's Valley of the Drums, reports on the near death of Lake Erie, outbreaks of occupational disease, threats of development in national parks and wilderness areas, and the accident at Harrisburg's Three Mile Island nuclear plant have contributed to the public's sense that there is still a long way to go before wilderness, environmental quality, and public health are adequately protected.

Congress responded to continuing public pressure by

filling many serious gaps in environmental and occupational health and safety protection: the Clean Water Act
(1972), enacted over President Nixon's veto; a strengthened Federal Insecticide, Fungicide and Rodenticide Act
(1972), which set guidelines for pesticide production and
use; Noise Control Act (1972); Black Lung Benefits Act
(1972), which broadened eligibility requirements for
black lung benefits; Safe Drinking Water Act (1974);
Toxic Substances Control Act (1976), which set federal
policy on the production and uses of toxics; Resources
Conservation and Recovery Act (1976); Surface Mining
Control and Reclamation Act (1977), which regulated the
stripmining of coal; Mine Safety and Health Amendments
Act (1978); the Alaska National Interest Lands Conservation Act (1980), which designated over 100 million acres
as national parks, preserves, and refuges; Superfund
(1980). These laws set national environmental-quality
standards, and established research, compliance, and
enforcement mechanisms to move the American industrial system toward attainment of those goals.

   These compliance standards and enforcement procedures gave people something which they had previously
lacked: the opportunity to pressure corporations and
administrative agencies to comply with clear guidelines
—and the ability to use litigation to force their compliance. Victor J. Yannacone, one of the founders of the
Environmental Defense Fund, frequently told environmental activists, "Don't just sit there and bitch—sue somebody."[55] Environmentalists found in lawsuits the kind of
disruptive tactic industrial workers in the 1930s had
pioneered in the sitdown strike. New litigation groups
—the Environmental Defense Fund, Natural Resources
Defense Council, and the Sierra Club Legal Defense
Fund—used the strategy of "suing the bastards" to inter-
vene directly in environmental protection disputes.
Through litigation citizens could force government and

corporations to comply with existing laws. They could win rulings broadening governmental responsibility and prompt the passage of new laws by pinpointing weaknesses in existing ones. Litigation also led to delays of certain ill-conceived projects until public education and lobbying campaigns could be organized to force improved design or cancellation.

Throughout the 1970s environmental activists made great gains, using public education, litigation, direct action, lobbying, organizing, and confrontational politics to win a redefinition of public rights.* Activism on environmental issues cut across a broad spectrum of the American public. As one observer has written:[56]

> One does not need to search very far to find cases of poor Chicanos fighting a highway on environmental grounds; Native Americans invoking NEPA (the National Environmental Policy Act) to contest a power plant location; or Chicago working-class groups effectively organized to stop air pollution (Campaign Against Pollution) or the location of an expressway (Anti-Crosstown Coalition). Moreover, some of the largest and most active of environmental groups are organized sportsmen, such as the National Wildlife Federation and its affiliates, which have a strong blue collar membership base, and the Izaak Walton League, whose membership seems to be located in small towns of America, and is clearly not upper class.

Environmental values became firmly established in the United States in the 1960s and 1970s. Today there are approximately 12,000 different environmental groups

*Llewellyn King, editor of *The Energy Daily*, wrote in 1977 that:

> The fact is that the environmentalists have won, and it has to be said that their achievements in a few short years have been massive. What they have achieved is an institutionalization of concern for the environment to every level of national life.[57]

across the country. A June 1981 Harris Poll revealed that an overwhelming majority of the American public supports continued—and even stricter—environmental laws. Eighty-six percent of Americans opposed weakening the Clean Air Act. By 93 to 4 percent, people almost unanimously opposed easing water pollution rules.[58]

Given the effectiveness of environmental activism in winning new rights and establishing new principles for industrial development in the past decade, it is not surprising that the business community launched its concerted effort to weaken environmental laws, regulations, and enforcement—and to undermine public support for these protections. Nor is it surprising the strategy has been based on job blackmail.

The likelihood is great that the coming years will see more and more efforts to use jobs as a wedge to split potential allies and reassert corporate dominance. Fighting job blackmail on environmental, health, and labor issues is a critically important challenge, one which will not be met unless both labor and environmental activists commit themselves to close cooperation. The final section examines the past decade's experience in fighting job blackmail, and suggests ways to make that fight easier and more successful.

PART IV

Beyond Blackmail: Organizing for Jobs and Environment

13
An End to "Business as Usual"

When people fail to organize to protect themselves, their rights are undermined and their needs ignored. Only the concerted effort of large numbers of people working together can force the kinds of changes won by workers in the 1930s and by environmentally-concerned citizens in the 1960s and 1970s. Only a willingness to overcome job blackmail by challenging corporate and government leaders' "business as usual" attitudes can yield significant gains and greater public empowerment.

Job blackmail would not be such an effective obstacle to mobilizing public activism if people felt more secure about their jobs and their employment prospects. When Vernon McDougall was a health and safety representative for the Paperworkers Union in the early 1970s, he learned first-hand the difference job security could make in people's attitudes and actions. For several years McDougall tried to involve workers in Maine's paper factories in protecting their own health and safety on the job. In the towns of Jay and Winslow, where the Scott and International Paper companies operated old, inefficient, heavily-polluting sulphite mills, he could not get workers to come to meetings or even acknowledge their workplace problems. But when the companies replaced the Jay and Winslow plants with new, expensive, state-of-the-art mills, McDougall noticed a significant change. Workers became eager to play a role in maintaining their well-being and more confident about what they could do. They created a Toxic Substances Committee and began devising ways to protect themselves on-the-job. "The company doesn't put this kind of money into these monsters and then walk away," explained George Lambertson, Paperworkers international representative in Maine since 1960.[1]

The best form of job security would be *full employment* —secure, safe jobs at decent wages for all who want to work. Full employment (or even movement toward full employment) would dramatically shift the balance of power between employers and workers. If employees felt they could afford to refuse unhealthy, unsafe, or environmentally-destructive work, they would be more likely to challenge employers on health and pollution problems—just as they would on low wages, poor benefits, and other grievances. As Leonard Woodcock wrote in 1976:[2]

> If we had a full employment economy in America today, corporate polluters would have a far more difficult time with environmental blackmail. The Union Carbides, the Allied Chemicals, the U.S. Steels, and the GMs would be far less successful in selling the myth that workers must sacrifice their jobs if we are to have a clean environment.

But the nation is far from full employment—or even a national commitment to that goal. Business leaders adamantly opposed full employment legislation in 1946 and 1976 and have consistently thwarted consideration of full employment as a serious policy option.

The challenge facing workers and other constituencies confronted with job blackmail—including environmentalists—is to lessen the impact of those threats *now,* when full employment is still a dream. Workers and environmentalists can begin to meet this challenge by working together to achieve: (1) economic protection for the small number of workers who actually do lose their jobs because of environmental legislation; (2) increased communication; and (3) mutual support for efforts to broaden democratic rights and challenge corporate power.

EMPLOYEE PROTECTIONS

Tony Mazzocchi, former vice-president of the Oil, Chemical and Atomic Workers, believes legislative protections are essential if workers and environmentalists are to minimize future conflicts:[3]

> Every single environmental measure should have a provision in it for the protection of a worker's income and benefits. That would go a long way toward undermining the jobs versus the environment argument. As it is now, the companies pick up the issue and run with it.

In June 1971 Leonard Woodcock and the United Auto Workers called for such protections during hearings on the economic impact of environmental regulation:[4]

> The problem, let me repeat, is not that [workers] are advocates of pollution, but that their economic circumstances require them to think first of jobs, paychecks and bread on the table.

Woodcock proposed that workers who lost their jobs because of employer pollution abuses should have the right to bring a class action suit against their employers and to recover lost wages and benefits, lost seniority, the cost of retraining, and moving expenses.[5]

Congress addressed Woodcock's concerns in Title VIII

of the proposed Public Works and Economic Development Act of 1972. The bill—which Congress passed but President Nixon vetoed—would have required the government to investigate all employment losses alleged to result from enforcement of any federal environmental law and to work with affected communities to devise alternatives to layoffs. Workers certified as unemployed because of pollution control standards would have been eligible for: 78 weeks of unemployment compensation at 60 percent of their former weekly wage, a year of mortgage and rent payments, and reemployment assistance. Employers would have been forbidden to discharge or discriminate against any employee who helped enforce pollution laws. If an employer were found to have fired a worker for environmental activity, the Labor Department could have ordered the worker reinstated and fined the employer. The bill would have also authorized the Department of Labor to make low-interest loans to help private industry meet pollution control standards. Senator Edmund Muskie (D-ME), a key sponsor of much of the major environmental legislation of the early 1970s, saw the bill as a way of assuring that the "jobs and livelihoods of workers, their families, and their communities are not used as pawns in industry efforts to undercut pollution control regulation."[6] But Nixon's veto killed the bill and corporate opposition prevented future attempts to pass similar legislation.*

It is important that workers threatened with an environmentally-related plant closing—or those who are victims of one—be protected from financial hardship and

*Both the Clean Air Act (Section 321) and the Clean Water Act (Section 507) have employee protection provisions lobbied for by the Steelworkers and other unions. Firms are prohibited from firing workers or discriminating against workers who file complaints of pollution-control violations against their employers. Workers who are threatened or who are laid off as a result of employer compliance with any part of either law can request an investigation and a public hearing from EPA. The administrator of EPA is required to conduct continuing evaluations of any shifts in employment resulting from compliance with both acts.

assisted in finding new work. But the nation's unemployment and plant-closing crisis extends far beyond the small number of plants shut down because of environmental regulations. Until workers and their communities can have greater control over and protection against *all* sudden, unannounced plant closings, job blackmail will remain a convincing threat. Currently only two state laws try to limit the ability of employers to move, but both are inadequate: Maine requires employers who close or move their plant to pay workers one week's salary for each year worked over three years; Wisconsin requires firms to give the state 60 days notice of "impending shutdown."[7]

Business leaders are opposed to any such laws, since they clearly restrain business ability to shift capital freely. Industry warns of dire consequences and raises the spectre of unemployment. A *Wall Street Journal* editorial claimed, "If anything, the [plant closing] bills would increase job loss."[8] And a corporate lobbyist in Massachusetts told the state senate, "Even serious consideration of [such a] bill would be raising a sign on the borders of this state that investment isn't welcome here."[9] The Ohio Public Interest Campaign, a coalition of labor unions, church groups, and civil rights, consumer, senior, and environmental organizations, has been fighting since July 1977 for passage of a state Community Readjustment Act. The Act, which would require two years advance notice, economic impact statements, severance pay, continued coverage of workers' health benefits, and community assistance funds, remains bottled up in the state senate. National legislation to protect workers adversely affected by plant closings would prevent one state's workers from being played against those of another. But the National Employment Priorities Act, first proposed in 1974 by Senator Walter Mondale (D-MN) and Representative William Ford (D-MI), was never even reported out of committee.

In many western European nations, employee protections are an accepted part of doing business. Employers in a number of countries are required to provide advance notice of shutdowns and conduct preclosing negotiations with employees so job loss is minimized. A group of American trade unionists representing the Auto Workers, Steelworkers, and Machinists visited England, West Germany, and Sweden in 1979 and concluded:[11]

> Without exception . . . all three [countries] had programs for coping with the adverse effects of economic dislocation upon workers and communities which are far in advance of anything yet tried on a large scale in a coordinated way in the United States.

The union representatives noted these laws have not caused economic ruin. In fact, "Many of the same corporations which can be counted on to oppose such programs in the United States have been investing heavily over the past thirty years and, for the most part, have operated profitably, in the three countries we visited."[12]

Environmentalists should join labor and other community activists in pressuring state and federal legislatures to pass employee protection laws with environment-related provisions. They should also support the efforts of unions to raise these issues at the bargaining table. Employee protections need to be seen as "environmental" issues as much as "labor" issues, since they strike at the root of fears which lead workers to oppose environmental-protection programs and environmental organizations.

KNOWLEDGE AND INFORMATION

Corporate control of knowledge and information gives job blackmail much of its power. But workers and environmentalists can help each other break the corporate monopoly on health and technical data. They can also mobilize public pressure for greater disclosure of corporate information. Such cooperation is not automatic; it requires a commitment to establishing close ties between organizations. And it means remembering, as president of the AFL-CIO's Industrial Union Department, Howard D. Samuel, has explained, that "the environmental and occupational safety and health issues are two sides of the same coin."[13]

Environmental researchers can sometimes help workers win better health protections on the job. In the late 1960s scientists found high levels of PCBs (polychlorinated biphenyls), then the most widely used synthetic organic chemical, in diseased fish. After careful studies they found PCBs do not degrade and, like DDT, can cause serious reproductive, neurological, respiratory, skin, and eye disorders.[14] In 1971 EPA banned most production of PCBs. In 1977 U.S. production of PCBs ceased.

Yet fifty years ago, industry and public health officials had evidence PCBs caused skin lesions, liver problems, impotence, and burning eyes among PCB factory workers. In 1933, 23 of the 24 workers in the first American PCB manufacturing facility had developed lesions. In 1943 the director of the New York State Division of Industrial Hygiene concluded that PCBs "are in general highly toxic compounds."[15] What was new in the late 1960s was that the information was reaching the public, that people became angry, and that they demanded action. For 30 years neither industry nor government had taken steps to protect PCB workers—until the problem surfaced *outside* the workplace. In effect, the environmental movement helped crack the conspiracy of silence that had surrounded workplace PCB contamination.

Just as environmentalists can provide workers with health data and pollution information which companies try to keep hidden, workers can provide environmental activists with useful in-plant knowledge. For example, workers in the receiving room at the Hudson Falls General Electric plant knew that no matter how harmless the company said PCBs were, their job required them to tear skull-and-crossbones labels off Monsanto barrels filled with PCBs.[16] Employees of the Hooker Chemical and Plastics Corporation in Burlington, New Jersey (members of Local 482 of the United Glass and Ceramic Workers Union), learned in February 1981 the company had secretly brought a highly toxic gas, nitric oxide, into the plant. They also knew they were occasionally ordered to vent vinyl chloride into the air. Standing on a picket line after the local decided to strike over Hooker's unhealthy procedures, Andrew Sinkerlis explained the strike was the union's way of fulfilling its "responsibility to the community" to alert people to the hazards.[17]

However, both workers and community residents currently have only limited access to the technical information they need in order to make informed choices about their welfare and safety. Employers intentionally restrict public access to information about products and processes, worker medical records, and corporate finances. Environmentalists and workers need to work together to broaden their knowledge of and access to this information, so workers can better protect themselves on the job—and be better able to challenge job blackmail.

In the early 1970s labor, community, and environmental activists in a number of cities and states set up Committees on Occupational Safety and Health (COSH groups), bringing together members of different local unions and environmental health activists for education and training. Usually set up outside the traditional union structure, some of these groups have been able to establish close ties between workers and the general community on issues of health, safety, and pollution.*

---

*It is important to note that many of the innovative occupational and environmental health and safety efforts of the late 1960s and 1970s were

COSH groups, labor, and environmental organizations have actively campaigned in recent years for legislation recognizing workers' "right-to-know" about job-related hazards. Connecticut enacted the first "right-to-know" law in May 1980. The law required employers to tell workers during their first month on the job about the carcinogenic substances present in the workplace, the health dangers they posed, and the proper ways to handle them.[18] One month later, employees in New York State won the right "to know the identity and hazardous effects of substances with which they work."[19]

The most impressive "right-to-know" campaign took place in Philadelphia. A broad coalition of community, environmental, and labor groups called the Delaware Valley Toxics Coalition was organized by Philadelphia's COSH group, PHILAPOSH, and other organizations. The coalition, which included the United Auto Workers, the Sierra Club, and the Philadelphia Council of Neighborhood Organizations, forced the city council to consider two amendments to the city's fire and air-pollution codes. These amendments required companies operating in Philadelphia to notify the city of all toxic substances used in their plants, emitted into the air, or stored on the grounds. They also stipulated that all this information be made available to the public.[20] After nine months of intense lobbying by the coalition's member groups, the city council passed the law unanimously on 22 January 1981.

Philadelphia's right-to-know law is unique, extending beyond the workplace and empowering both workers and

---

initiated outside the union structure, often as a result of union inaction. The movement to win Black Lung benefits was initiated in the West Virginia coal fields by a loose coalition of public health physicians, retired miners, VISTA workers, and union members. The Brown Lung Associations, which organized retired textile workers to win compensation benefits and strict controls on cotton dust exposure, also developed independently of the unions. Only after these groups achieved some success and mobilized thousands of people did the unions come to their defense and incorporate their demands into the unions' own programs.

community residents. According to PHILAPOSH director Jim Moran, bridging the labor-environmental-community gap was critical to the campaign's success. The diversity of support received from both within and outside labor insured "the legislation couldn't be dismissed simply as a labor question"—or an environmental one.[21]

In the waning days of the Carter administration, OSHA issued a federal "right-to-know" regulation. Lobbied for primarily by organized labor and COSH groups, the regulation challenged three distinct areas of management prerogative. Employers had to inform workers of the health hazards of materials with which they worked; hazardous substance containers had to be labeled with chemical names and hazard information; workers, their physicians, and (with workers' permission) their unions, were guaranteed access to company medical records.

Business, particularly the chemical industry, vigorously resisted these regulations. It did not take long for the Reagan administration to respond. Within a month after becoming OSHA administrator, Thorne Auchter withdrew the labeling standard and the requirement that workers be informed of potential health hazards. The third provision, access to medical records, survived, but it is being challenged in the courts.

There is another area of closely guarded corporate data which should also be opened. The right-to-know concept should be expanded to include greater access to corporate financial data. When companies claim they cannot afford to clean up or, as they often say, "remove the last two percent" of unhealthy emissions, the burden of proof should be on the firm.*

---

*Corporations have always resisted opening their books, although in recent contract negotiations, in exchange for wage and other concessions, some firms have agreed to show unions financial data on plants which they decide to close. There are mixed feelings in labor about these agreements. John Yolton of the United Auto Workers is skeptical. "For all those years that the companies were doing fine, they didn't want to show us the books or share the profits. Now they want to force the books on us so they can justify more concessions."[22]

In Europe the 10-nation European Economic Community (EEC) has been considering a proposal to require extensive disclosure of financial data to workers and the public. The "Vredeling Initiative," introduced in 1980, would require multinational corporations doing business in EEC nations to give workers a semiannual "clear picture" of the corporation's financial situation, development and employment plans, marketing strategies, new products and technologies, and "all procedures and plans liable to have a substantial effect on employees' interests."[23]

The U.S. Chamber of Commerce, the National Foreign Trade Council, and many individual corporations have protested. Some have threatened the EEC with retaliations. The former general counsel in Europe for International Telephone and Telegraph warned that his company would find it "very difficult" to live with the proposal: "I just don't see how we could operate under this regulation."[24] There has even been legislation introduced in Congress that would allow the U.S. government to prohibit American corporations from complying with European disclosure regulations.

American corporations and the current administration are no less hostile toward worker access to management information in this country. The less people know, the less they can interfere—and the more easily they can be won over. The "right-to-know" about both health and financial data—whether won in Congress or the regulatory agencies, by state and local legislation or through collective bargaining—weakens the clout of job blackmail threats and reduces worker and community vulnerability. That is a major reason why corporations oppose greater disclosure. That is also why environmental and labor activists must work together to secure these rights.

CHALLENGING MANAGEMENT PREROGATIVE

Greater knowledge about products and processes, personal medical histories, and corporate finances is critically important in the fight against job blackmail. But as Charlie Richardson, a Philadelphia shipyard worker and chair of the PHILAPOSH political action committee, explained, "Just having the knowledge isn't enough. You can confront the companies with all the knowledge you want, but that's not what turns them around. After you get the knowledge, you have to do something with it."[25] Workers, especially if they are organized, have the power to "do something" to defend public health and environmental quality.

In 1969 Gilbert Pugliese, a worker at the Jones and Laughlin Steel Corporation in Cleveland, refused to follow his foreman's instructions to dump several hundred gallons of waste oil into the Cuyahoga River. Pugliese felt the oil could just as easily be pumped into drums. He was immediately suspended for five days, then reinstated because of strong support from his union local. Two years later the foreman again insisted Pugliese dump oil into the river. He again refused, risking 18 years seniority and his job. Pressure from the local led the Steelworkers International office to support Pugliese. The company backed down. Pugliese kept his job and the company agreed to pump the oil into drums.[26]

Eleven years later Ken Willet, a member of Canadian Paperworkers' Union Local 574 working for Consolidated Bathurst Incorporated, was suspended and fined a day's pay when he refused to send some 80 tons of chemical pulp stock into the Little Cascapedia River in Quebec. Because of Willet's action, and a grievance filed by the union, the company changed its system of disposing of pulp wastes. Willet explained, "If you work in a mill for 15 years, you see pollution first-hand. Eventually you have to do something about it."[27]

Environmental whistleblowing is not restricted to blue collar production workers. Biologist Morris Baslow was employed by a consulting firm hired by three New York State electric utilities to rebut EPA claims that power plant discharges of warm water were endangering Hudson River fish life. Baslow's research convinced him that EPA was right; but his employer was only interested in giving the utilities what they wanted. In 1979 Baslow sent information to EPA showing how his employer had distorted data. He was fired that same day and sued for stealing company documents. In December 1980 the New York utilities agreed to a number of concessions, including the endowment of a foundation to finance research into the impact of power plants on aquatic life. "I am still not sure any one individual can fight big utilities or businesses," said Baslow, "but I knew I had to try."[28]

Most environmental legislation prohibits employers from firing or discriminating against workers like Baslow. But, in reality, individuals acting alone do not have much power in relation to their employers. Unions have a better chance than individuals of forcing management to improve environmental and health/safety protections.

Perhaps the most well-known employee action on health and safety issues was the five-month 1973 strike by the Oil, Chemical and Atomic Workers (OCAW) against Shell Oil Company. In January 4000 OCAW workers walked out in California and four other states. The union made four key demands: (1) establishment of a joint union-management health and safety committee in every plant; (2) periodic inspections of plants by independent consultants to determine whether workers were being exposed to hazards; (3) medical examinations of workers, at company expense, when indicated by plant inspections; and (4) the availability to the union of all company records on workers' sickness and death.[29] Shell initially refused to bargain on these demands because they were part of "management prerogative." But the union, primarily because of Tony Mazzocchi's years of building labor-environmental cooperation, was able to win endorsements of the strike and a boycott of Shell products from more than a dozen environmental and public interest groups.* A group of 25 scientists and educators published a statement in the 3 May 1973 *New York Times* supporting the strike and boycott and emphasizing the connection between workplace and outside environments. Shell eventually bowed to the pressure and negotiated a settlement. Although the union was only partly successful in winning its demands, the strike made clear to the public and to other unions that workers were willing to confront employers on health and safety issues, that they could develop significant public support for such actions, and that such public support could help the union in negotiations with management.

Environmentalist support for worker health and safety struggles can make a difference. But environmental organizations should also be ready to lend their support to unions on "labor issues" which do not have direct connections to health and safety or environmental protection. Strong unions provide protection against the arbitrary power of employers. Morris Baslow was not a union member. He was fired for taking a principled environmental stance. Gilbert Pugliese and Ken Willet were union members, and although both were temporarily suspended for their refusal to pollute, they did not lose their jobs. It is almost impossible for workers who are not

---

*Center for Science in the Public Interest, Ecology Center Council, Environmental Defense Fund, Environmental Policy Center, Friends of the Earth, Health Research Group, Institute for Public Transportation, National Tenants' Association, National Parks and Conservation Association, National Welfare Rights Organization, Natural Resources Defense Council, Public Interest Economics Center, the Wilderness Society.

represented by a union to challenge their employers on management policies without being fired. Unorganized workers also have a much harder time than union members just knowing their rights under OSHA, the Clean Air and Water Acts, and other legislation.

It was with an understanding of this interconnection of environmental and labor struggles that, in 1980, several environmental groups organized to support the year-old strike for a union contract and improved working conditions by 200 employees of Sanderson Farms, a chicken processing plant in Laurel, Mississippi. The workers, most of whom were black women, earned little more than minimum wage—even those who had been at the plant for 12 years. In a letter circulated to environmental groups around the country, Environmentalists for Full Employment urged people to attend a national march in Laurel in support of the International Chemical Workers Union organizing drive:[30]

> Over the years, the environmental movement has learned the importance of organized labor to a clean and safe environment. . . . In recognition that working people and environmentalists are part of the same struggle for the right to organize and for safe and healthy workplaces and communities, we urge you to take to the streets on May 17 to support justice and dignity.

Just as strong active unions are important to the environmental movement, strong democratic environmental groups are an asset to the labor movement. The health and safety activism of the past decade emerged from the broader environmental movement. According to the UAW's Frank Wallick, the Occupational Safety and Health Act would never have had a strong emphasis on health protections had it not been for the environmental awakening of the late 1960s. Environmental organizations can provide research, lobbying, and strike support and can put public pressure on corporations and the government in support of workers and their unions. Most importantly, effective environmental activism can insure that environmental quality does not deteriorate to the point where the viability of whole industries and the national economy is jeopardized. As Leonard Woodcock has said, "A strong and healthy economy cannot exist within an unhealthy environment, just as only a strong economy can enable us to achieve that healthy environment."[31]

The more solid the groundwork of mutual support and sensitivity to each other's priorities and fears, the better the chance of being able to push back the boundaries of management prerogative and expand democratic rights in both the workplace and the community. When labor and environmentalists agree to confront the business community together, they can effectively demand both jobs *and* environment and reject the false choices posed by employers. It is not an easy process, but there are examples of impressive movement toward that goal. Two significant models come from abroad: the Alternate Corporate Plan campaign launched by workers at Lucas Aerospace in Britain; and the Green Bans movement of the Builders' Labourers Federation of New South Wales, Australia.

Lucas Aerospace: Lucas Aerospace is one of the leading high-technology aerospace equipment manufacturers in Britain. But during the 1970s the company was losing money. As early as 1970 many trade unionists at Lucas saw the company was likely to cut employment drastically, or move abroad in search of cheaper labor, in order to stay in business. They decided to fight future layoffs by forming a Combine Shop Stewards Committee representing all 13 trade unions at 17 Lucas Aerospace sites—and by demanding a role in determining the fate of the company. In 1974 the Stewards Committee began campaigning for what its members called "the right to work on socially useful products." Questionnaires were sent to every Lucas plant asking that workers survey their job skills and the equipment at the site, and give concrete suggestions for alternative products that could be made at Lucas. Workers suggested over 150 ideas for products which were environmentally benign, conserved natural resources, could help the ill and handicapped, and could keep Lucas workers employed. These included kidney machines, low-cost solar collectors, wind generators, road/rail vehicles for cheap, efficient public transport, and hybrid electric/internal combustion engines. The Alternative Corporate Plan grew to six volumes of detailed engineering drawings and economic calculations.[32] It also included plans for retraining programs and for restructuring the work process.[33]

When the Stewards Committee presented the plan to the company in 1976, management flatly rejected it, suggesting it would be best for the Lucas workforce to let management make product policy. But the Stewards Committee did not give up. It chose instead to take the Plan to the public in a highly visible media campaign and to seek—and win—support from many groups outside labor. Today the company still refuses to acknowledge the Alternate Corporate Plan or to involve its workforce in determining the company's future. But the very existence of the Plan, its public challenge to management, and the process of self-education which workers underwent in preparing it, has made the company hesitate to initiate new layoffs. The company cannot simply tell employees, "We have no choice." The employees themselves have shown choices exist. And they are stronger and better organized than before the campaign began.

Green Bans: In the United States the building trades have traditionally been among the most anti-environmental labor unions. In Australia, however, under the brash leadership of Jack Mundey in the early 1970s, the New South Wales branch of the Builders'

Labourers Federation embarked on a unique program of labor-community cooperation for environmental protection. The Builders' Labourers introduced "Green Bans," democratically-decided vetoes of development which building trades' workers considered socially and environmentally unsound.

In the late 1960s Sydney and other cities were experiencing a building boom that was uprooting whole neighborhoods, threatening parklands and the quality of urban life. Instead of simply doing whatever work they were given, the Builders' Labourers issued a public statement in 1970 declaring that workers who built the urban environment had a right to express their opinions on what they were building and how it was being built. Soon thereafter a group of citizens from a neighborhood adjacent to the last remaining area of original bushland in Sydney approached the union, challenging it to put its principles into practice.

A developer was ready to build 25 luxury homes on the bush, and the residents had run out of ideas on how to stop them. As a last resort, and somewhat hesitantly, they turned to the union. After organizing a debate in which both the developer and local residents made presentations, the workers voted to back the citizens' group and refused to build. When the developer threatened to go ahead with nonunion labor, the Builders' Labourers vowed to do no further work on any of that developer's projects. The developer gave in and the first Green Ban went into effect. In the next three years, over 40 Green Bans were proclaimed. The union's actions stopped highway and park destruction, and the demolition of historic buildings and low-income inner-city housing. Often developers had to compromise with local residents by revising their plans to minimize environmental damage before the union would agree to build.

The campaign gave workers a new sense of their own

power and their ability to challenge their employers. According to Mundey:[34]

> The more the controversy developed, the more that workers could see the need to stop the freeway or stop the destruction of houses. And the more they could see that they had the right to make some of those decisions. . . . It was their city, their history, their heritage. And they had the right to make some of the decisions about its future.

The Green Bans had a similar impact on the residents of Australian cities. They saw that, with union help, they might be able to stop and reshape development that was ruining their cities. People found new courage. According to a local priest, residents of one low-income neighborhood slated for demolition who had been pushed around all their lives, revolted: "They came out with old cars and lemonade boxes and set up a wall of defiance against the demolishers and said NO." [35]

The union placed great emphasis on listening to all sides and opening each controversy to the democratic process. "Our strength was that we always called public meetings," explained Jack Mundey. "We always said, 'We'll only accede to your request if you call a public meeting and ask us to do so—and if the membership votes for it.' " [36]

The union was also determined to challenge what Mundey and others perceived as the false distinction between workers and environmentalists:[37]

> For instance, it is said that workers have "no right in" or "are not interested in" environmental issues. This is a myth, dangerous as well as wrong . . . If the New South Wales Builders' Labourers Federation did anything, it killed this myth. It showed that workers are the section of the community first and most affected when the environment is ravaged.

There have been only a few new Green Bans in Australia since 1974.* But not one of the 40 Green Bans of the early 1970s has been overturned. Although Mundey and his supporters could not maintain their political power within the union, the years of their leadership left an important legacy. The nation's historic preservation laws have been rewritten to include greater citizen participation. More importantly, the Green Bans movement, like the Lucas Corporate Plan campaign, advanced the idea that workers have the right and the ability to participate—as workers—in social decisions which affect their lives on-the-job and at home. And the Green Ban movement showed that effective worker-community alliances strengthen the ability of each constituency to challenge corporate control over what should be public decisions. Like the Lucas campaign and any other effective challenge to job blackmail, the New South Wales Builders' Labourers Federation showed that people need not accept management's definitions and choices. As Mundey explained, "Though we all want our members employed, we will not just become robots directed by developers-builders who value the dollar at the expense of the environment."[38]

---

*In 1975 the national leadership of the Builders' Labourers Federation took control of the New South Wales branch of the union away from Mundey and his allies. The new leadership adopted a policy of greater accommodation with the construction industry and no longer advocated Green Bans. At the same time, sharply rising unemployment in the construction industry made workers more reluctant to refuse work.

14
"Don't Tell Us
Who Our
_____Friends Are"

Cooperation between labor and environmental activists in the United States goes back at least to 1948, when the Steelworkers requested the Public Health Service to study the deadly air inversion that killed 20 people in Donora, Pennsylvania. In the late 1950s the United Auto Workers led the unsuccessful fight to prevent construction of Detroit Edison's fast-breeder reactor. A Long Island local of the Gas, Coke, and Chemical Workers (which later merged into the Oil, Chemical and Atomic Workers) collected thousands of baby teeth for the campaign which made strontium 90 contamination a national issue and mobilized public support for the 1963 limited Nuclear Test Ban Treaty.

In the late 1960s and early 1970s, there was strong support from some unions for strict environmental legislation. Workers realized that they suffered doubly from uncontrolled pollution—at work and at home. Many trade unionists were questioning the postwar labor strategy of restricting most bargaining sessions to wages and benefits. As Mike Olszanski of Steelworkers Local 1010 asked, "What good is a better pension plan if you aren't going to live long enough to enjoy it?"[1]

A variety of unions went on record demanding action against pollution and environmental degradation. In 1967 the Auto Workers established a Conservation and Resource Development Department, headed by Vice-President Olga Madar. In January 1970, shortly before his death, Walter Reuther challenged his and other unions to make environment an issue not just for annual resolutions but also for collective bargaining:[2]

> I think the environmental crisis has reached such catastrophic proportions that I think the labor movement is now obligated to raise this question at the bargaining table in any industry that is in a measurable way contributing to man's deteriorating living environment.

A month later the union sent an "Environmental, Occupational Health and Safety Questionnaire" to more than 400 locals and also sponsored the nation's first environmental teach-in, two months before Earth Day, at the University of Michigan. In 1970 bargaining UAW locals initiated about 750 environmental protection demands. Even though the vast majority were related to ventilation and in-plant pollution, union leaders and members were making the connection between the right to negotiate on health and safety and the right to bring other pollution control demands to the bargaining table.[3]

The Auto Workers membership questionnaire was modeled on one which the Oil, Chemical and Atomic Workers (OCAW) circulated to its locals in 1969. OCAW was one of the first unions to make health and safety education a top priority, passing a resolution to that effect at its 1967 convention and holding a series of regional conferences in 1969 on "Hazards in the Industrial Workplace." OCAW was also one of the first unions to stand up to environment-related job blackmail, forcing Union Carbide to back down at its Marietta, Ohio, plant in 1971. At the 1971 AFL-CIO convention OCAW introduced a resolution calling for Federation support of legislation to put the burden of proof for environment-related layoffs on the employer, "with public hearings and opportunity for cross-examination of employer witnesses provided."[4]

In early 1970 the International Brotherhood of Pulp, Sulphite and Paper Mill Workers* successfully negotiated with the Kamloops Pulp and Paper Company in British Columbia for the establishment of a joint union-management environmental protection committee to educate employees on in-plant and community pollution. Later that year the union sponsored a workshop on "Man and his Environment" for more than 250 local union leaders. The Paperworkers' 1971 environmental position paper went so far as to suggest local unions should make the term "unfair environmental practice" as much a byword as "unfair labor practice."[5]

The International Association of Machinists secured the guarantee that workers in a shop temporarily closed because of an alleged pollution violation would receive full compensation at their regular rate of pay for all lost time.[6] The Machinists, the Auto Workers, and other industrial unions—most prominently the United Steelworkers of America and their legislative director Jack Sheehan—helped shape and pass the 1970 Clean Air Act amendments and the 1972 Clean Water Act amendments. These unions were also active supporters of Earth Day.

Many other unions expressed at least symbolic support for pollution controls. The Amalgamated Clothing Workers resolved in 1972 that "through its publications, legislative activities and educational activities, [the union] will continue to fight for a cleaner environment."[7] The Indus-

---

*Merged in 1972 with the United Papermakers and Paperworkers to form the United Paperworkers International Union.

trial Union Department of the AFL-CIO adopted a resolution condemning and rejecting "the environmental blackmail of those who would intimidate the worker with economic threats."[8] The Plasterers Union, one of the AFL-CIO's Building and Construction Trade unions, also expressed concern. President John T. Power wrote in late 1971:[9]

> In my opinion, organized labor has every justification to interject themselves into . . . concern over the establishment and functioning of environmental programs. Organized labor has the same moral responsibility that was evident in spearheading other social legislation and the implementation thereof, such as social security, health, education, safety in the workplace, etc.

Other unions facing serious health and environmental problems were less sympathetic. The Teamsters conducted a 3-year study of environmental and occupational health and safety problems associated with trucking—and kept the findings confidential. The construction unions were enthusiastic about the Clean Water Act, since it was primarily a public works program building sewage treatment plants. But they balked at the Clean Air Act or other environmental legislation which corporate interests warned would lead to cancellations, delays, and less new construction. On "growth" and related questions of energy development, the AFL-CIO's hostility to environmentalists, which became acute in the mid-1970s, was already quite evident. And there were limits to how aggressively the AFL-CIO was prepared to challenge job blackmail and demand strict environmental protections. In 1971 the AFL-CIO executive board, dominated by President George Meany and other union leaders from the building trades, did not approve the strong resolutions proposed by the Oil, Chemical and Atomic Workers on job blackmail and environmental quality.

During this time, environmental groups differed in their

commitment to effective occupational health and safety protections. Although most environmental and conservation organizations supported OSHA legislation in 1970, the older wildlife and wilderness groups shied away from lobbying and public statements. Many of Ralph Nader's organizations played an extremely important role in shaping the legislation and building public support, along with the Sierra Club and Environmental Action. After OSHA was enacted several organizations, including Environmental Action and Friends of the Earth, made a conscious effort to make their members aware of the critical relevance of workplace pollution control to the environmental movement. In 1971 Senator Philip Hart (D-MI) established the Urban Environment Conference to help broaden the way the public defined environmental issues and to focus on the particular environmental problems of urban minorities. The Conference established three task forces: one on minorities; another on clean air (which later became the independent National Clean Air Coalition); and a third, with financial support from the United Auto Workers, on environment-related job blackmail.

The most important impetus for increased environmental sensitivity and support for labor was the 1973 strike against Shell Oil by the Oil, Chemical and Atomic Workers. Sierra Club chapters went through lengthy and heated debates over whether or not to support the strike: the decision to do so resulted in the resignation of several hundred members, primarily from the oil states, who felt the group had gone too far.[10] For other environmental groups the Shell strike marked the first time they directed their educational and organizing resources to a workplace health and safety issue. According to UAW Washington representative Frank Wallick, "The Shell strike, like the passage of OSHA, was a tremendous catalyst to increased awareness and support among labor and environmental groups."[11]

COOPERATION AND CONFLICT AFTER 1974

When the price of oil quadrupled in 1974, energy and growth moved to center stage as the most controversial environmental issues. While broad labor-environmental agreement had emerged about the close connection between in-plant health problems and general environmental quality, energy and development policy intensified deep divisions between segments of the labor and environmental movements.

The business community claimed environmentalists were threatening the entire economy by raising questions about nuclear safety, the Alaska Pipeline, and other energy and resource development projects. As *Fortune* explained:[12]

> It appears that if [environmental] laws were actually to be enforced as they are written or as courts have interpreted them, the end result might be a no-growth economy, if not a bankrupt nation.

By 1977 *Forbes* and *U.S. News and World Report* both announced the beginning of an "environmental backlash."[13]

Many unions sided with employers. The nation needed more domestic energy production in order to keep growing and create jobs, they argued. And environmentalists were making that impossible. The most vigorous proponents of this position were the unions in the Building and Construction Trades Department of the AFL-CIO. These unions saw environmental resistance to highways, dams, power plants and other large construction projects as a direct attack on their member's jobs. Although the Business Roundtable and other employer organizations were engaged in an aggressive (and fairly successful) campaign to increase the nonunion share of large-scale construction contracts, including nuclear plants, the leadership of the construction unions continued its traditional policy of accommodation with employers and large contractors.*

The Laborers International Union ran a cover story in its membership magazine entitled "The Clean Air Act: An Attack on the Construction Industry?" The Carpenters in northern California blamed environmentalists for the loss of 2,000 jobs in the timber industry. On nuclear power, the construction unions were particularly combative. When utility companies and other major industries campaigned against anti-nuclear ballot initiatives in seven states, the building trades led the labor opposition to the initiatives and gave credibility to the utilities' "jobs versus the environment" formulation. In 1978 and 1979, beginning at the Seabrook, New Hampshire, site, nuclear construction workers participated in a number of counter-demonstrations against antinuclear activists.

But the building trades were not the only unions which differed with environmental groups in the difficult period after 1974. Many unions outside the building trades opposed the antinuclear ballot initiatives. The United Mine Workers were not officially opposed to 1977 strip-mining legislation, but the union also did not offer much support. When Congress considered amendments to the Clean Air Act in 1977, the United Auto Workers sided with the industry's request for relaxed standards on auto-emissions.

*In a 1979 letter to the Edison Electric Institute and the Atomic Industrial Forum, Robert A. Georgine, president of the Building and Construction Trades Department, expressed his displeasure with the industry's attack on labor:[14]

> We have always argued that nuclear energy was a symbol of how labor-management cooperation could serve our nation's needs while creating well-paid jobs for workers. Today we are having some difficulty defending this concept in light of recent attacks on the trade-union movement. . . . Indeed, several of our own presidents have begun to question the role of the Roundtable and NCA in encouraging the open-shop and non-union hiring and referral service.

Environmentalists were not oblivious to the growing disagreement and conflict. When environmental organizations were not represented at the founding meeting of the National Committee for Full Employment in 1975, a number of environmental activists decided to try to reverse the trend. They organized hundreds of national, regional, and local environmental groups to help sponsor the creation of Environmentalists for Full Employment (EFFE). By drawing environmentalists into the full employment fight, EFFE prompted *Business Week* to observe that "even environmentalists" were supporting the Humphrey-Hawkins Bill.[15]

In the spring of 1976 the Auto Workers, the Steelworkers, the Urban Environment Conference, EFFE, and more than 100 other labor, environmental, and community organizations sponsored a conference on job blackmail. "Working for Environmental and Economic Justice and Jobs" attracted over 300 activists to the Auto Workers education center in Black Lake, Michigan. The conference helped establish a network of environmental and labor activists which still exists today. But the momentum of the Black Lake meeting did not carry very far. Although delegates were committed to organizing state labor-environmental conferences and coalitions, few materialized. One New York State Paperworkers' official told EFFE organizers, "It's the wrong time. My members are so angry at environmentalists, I wouldn't recommend they be in the same room together."[16]

Despite considerable tension and conflict, unions and environmental organizations continued to cooperate on legislative initiatives which were important to both throughout the middle and late 1970s. The AFL-CIO and many individual unions backed the Safe Drinking Water Act of 1974 and worked hard for passage of the Toxic Substances Control Act of 1976. Environmentalists lobbied for passage of mine safety legislation and for improved regulation and enforcement of workplace safety and health. In 1978 environmental groups (including the Clamshell Alliance and other newly formed antinuclear alliances) provided support to organized labor during the fight for Labor Law Reform, lobbying members of Congress in Washington and their home districts. In 1979 dozens of the same groups joined to support the United Mine Workers' strike for the right to refuse hazardous and unhealthy work.

Working together contributed to greater mutual understanding and appreciation. In contrast to labor's general coolness to environmental groups at the start of the fight for full-employment legislation in 1975, Lane Kirkland, president of the AFL-CIO, specifically welcomed environmentalists to participate in Solidarity Day, the fall 1981 anti-Reagan demonstration which brought more than 250,000 union members and supporters to the nation's capital:[17]

> We in labor have long recognized that a job which kills and cripples is not much of a job, that a clean workplace is not worth much if our homes and communities lie in the midst of poisoned air and poisoned water. We have been pleased to work with the environmental movement to enact and defend clean air and water legislation, toxic substances control and strict stripmining legislation. And we have appreciated environmental support during our struggle for Labor Law Reform, to defend OSHA and for effective full employment legislation.

In recent years cooperation between organized labor and environmental groups on the national policy level has grown steadily more sophisticated and extensive. One clear indication was the formation in February 1981 of the OSHA/Environmental Network, an alliance of labor, environmental, and other citizen's organizations created to fight for continued and improved workplace and environmental health protections. Spearheaded by the Steelworkers, the AFL-CIO Industrial Union

Department, and national environmental groups such as Friends of the Earth, the Sierra Club, the Wilderness Society, the Urban Environment Conference, and the National Clean Air Coalition, the Network has established a presence in more than half the states. Its principal activity has been organizing grassroots labor-environmental lobbying in support of a strong OSHA and Clean Air Act. According to Network field director Bill Wilson:[18]

> We've had some comments from Congresspeople saying they were surprised to see labor and environmental people together, and at times they tried to meet with each group separately, but the delegations refused to be separated.

The OSHA/Environmental Network is also helping local labor-environmental coalitions recognize and challenge job blackmail. The organization's Statement of Principles reads:[19]

> The existence of the Network symbolizes the historic refusal of the people of this country to be divided on environmental and health and safety goals that must be held in common. We recognize the importance of working together to resolve our differences and to resist those who would divide us into separate camps in order to weaken our laws or undermine enforcement.

This is an important step. National legislative cooperation by labor and environmental lobbyists in Washington is of course essential; but the most explosive labor-environmental conflicts usually occur at the local level, where both workers and environmental activists have an immediate tangible stake in the outcome. Fear and anger can mount quickly on both sides, bolstering the employer's power unless there is an organized group willing and able to expose the blackmail, seek alternatives, and resist manipulation by employers. State coalitions run by union *and* environmental organizers can play such a role.

Two years before the Network was formed, a coalition

of seven national environmental organizations provided important support to 1,600 nuclear workers at the Portsmouth Gaseous Diffusion Plant in Piketon, Ohio. Workers at the uranium enrichment plant, owned by the Department of Energy but operated on a cost-plus basis by Goodyear Atomic, struck in 1979 over economic, health, and safety issues. The workers, represented by OCAW, charged the company with falsification of plant records on radiation leaks, refusal to provide safety equipment requested by workers, failure to replace faulty radiation-leak alarms, discrimination against health and safety activists, and planned takebacks of economic benefits. After the strike had lasted seven months, a number of Washington-based environmental and antinuclear groups —SANE, the Urban Environment Conference, Environmentalists for Full Employment, Environmental Policy Center, Environmental Action Foundation, Mobilization for Survival, and Friends of the Earth—formed a Strike Support Group. The group helped the striking workers generate publicity and political pressure, arranging for about 100 workers to come to Washington, hold a press conference with Ohio Senators John Glenn and Howard Metzenbaum, and meet with Department of Energy officials.

At the press conference Senator Glenn tried to split apart the labor-environmental coalition. Turning to the workers he reminded them of SANE's antinuclear stance and warned that the environmental groups were not there to support health and safety demands, but rather to shut down the nuclear industry and throw them all out of work. But the strikers stood firm. They hooted and jeered, demanding Glenn respond to their complaints. Finally, local President Denny Bloomfield stood up, slammed his fist on the table and said:[20]

> Listen, these folks have at least responded to our problem more effectively than anyone else in Wash-

ington. The fact that we may have political differences
doesn't matter. So don't tell us who our friends are.

The alliance survived and the workers finally won
(primarily because of Energy Department pressure on
Goodyear Atomic after the workers' Washington visit).
The ability of antinuclear environmentalists to team with
nuclear workers, and not be perceived as a threat to their
jobs, revealed an impressive level of political sophistica-
tion among both groups. Environmentalists were willing
to avoid the polarizing, sensitive issue of whether or not
the nation should pursue nuclear energy development.
They stuck to the issues of health and safety in the plant
and the importance of strong unions. Consequently the
workers were willing to ally with the environmental
support group.

Even on the divisive issue of nuclear power, there has
been progress building labor-environmental coalitions to
promote safe energy alternatives and an end to depen-
dence on nuclear power. Before the accident at Three
Mile Island in March 1979, only the United Mine Workers, the Graphic Arts International Union, and the International Longshoremen's and Warehousemen's Union
had deviated from the AFL-CIO pronuclear position. Few
efforts had been made by environmental activists to
engage labor on the nuclear question. One notable exception was Barry Commoner who, throughout the 1970s,
advised union locals and internationals that nuclear power
was not only bad for health and safety, but also for jobs
and the economy. In 1977 Environmentalists for Full
Employment published *Jobs and Energy,* a synthesis of
available evidence on the employment impact of nuclear
versus other energy sources. The pamphlet and the November 1978 Joint Economic Committee hearings on
"Creating Jobs through Energy Policy" helped expand the
dialogue on energy and jobs within the labor movement.
The Machinists, Sheet Metal Workers, and Auto Workers
internationals moved toward strongly prosolar positions

and were active participants in Sun Day on 3 May 1978. By late 1978 Machinists' president Winpisinger had publicly taken an antinuclear position. Some locals and districts in the Steelworkers, the Meatcutters, and a few other unions went on record opposing further construction of nuclear plants.

After Three Mile Island a flurry of antinuclear resolutions were passed by locals and districts of the UAW, Steelworkers, and the American Federation of State, County and Municipal Employees (AFSCME). They were joined by three international unions of the AFL-CIO—the Machinists, International Chemical Workers, and Woodworkers. In November 1979 the Machinists brought representatives from over 50 international unions, including many in the building trades, to a conference called "Labor/Science Dialogue on Energy, Jobs and Environment." There unionists heard environmentalists, safety and health officials, and economists who were supportive of labor, talk in a union hall about nuclear economics, energy alternatives, radiation, and jobs.[21] For many, this was the first time they had been exposed to a comprehensive view of the energy situation different from that put forward by the energy giants and endorsed by the AFL-CIO.

In April 1980 a group of trade unionists gathered at the Machinists' headquarters in Washington, D.C., to form the Labor Committee for Safe Energy and Full Employment. The Labor Committee's goal was to raise issues of nuclear dangers, safe energy options, and jobs within the labor movement. The group spurred nine international unions and the Coalition of Labor Union Women to issue a call for a national conference.* Over 850 union mem-

---

*United Mine Workers, United Auto Workers, International Association of Machinists, Service Employees International Union, Graphic Arts International Union, International Chemical Workers Union, United Furniture Workers, International Woodworkers of America, International Longshoremen's and Warehousemen's Union.

bers and about 150 environmentalists attended the First National Labor Conference for Safe Energy and Full Employment held in Pittsburgh in October 1980. They shared information and experiences and heard energy and employment experts from both the labor and environmental movements. The conferees passed resolutions opposing nuclear power and denouncing job blackmail on energy and other environmental issues. As one report noted, "The conferees made it quite clear they opposed nuclear power because they were *for* jobs, *for* strong trade unions, *for* economic progress, *for* public health and *for* the ability of working people and communities to control their own destinies."[22]

Six months later, on 28 March 1981 the Greater Harrisburg Labor Committee for Safe Energy and Full Employment (one of several local committees which were founded after the Pittsburgh Conference) organized a march to commemorate the second anniversary of the Three Mile Island accident. Initiated by trade unionists from six different Harrisburg area locals, the march had support from 12 international unions and attracted over 15,000 union members, local residents, and concerned citizens. It was the largest labor-organized nuclear protest in the United States. The marchers had two demands: that Three Mile Island I remain shut down, and that radioactive water from the crippled plant not be dumped into the Susquehanna River. Today the plant remains closed and plans to dump the water have been shelved.

There has been significant progress, particularly since 1978, in bridging the labor-environmental gap. But the effort to develop closer cooperation between workers and environmentalists on energy and development issues still runs into vigorous opposition from the building trades unions. At the Pittsburgh conference about 200 members of Local 5 of the militantly pronuclear International Brotherhood of Electrical Workers demonstrated, bearing signs that read, "No Power, No Employment," and "Anti-Nukes are Kooks." After the Harrisburg march the Building and Construction Trades Department of the AFL-CIO bought full-page ads in the *Harrisburg Patriot* and the *Washington Post* denouncing the march and denying that involvement of 12 international unions indicated organized labor's support of nuclear power might be weakening. The ads proclaimed, "Is Organized Labor Opposed to Nuclear Power? No Way! Electricity Means Jobs."

TWO CASE STUDIES

People working together can expand the boundaries of industrial and economic democracy. This does not mean that groups which organize to challenge corporate power will always win. Such challenges are often defeated. But power, control, and greater democracy are not won without a fight. Even an unsuccessful fight provides experience, political education, and strategic lessons for those that follow.

The outcome of the ongoing battle for decent jobs, safe workplaces, and a clean environment depends upon the ability of workers and environmentally-concerned citizens to defend themselves, defend each other, and work together to challenge "business as usual." As this book has shown, there has been much experience in this country resisting job blackmail and forcing alternatives to corporate dominance of work and community life. Some have been more successful than others. The following case studies examine two different models of labor-environmental interaction and show that the ways the two groups work together profoundly affect their combined ability to overcome job blackmail.

The Redwoods National Park Expansion: One of the most bitter conflicts between workers and environmentalists in the late 1970s centered around plans to expand the Redwoods National Park in northern California. A classic example of corporate job blackmail, the ensuing battle ended in an innovative compromise. But because the compromise was reached without significant involvement of the people pitted against each other at the local level, the solution was seriously flawed.

When Redwoods National Park was created in 1968 to protect the oldest and tallest trees in the world, the land directly upslope was left in private hands, open to logging by three timber companies: Louisiana-Pacific, Simpson, and Arcata Redwood. The clearcutting above the tall trees washed silt, sand, gravel, and rock down the hillsides into Redwood Creek. The creek flooded often and there were occasional landslides. Soil conservationists and forestry experts generally agreed that if the park were not expanded to stop the logging and reduce the runoff, the tall trees would be lost.

The Natural Resources Defense Council and the Sierra Club filed suits to protect the Park from further abuse. When the courts ruled that the Interior Department had failed to protect the Park and that environmental impact statements would be required for all nearby logging plans, momentum built for expanding the Park. And the conflict between environmentalists and affected loggers exploded.

Representative Philip Burton (D-CA) proposed legislation to expand the Park by 48,000 acres. The companies protested that the expansion would throw 2,000 local loggers and millworkers out of work. Timber workers and their unions, led by the United Brotherhood of Carpenters and Joiners, followed industry and blamed environmental "preservationists" for stealing their jobs. John Henning, president of the California AFL-CIO, charged environmental "cultists" were "absolute death and destruction to the economic growth and future of this state."[23] Loggers denounced environmentalists who were "overwhelmingly white and upper class" and who didn't "give a damn about working people."[24] They took their protest to Sacramento, driving 500 logging trucks for two hours around the state capitol, blowing their horns, and tying up traffic. Representative Burton, generally supported by California's labor unions, was booed and cursed in a public hearing in Eureka. "I've conducted a lot of hearings," he said, "but seldom have I seen the fear I saw in Humboldt County related to the loss of jobs."[25]

That fear had been building for many years throughout the Pacific northwest—and it was quite legitimate. Tens of thousands of jobs in the northwest timber industry disappeared in the 1960s and 1970s. But the steadily rising unemployment had nothing to do with environmentalists. The timber companies had heavily overcut their forests, leaving what one unemployed worker called "lumber towns with no lumber."[26] A 1977 U.S. Forest Service study concluded that because of overcutting of corporate-owned forests in northern California, timber harvests would decline by two-thirds by 1985—whether or not the park expansion was approved.[27] The companies had taken most of the timber and profits they could from the northwest: the next stop would be the southeastern states, where they were already buying private land at a fever pitch and employing nonunion workers at lower wages.

Unfortunately, little effort had been made by either the timber workers or local environmental activists to address these questions together *before* the park expansion issue split them apart. The groundwork for cooperation had not been laid. There were few personal contacts or formal organizational links between the two groups. So when the antagonism mounted, there was no way to bring loggers and environmentalists together in a noncombative atmosphere to seek ways to reject the "jobs versus the environment" formulation and place responsibility on the companies whose policies had created the employment crisis. As a result the companies were able to manipulate the way the conflict was defined, to escape any challenge to their right to come and go, and to reaffirm their prerogative to abuse workers and the nation's natural resources as they pleased.

A compromise solution to the Redwoods National Park controversy was achieved, but not because of any rapprochement at the local level. The compromise was hammered out in Washington. The AFL-CIO and the Carpenters understood that national public support for the Park expansion was strong. Opposition to Burton's bill would be futile and would only alienate many political allies. So the AFL-CIO decided on a *quid pro quo:* the labor federation would support the Redwoods Park expansion only if displaced workers would be protected from income loss and offered retraining opportunities.

The AFL-CIO, in fact, was on the right track. The workers deserved compensation. The federal government was going to pay the timber companies $300 million compensation for the new acreage (besides the $170 million and 10,000 acres of federally-owned timberland given them in 1968 for the original Park lands). As Jay Power, then a lobbyist for the Carpenters, explained, "We wanted to put in there the principle that the government can't ride in, destroy a whole community, pay off the companies, and let the workers jump in the river."[28]

The result was the Redwood Employee Protection (REP) program. All local timber workers laid off between 31 May 1977 and 30 September 1980 were guaranteed full salary, health and welfare benefits, and pensions (to be paid by the government) until 30 September 1984, or their sixty-fifth birthday, or their acceptance of a severance payment, or for as many weeks as they had worked in the industry—whichever came first. Eligible workers also qualified for government-funded training and relocation benefits. As of July 1981 $41 million had been spent on these worker protections, which were claimed by over 2,500 workers.[29]*

Both labor and environmentalists got something in the legislative package. The Park was expanded, preserving the redwoods and providing a more appealing area for tourists and hikers. Unemployed loggers protected their incomes for at least a few years. The mutual distrust and hostility subsided somewhat. According to Al Lasley, a local Carpenters' Union representative who had been vociferously anti-environmentalist at early public hearings:[30]

> We got a trade-off. And environmentalists were helpful in getting it through. This shows that there are ways for labor to work with environmentalists. In the end, it is easier for labor to work with environmentalists than it is to work with the companies.

Once the program went into effect and the timber companies received their payoffs, workers found their support from employers and government began to erode. In early 1981 the Department of Labor issued revised eligibility guidelines which led to the temporary suspension of benefits to 930 people. The companies were uncooperative in helping ex-employees establish proof of their eligibility. "It's kind of funny," said Tim Skaggs, president of the International Woodworkers of America, Local 3-98. "When we were fighting the Park expansion, we were shoulder to shoulder with the industry, but now that we have to retain benefits for displaced working people, the industry has forgotten us."[31] Much of the support which laidoff Redwoods workers have received

---

*Only 251 workers enrolled in any training programs. Neither the government, the private sector, nor the unions tried to initiate innovative training programs that could address the needs and use the skills of the unemployed timber workers.

has come primarily from citizen and environmental groups. "We've been able to defend REP so far," explained Skaggs in February 1981, "because we've had great support from the general public and a lot of community organizations. In fact, some of our strongest support has come from the environmental groups."[32]

The problem with the Redwoods compromise is that what should have been only a back-up program—income maintenance for displaced workers—was the only program. Consequently, a large number of former lumberjacks and millworkers have been left to grow hopeless on the government dole. Despite their many profitable years of logging the area, the companies were not required to contribute a penny to the programs. And no provisions were made for bringing new jobs to the lumber towns. According to Tim McKay of the North Coast Environmental Center in Arcata, California, "The park legislation was good in concept, but labor went along with the timber companies without looking down the road." The unions proposed no alternatives to the continued dislocation of timber workers resulting from automation and depletion of resources. They did not even raise the question in a serious way. McKay concluded:[33]

> By focusing all the attention on the park as the cause
> of dislocation, we've taken attention away from the real
> issue: how can we diversify the economic base of this
> region?

Today many Humboldt County "timberbeasts" remain frustrated and angry. According to 43-year-old Jack Roby, "I don't want a handout! I want a job!" Many still blame the "Park people," that is, the government and environmentalists. One former Louisiana-Pacific employee told a reporter, "Hell, yes, I'm bitter about the government taking our jobs. You can't eat park! We need work!"[34] Today the entire county is paying the price for capitulating to the timber companies' blackmail, and for not challenging the corporate formulation of the conflict. That many unemployed loggers still maintain their loyalty to their former employers, even though that loyalty was never reciprocated, is revealing testimony to the failure of both the unions and environmental activists to see the Redwoods Park controversy in the broader context of corporate power versus democratic participation in economic and environmental planning.

Steelworkers Local 1010 and the Bailly Alliance: In sharp contrast stands a unique model of labor-environmental activism and cooperation in northwest Indiana, along the shores of Lake Michigan. There, Steelworkers Local 1010, which is the largest steel-making local in the nation, representing 18,000 workers at the mammoth Inland Steel plant in East Chicago, has been challenging the inadequacy of in-plant health and safety protections and pollution control for the last 11 years. Throughout those years Local 1010 has concentrated on developing contacts and working relationships with local environmental organizations. The result has been labor and environmental unity which has been able to resist job blackmail and make significant strides toward preserving jobs and protecting the environment.

Local 1010's environmental involvement began in 1971. The Army Corps of Engineers was dredging the Indiana Harbor Ship Canal near the Inland Steel plant, removing the oily, greasy sludge built up from dumping by steel companies and refineries located along the shore. This time some of the dredged materials were hauled by barge to Inland Steel to be used as landfill. Recreational fishermen began to complain: their lures were coming up covered with sludge, their weights were corroding, and the fish were disappearing.

Many of these fishing enthusiasts were employees of Inland Steel. Mike Olszanski, Joe Frantz, and several other workers who were active in the local union demanded at a union meeting that the local take some action. The president of the local responded by establishing an Environmental Committee. But he appointed one of his own supporters as chairman, hoping Olszanski and his friends would stop making trouble.

They did not stop. First, they went to state officials demanding the lake be cleaned and the dredging stopped. When they got no response, they decided on independent action. They got a boat, found somebody who knew something about collecting water samples, and filled several 4-gallon glass jars with the foul lake water. Analysis of the samples showed concentrations of oil, grease, and chemicals several thousand times greater than EPA and state standards allowed. Olszanski contacted the media, which played up the story because it shattered some common stereotypes. Here were trade unionists challenging pollution caused by their own employers, steelworkers who were not supposed to care about such things.

The Environmental Committee decided it needed help, so it began to work with local organizations. Local 1010 invited EPA and state pollution control officials to the union hall, as well as representatives from the Lake Michigan Federation and the Save the Dunes Council. According to Olszanski, "It was the first time that a lot of these people had ever been in a union hall before. And they were pretty excited to see a union coming out against the company and for the environment."[35] EPA forced the Corps of Engineers to prepare an Environmental Impact Statement and develop alternatives to using sludge as landfill.

In 1974 the Local 1010 Environmental Committee helped its district leadership challenge a job blackmail attempt by U.S. Steel at the nearby Gary Works. The U.S. District Court had finally ruled that the company, which had intentionally avoided cleaning up its open hearths because it planned to replace them with new technology, could no longer delay compliance and would have to begin paying fines of $5,000 a day until standards were met. The company announced it would not pay the fine and would shut down the hearths if forced to pay—at a cost of 2,500 jobs. Olszanski and District 31 Director Ed Sadlowski knew the company was lying. There were fewer than 500 people employed in the old open hearths. Many would have jobs in the new basic-oxygen-process furnaces and contract provisions protected any who might be displaced. Sadlowski publicly challenged the company's effort at intimidation. According to Olszanski:[36]

> Sadlowski's statement made the difference. The blackmail attempts did not have any lasting effect on our membership because we were able to take the offensive and say, "You are lying to the workers and you are lying to the community."

In 1976 Jim Balanoff, a member of the rank-and-file caucus to which Mike Olszanski and Joe Frantz belonged, was elected president of the local. He gave the Environmental Committee his full support and appointed Olszanski as its chairman. Since then Local 1010 has been at the forefront of efforts to improve both in-plant and community environmental protections, deliberately challenging traditional rights of management and seeking to unite workers and the community against corporate job blackmail.

The Environmental Committee immediately began a campaign to force Inland Steel to reduce cancer-causing coke oven emissions, the most serious health and environmental problem in basic steel production. Committee members contacted EPA and demanded to know what EPA was doing about making the company comply with the law. They intervened against the company in EPA hearings and proposed their own solutions. The local joined the Lake Michigan Federation and renewed their contact with other environmental groups. And the Environmental Committee began to educate Local 1010 members to the dangers and the alternatives.

In 1978 Inland Steel warned that if its application to build a new boiler were held up until coke oven and other existing emissions were reduced, the company's modernization program would be disrupted, which "could result in loss of jobs which would be created by the program."[37] The Environmental Committee responded by demanding that modernization should lead to *less* pollution, not more. It emphasized that the issue was not just an in-plant problem: residents of communities near coke plants have twice the rate of lung cancer as the general population. Olszanski invoked the employee protection provision of the Clean Air Act, requesting that EPA administrator Douglas Costle investigate Inland's threat, hold a public hearing, and force the company to substantiate its position. Costle refused the request. But the publicity Local 1010 obtained as a result of its open challenge, combined with the threat of EPA intervention and the strong community support for the union, influenced the company's decision to sign a consent decree in which it agreed to faster and better cleanup—with no job loss.

At hearings on the consent decree in 1979, Local 1010 kept up the pressure by making a series of proposals as to how the company could reduce coke oven emissions—if it wanted to. The union emphasized that the only way to clean up the coke oven batteries was to double or triple the size of maintenance and operation work crews and to allow the crews enough time to clean the doors after each coke charge so the seal would be tight. Local 1010 charged this was precisely why the company did not want to clean up: the company did not want to hire more workers and slow production even the 5 to 10 percent that would be needed to maintain the equipment. While the company talked a lot about "jobs versus the environment," it seemed interested in preserving neither. The union demanded that the consent decree include language specifying minimum crew size and coking schedules. The judge refused, explaining it was not his role to dictate to a firm on such procedures. The union made another proposal the judge refused to act on, one which challenged EPA to give workers a much more active role in protecting their own health and environment. Local 1010 suggested EPA train union members to be smoke readers so they could inspect company compliance and submit regular reports to the agency. As Mike Olszanski explained:[38]

> We see violations every day. But we can't give you exact figures. We just see a lot of smoke. EPA can't get the inspectors to the plant often enough. But we're there every day. Why not train us to do the work?*

In October 1981 Inland Steel's "C" Coke Oven Battery passed an EPA inspection—the first time in history for any of the plant's coke ovens. The company did it by doubling the crew size on top of the ovens and giving them more time to do the work. In other words, they adopted the union's proposal. According to Mike Olszanski:[39]

> This had an effect on workers. Many had never really thought it possible that a coke oven could be operated cleanly, because they had never seen it happen. Now they've seen it—and they know we were right. The company put in a lot of new pollution control equipment. Now they have to make the commitment to use it.

*The idea of workers having greater control over monitoring health hazards and improving workplace conditions would certainly make government regulation more efficient. OSHA has 1,200 inspectors, EPA not many more. But there are 100 million Americans who work for a living and who, with a minimum of training, could make great contributions to their own health and safety and to environmental quality. For two good presentations of this argument, see Witt and Early, "The Worker as Safety Inspector," *Working Papers,* September 1980; and Boden and Wegman, "Increasing OSHA's Clout: Sixty Million New Inspectors," *Working Papers,* May 1978.

But once the inspection was over, the company cut back the crew size, speeded up the process, and resumed its pollution.

Since then, Inland Steel has asked EPA for permission under the 1981 Steel Stretch-out Amendment to the Clean Air Act to postpone $30 million slated for pollution control spending and invest the capital in plant modernization. Local 1010, able to move quickly because of its organizational base and experience, intervened with EPA, charging the "stretch-out" should not be granted until the coke oven batteries are consistently in compliance.

In 1976, at the same time Local 1010's Environmental Committee was beginning to challenge Inland Steel's coke oven pollution, the workers were also getting involved in a campaign against the construction of the Bailly nuclear plant. Environmental and antinuclear groups had been in court for several years trying to stop construction of the plant being built next to the Indiana Dunes National Lakeshore Park, six miles from Gary. Some of the members of Local 1010, including Joe Frantz and Mike Olszanski, had been personally concerned for some time about the Bailly reactor. In 1976 the local's leadership raised the issue at a union meeting and the 150 members present voted unanimously against its construction. That began a process of education within the union on nuclear power in general, and the Bailly plant in particular. Local 1010 began to meet with the antinuclear Bailly Alliance to plan greater public involvement in their effort. In spring 1978 a conference on energy policies for Northwest Indiana was sponsored by Gary's Mayor Richard Hatcher, the Save the Dunes Council, the Izaak Walton League, the Bailly Alliance, and Local 1010. Unions, environmental groups, the League of Women Voters, community organizations, and fish and game clubs were all represented.

Local 1010's Environmental Committee focused on

showing its members that the Bailly nuclear plant was not necessary for jobs and that a coal-fired generating plant, energy conservation, and solar power were viable alternatives. Members of the Bailly Alliance and Local 1010 went to workers around northwest Indiana and explained what was wrong with the proposed plant. Together, they publicized the intention of Bethlehem Steel, whose plant was adjacent to the Bailly site, to have 170 workers remain on the job in the event of a reactor accident—a "suicide squad" whose task would be to save the company's costly coke ovens and blast furnaces. Local 6787, representing workers at the Bethlehem Steel plant, formally joined the anti-Bailly forces after the near-meltdown at Three Mile Island.

The importance of union involvement in community environmental campaigns was illustrated most clearly by the role Local 1010 played in spurring the unions representing workers at Northern Indiana Public Service Company (NIPSCO) to oppose the plant their employer wanted to build. Local 1010 met with NIPSCO workers and provided questions to ask management about the plant: How would employee exposure to radiation be monitored? Would employees be kept informed of their exposure levels? What would happen to workers who exceed their annual maximum dose? When the NIPSCO locals saw that management did not have adequate answers, their doubts multiplied. In the context of an 8-month strike against the company on economic and non-nuclear workplace safety issues, the union members began to see, as Mike Olszanski put it, "that the company interest was not the same as their interest. And if the company is trying to cheat you on your paycheck, there's every reason to believe that they'll try to cheat you on nuclear safety standards."[40] That education process was critical to solidifying District 31's opposition to the Bailly plant. And it probably would not have happened if the

NIPSCO workers had not been approached by other unionists.

In April 1981 the Nuclear Regulatory Commission gave NIPSCO authorization to resume construction of the Bailly plant. But over 1,000 local workers and their families demonstrated their disapproval—led by the NIPSCO locals' presidents, the president of Local 6787, and Jim Balanoff, then the director of District 31. In August, tired of delays, afraid the plant had become an economic albatross, and faced with a situation where job blackmail had no impact due to unified opposition from both workers *and* environmental organizations, NIPSCO abandoned the Bailly project forever.

Together Local 1010 and the Bailly Alliance have built a strong regional network of workers *and* environmentalists committed to jobs *and* environmental protection. The Bailly Alliance, almost from its inception, tried to avoid the trap of being labeled solely "environmentalist." As Alliance member Brenda Frantz explained:[41]

> We were steelworkers, journalists, a mechanic, house-wives, professors, an architect, secretaries, all work-ing people and all working full-time, some of us parents as well, living in the industrial heartland of the country.

The members of Local 1010 had used the resources of their organization and their personal contacts throughout the labor community to lend credibility to the concept that environmental activism was a necessary and legiti-mate labor priority. As Mike Olszanski often told people in the Gary area, "If you are pro-labor, then you are pro-environment." These labor and environmental orga-nizers were clear about what they had to do, unlike the loggers and environmentalists in Northern California. Olszanski explained:[42]

> The only thing which works is the adversary system. If we are not as powerful as they, it's not going to work

and we won't get clean air. With enough political
force, though, you can make them change.

FIGHTING FOR JOBS, ENVIRONMENT AND
DEMOCRACY

Not all environmental or health problems are as amena-
ble to close labor-environmental cooperation as those
faced by Local 1010, the Bailly Alliance and other residents of northwest Indiana. The concentration of steelworkers who lived in the surrounding community and
were afraid of living near a nuclear plant provided a
strong base of local labor opposition. And the fact that
Inland Steel's East Chicago plant is both modern and
profitable made Local 1010's workers less susceptible to
job blackmail on environmental issues both within and
outside the mill.

But across the country, many workers are employed by
companies that will close or move their plants if more
profitable uses can be found for their capital. Workers in
these plants, especially unorganized workers, are indeed
vulnerable. And the ability of these workers to defend
their rights is becoming more difficult as high unemployment, rapid industrial flight and job-threatening technological change increase their insecurity. The most heated
conflicts between unions and environmental groups developed in the first few years after the shock of the 1974-75
recession. The current deep recession may lead to another
wave of panic and conflict, as companies intensify their
efforts to force workers to choose between their jobs and
their health.

The fight for both jobs *and* environment is a struggle
over the allocation and use of the nation's wealth, resources and labor—and over who should decide national
investment priorities. These are critically important ques-

tions which should be decided publicly, that is, democratically. If the nation wants to provide jobs for everyone who wants to work, then the public will have to make sure that adequate resources are devoted specifically to creating jobs. If people want protection from industrial hazards and unwise development in the workplace, their communities and the wilderness, then they will have to demand that employers operate within environmental constraints. And they will have to force the government to use its power to keep industry in line rather than keep workers in their place. This can happen only if debate over national priorities and development is conducted by an active public that is aware of the many choices still available to this wealthy and resource-rich nation, a public that is resistant to economic and political intimidation.

At stake is the future of democracy—economic and political democracy. As is evident from this book, there is a conflict between increased democratic rights and the desire of business to operate with minimal public accountability. All the false choices served up by the business community—of which "jobs vs. environment" is only one—are designed to mask this fundamental conflict. At various times in this nation's history, when people have experienced the failure of business and government to meet their basic needs, they have mobilized in opposition. And they have been able to force redefinitions of what constitutes "business as usual."

The basis for the redefinition which must be achieved today has been stated succinctly by Steelworkers legislative director John Sheehan:

> Now is not the time to make [environmental protections] ineffective because of some political objective to "get the government off our backs." What we need is to get carcinogens out of our lungs and put good jobs in our community.[43]

Jobs *and* environment—inseparable and interrelated. If both workers and environmentalists begin from this premise and fight for its acceptance as national policy, then the "jobs vs. environment" and "labor vs. environmentalists" formulations will be finally and totally discredited. It will become impossible for employers or government officials to get away with threats like "What are you trying to do, shut down the plant?" and "You've got no choice: it's either pollution or no job at all." Were this to happen, people could move beyond job blackmail to the difficult but critical task of preserving and extending democracy in America. People could live their lives not as "workers" or "environmentalists," but as citizens willing to fight together for decent jobs, safe workplaces and a clean, healthy environment.

Notes

1

1. The story of the Anaconda shut down is from daily articles in five local newspapers: *Montana Standard, Missoulian, Great Falls Tribune, Billings Gazette, Helena Independent Record,* 28 September–29 October 1980.
2. Leonard Woodcock, "Labor and the Economic Impact of Environmental Control Requirements," in *Jobs and the Environment: Three Papers* (Berkeley: University of California Institute of Industrial Relations, 1972), p. 5.
3. John Quarles, *Cleaning Up America: An Insider's View of the Environmental Protection Agency* (Boston: Houghton Mifflin Company, 1976), pp. 63–64.
4. Morton Mintz and Jerry S. Cohen, *America, Inc.* (New York: Delta Books, 1971), p. 294.
5. David D. Doniger, *The Law and Policy of Toxic Substances Control* (Baltimore: Johns Hopkins University Press, 1978), pp. 53n–54n.
6. Press Release from Governor Edmund G. Brown, Sr., at a press conference for the Citizens for Jobs and Energy, Los Angeles, 6 May 1975.
7. Lynton K. Caldwell, Lynton R. Hayes, and Isabel M. MacWhirter, *Citizens and the Environment* (Bloomington, Indiana: Indiana University Press, 1976), p. 260.
8. Letter from Sigmund Arywitz to all unions and councils, 22 January 1975, Los Angeles County Federation of Labor, Los Angeles, California.
9. Leonard Woodcock, "Labor and the Economic Impact," p. 5.
10. Quarles, *Cleaning Up America,* p. 65.
11. Doniger, *The Law and Policy of Toxic Substances Control,* pp. 62–64.

12. For further reading:
    U.S. Congress Joint Economic Committee, *Creating Jobs Through Energy Policy* (Washington, D.C.: U.S. Government Printing Office, 1978);
    U.S. Congress Subcommittee on Energy of the Joint Economic Committee, "Employment Impact of the Solar Transition" (Washington, D.C.: U.S. Government Printing Office, 1979);
    Richard Grossman and Gail Daneker, *Energy, Jobs and the Economy* (Boston: Alyson Publications, Inc., 1979);
    Nancy Irwin, ed., *A New Prosperity: Building a Sustainable Energy Future,* SERI Solar Conservation Study (Andover, Massachusetts: Brick House Publishing, 1981).
13. Charles Komanoff, Energy Consultant, Komanoff Energy Associates, New York, New York, in remarks to the First National Labor Conference for Safe Energy and Full Employment, Pittsburgh, Pennsylvania, 11 October 1980.
14. Nancy Irwin, ed., *A New Prosperity*, p. 1.
15. Ibid.
16. Brian Turner and Iris J. Lav, *Energy for a Working America* (Washington, D.C.: Industrial Union Department Energy Project, AFL-CIO, 1981), p. 55.
17. William Winpisinger, "Proceedings of the Hawaii Conference on Jobs and the Environment" (Honolulu, Hawaii: The LOL Foundation, 1978), p. 21.
18. Marc S. Miller, ed., *Working Lives: The Southern Exposure History of Labor in the South.* (New York: Pantheon Books, 1980), p. 32–39.
19. J. W. Marriott, Jr., President and Chief Executive Officer of Marriott Corporation, keynote address to American Marketing Association, St. Louis, Missouri, 24 February 1978.
20. Steve Max, "The Economy and the Energy Crisis" (Chicago: Midwest Academy, 1977), p. 7.
21. August Meier and Elliott Rudwick, *Black Detroit and the Rise of the UAW* (New York: Oxford University Press, 1979), p. 88.
22. Miller, *Working Lives*, p. 313.
23. Winpisinger, "Hawaii Conference," p. 21.

2

1. Memo to Economic Dislocation Early Warning System regional staff from Donald F. Wood, Economic Analysis Division, Environmental Protection Agency, 3 February 1979.
2. Maurice H. Stans, "Wait a Minute," *Business and Environment: Toward Common Ground,* H. Jeffrey Leonard et al., eds. (Washington, D.C.: Conservation Foundation, 1977), pp. 124–131.

3. Phone conversations with economists at the National Association of Manufacturers, the Business Roundtable, the U.S. Chamber of Commerce, and the Heritage Foundation, December 1981.
4. Phone conversation with an economist at a national business organization, who asked to remain anonymous, 21 December 1981.
5. Eckardt C. Beck, "Ending Pollution Blackmail," *New York Times*, 8 May 1978.
6. Economic Dislocation Early Warning System, U.S. Environmental Protection Agency, 2nd Quarterly Report 1981, issued 13 October 1981.
7. Michael Kieschnick, *Environmental Protection and Economic Development* (Washington, D.C.: U.S. Department of Commerce Economic Development Administration, October 1978), p. 26.
8. Oil, Chemical and Atomic Workers International Union, *Health, Safety and Environmental Considerations as Factors in OCAW Plant Closings, 1970–75* (Denver, Colorado: Research Department, OCAW, 1976), p. 10.
9. These examples were selected from ten years of EPA Economic Dislocation Early Warning System Quarterly Reports.
10. Department of Information, AFL-CIO, "Labor News Conference" radio series, Program 51, Series 18, 3 April 1979.
11. Phone conversation with Robert Crandall, senior economist, Brookings Institution, 24 December 1981.
12. Memo from Donald Wood, EPA, 3 February 1979.
13. U.S. Congress Joint Economic Committee, *Environmental and Health/Safety Regulations, Productivity Growth and Economic Performance: An Assessment,* 96th Congress, 2nd Session, 1980, p. 62.
14. Howard D. Samuel, "The Role of States in Air Pollution Control," testimony before the U.S. Senate Committee on Public Works, 9 July 1981, p. 2.
15. "New Study Agrees—U.S. Is Losing Jobs," *Viewpoint: An IUD Quarterly,* Fourth Quarter, 1975.
16. "Computerizing Your Job," *Dollars and Sense,* December 1979: 15–17.
17. AFL-CIO Department of Economic Research, *Job Loss Impact of President Reagan's Budget Cuts* (Washington, D.C.: AFL-CIO, February 1981).
18. Conversation with Robert Michel, Office of Water Program Operations, Environmental Protection Agency, 25 February 1981.
19. Environmental Industry Council public relations materials, 1981.
20. Interview with Michael Olszanski, Local 1010, United Steelworkers of America, 22 November 1981.
21. Michael Olszanski, "New Jobs Vital to Stop Inland Pollution," *Local 1010 Steelworker,* November 1976: 3.

22. National Research Council, *Manpower for Environmental Pollution Control* (Washington, D.C.: National Academy of Sciences, 1977), p. 65.
23. Arthur D. Little, Inc., *The Economic Effects of Environmental Regulations on the Pollution Control Industry: Executive Summary* (Cambridge, MA: Arthur D. Little, Inc., 1978), p. xi.
24. Walter G. Gilbert, "Perspective on Training Needs," in *Meeting Environmental Workforce Needs* (Silver Spring, Maryland: Information Dynamics, Inc., 1981), pp. 49–51.
25. Robert Goldberg, "Manpower Requirements and Training to Control Air Pollution," in *Meeting Environmental Workforce Needs* (Silver Spring, Maryland: Information Dynamics, Inc., 1981), pp. 141–46.
26. Kenneth Leung and Jeffrey Klein, *The Environmental Control Industry: An Analysis of Conditions and Prospects for the Pollution Control Equipment Industry* (Washington, D.C.: Council on Environmental Quality, 1975), p. 22.
27. Chase Econometrics, *The Macroeconomic Impacts of Federal Pollution Control Programs* (Washington, D.C.: The Council on Environmental Quality and the U.S. Environmental Protection Agency, 1975), p. 1.
28. Data Resources, Inc., *The Macroeconomic Impact of Federal Pollution Control Programs: 1981 Assessment* (Washington, D.C.: U.S. Environmental Protection Agency, 1981), p. 2.
29. H. Jeffrey Leonard and Christopher S. Duerksen, "Environmental Regulations and the Location of Industry: An International Perspective," Conservation Foundation Conference on the Role of Environmental and Land Use Regulation in Industrial Siting (Washington, D.C.: Conservation Foundation, 1979).
30. Gus Tyler, *Scarcity: A Critique of the American Economy* (New York: Quadrangle Books, 1976), p. 176.
31. Phone conversation with Jeffrey Leonard, Conservation Foundation, 2 February 1982.
32. Victor Cohn and Joanne Omang, "Cancer Outbreak Found at Two Texas Plants," *Washington Post,* 24 July 1980: A1, A7.
33. Harvey Wasserman, "Unionizing Ecotopia," *Mother Jones,* June 1978.
34. Council on Environmental Quality, *Environmental Quality—1979* (Washington, D.C.: U.S. Government Printing Office, 1979), p. 377.
35. Council on Environmental Quality, *Environmental Impact Statements: An Analysis of Six Years' Experience by Seventy Federal Agencies* (Washington, D.C.: U.S. Government Printing Office, 1976), p. D1.
36. Council on Environmental Quality, *Environmental Quality—1979,* p. 377.
37. Ibid.

38. David Moberg, "Unions Are of Three Minds on Clean Air," *In These Times*, 11–19 November 1981: 2.
39. Council on Environmental Quality, *Environmental Quality—1979*, p. 590.
40. Mitchell Lokiec, *Labor and Technology in the Postwar Era* (Columbia, South Carolina: Bobbin Publications, 1972), p. xv.

3

1. Leonard Woodcock, "Jobs and Environment—No Conflict," *Not Man Apart*, January 1976.
2. Irving S. Shapiro, "The Future Role of Business in Society," *Business and Environment: Toward Common Ground*, H. Jeffrey Leonard et al, eds. (Washington, D.C.: Conservation Foundation, 1977), p. 424.
3. "Proceedings of the Hawaii Conference on Jobs and the Environment" (Honolulu: The LOL Foundation, 1978), p. 21.
4. Herbert J. Muller, "Human Values and Modern Technology," *Technology and Social Change in America*, Edwin T. Layton, Jr., ed. (New York: Harper and Row, 1973), p. 169.
5. Gus Tyler, *Scarcity: A Critique of the American Economy* (New York: Quadrangle Books, 1972), p. 199.
6. Lester Thurow, *The Zero-Sum Society: Distribution and the Possibilities for Economic Change* (New York: Basic Books, Inc., 1980), pp. 203–204.
7. *Wall Street Journal*, 7 August 1978.
8. Testimony by Alfred Kahn before the Subcommittee on Environmental Pollution of the Senate Committee on Environment and Public Works, 27 February 1979.
9. U.S. General Accounting Office, *Government Regulatory Activity: Justifications, Processes, Impacts and Alternatives*, Report to Congress, 3 June 1977.
10. David Montgomery, *Workers' Control in America* (New York: Cambridge University Press, 1979), p. 1.
11. Jeremy Brecher, *Strike!* (Boston: South End Press, 1972), p. 60 (emphasis added).
12. David Moberg, "The Great Computer Heist of Jobs, Skill and Power," *In These Times*, 19–25 September 1979: 4.
13. E. J. Mishan, *Technology and Growth: The Price We Pay* (New York: Praeger Publishers, Inc. 1969), p. 40.
14. Edwin McDowell, "OSHA, EPA: The Heyday Is Over," *New York Times*, 4 January 1981: Section 3, p. 1.
15. Kenneth J. Arrow, "The Limitations of the Profit Motive," *Challenge*, September-October 1979: 23.
16. David M. Gordon, *The Working Poor: Towards a State Agenda* (Washington, D.C.: Council of State Planning Agencies, 1980), p. 18.

17. Bureau of Labor Statistics, U.S. Department of Labor.
18. Gordon, *The Working Poor*, p. 8.
19. Ibid., pp. 8–9.
20. Ibid., p. 9.
21. National Advisory Council on Economic Opportunity, *Critical Choices for the 80s*, Twelfth Report (Washington, D.C.: U.S. Government Printing Office, 1980), p. 59.
22. Ibid., pp. 45–63.
23. Ibid.
24. Steve Sheffrin, *The Costs of Continued Unemployment* (Washington, D.C.: Exploratory Project for Economic Alternatives, 1977), p. xii.
25. Research Department of the AFL-CIO, Washington, D.C.
26. National Advisory Council, *Critical Choices*, p. 61.
27. Bureau of Labor Statistics, U.S. Department of Labor.
28. Gordon, *The Working Poor*, p. 6.
29. Ibid., p. 8.
30. George McAlmon, "A Storm Warning," advertisement sponsored by The American Income Life Insurance Company, *The Texas Observer*, 6 November 1981: 21.
31. "Economic Policy Hearings Start," *Focus on Full Employment*, December 1975: 3.
32. National Institute for Occupational Safety and Health, *President's Report on Occupational Safety and Health* (Washington, D.C.: NIOSH, 1972), p. 111.
33. Barry Weisberg, *Beyond Repair* (Boston: Beacon Press, 1971), p. 163.
34. Statement of the Ohio AFL-CIO on "Exposures to Toxic Substances in the Workplace and Compensation of Diseased Workers."
35. Council on Environmental Quality, *Environmental Quality—1979* (Washington, D.C.: U.S. Government Printing Office, 1979), p. 534.
36. Kenneth Bridbord et al., eds., *Estimates of the Fraction of Cancer in the United States Related to Occupational Factors* (Washington, D.C.: National Cancer Institute, National Institute of Environmental Health Sciences, National Institute for Occupational Safety and Health, 1978), p. 24.
37. Phyllis Lehmann, *Cancer and the Worker* (New York: The New York Academy of Sciences, 1977), p. 4.
38. Bridbord et al., *Fraction of Cancer*, pp. 9–10.
39. Ibid., p. 24.
40. Shelby Marshall, "Labor Education Day for Public Interest Groups," *A Report to the Steering Committee of the New York State Alliance on Jobs and the Human Environment*, September 1977.
41. Barbara Blum, *Cities: An Environment Wilderness* (Washington, D.C.: U.S. Environmental Protection Agency, 1978), p. 3.
42. Robert M. Solow, "The Economics of Pollution Control," *Jobs and*

the Environment: Three Papers (Berkeley, California: Institute of Industrial Relations, University of California, 1972), p. 13.

43. Deborah Bouton, "In Spring, Some People's Thoughts Turn to Pesticides," *In These Times,* 27 May–3 June 1981: 6.
44. Michael Brown, *Laying Waste: The Poisoning of America by Toxic Chemicals* (New York: Pantheon Books, 1980), p. 123.
45. Council on Environmental Quality, *Environmental Quality—1979,* p. 174.
46. Joanne Omang, "EPA Names 115 Toxic Waste Dump Sites Slated for Clean-up," *Washington Post,* 24 October 1981: A4.
47. Fred C. Shapiro, "A Reporter at Large: Radioactive Waste," *New Yorker,* 19 October 1981: 57–58.
48. Lester R. Brown, *Building a Sustainable Society* (New York: W. W. Norton and Company, 1981), p. 27.
49. Ibid., p. 18.
50. Ibid., p. 43.
51. Ibid., pp. 84-85.
52. Dianne Dumanoski, "Acid Rain," *Sierra,* May–June 1980: 38–40.
53. "Dropping Acid," Editorial in the *Washington Post,* 16 October 1981: Section A.
54. Daniel R. Fusfeld, "Some Notes on the Opposition to Regulation," *Journal of Post-Keynesian Economics,* Spring 1980: 365.

4

1. John Stanton, "Packard, Wilson Issue An Energy Warning," *The Peninsula Times Tribune,* Redwood City, CA, 19 July 1979: E1.
2. Ibid.
3. Steve Max, "The Economy and the Energy Crisis" (Chicago: Midwest Academy, 1977), p. 5.
4. Milton Moskowitz, Michael Katz, and Robert Levering, eds., *Everybody's Business: An Almanac* (San Francisco: Harper and Row, 1980).
5. Richard Edwards, *Contested Terrain: The Transformation of the Workplace in the Twentieth Century* (New York: Basic Books, 1979), p. 77.
6. Ibid.
7. C. Wright Mills, *The Power Elite* (New York: Oxford University Press, 1956), p. 7.
8. Ralph Miliband, *The State in Capitalist Society* (New York: Basic Books, 1969), p. 164.
9. "Ford: Concession at Three Locals," *Labor Notes,* 23 November 1981: 8.
10. Interview with Anne Cassin, Environmental Protection Agency Office of Economic Analysis, 28 June 1981.
11. Ibid.

12. Marc S. Miller, ed., *Working Lives: The Southern Exposure History of Labor in the South* (New York: Pantheon Books, 1980), p. 237.
13. Ibid.
14. Ibid., p. 318.
15. Andrew Rowland, "Tanning Leather, Tanning Hides: Health and Safety Struggles in a Leather Factory," *Radical America*, November–December 1980: 26.
16. Leonard Woodcock, president of the United Auto Workers, keynote address to "Working for Environmental and Economic Justice and Jobs" conference, Black Lake, MI, 2 May 1976.
17. Lee Bandy, "Textile Official Says Brown Lung Does Not Exist," *The State*, Columbia, S.C., 4 October 1978: B1.
18. Iver Peterson, "Cancer Studies Only Reinforce Fears of Employees in GM's Model Shop," *New York Times*, 7 December 1981.
19. Ibid.
20. Frank B. Shants, "Countering the Anti-Nuclear Activists," *Public Relations Journal*, October 1978: 10.
21. Michael D. Reagan, *The Managed Economy* (New York: Oxford University Press, 1963), p. 83.
22. Paul Brodeur, *Expendable Americans* (New York: The Viking Press, 1974), p. 250.
23. U.S. Congress Joint Economic Committee, *Mid-Year Review of the Economic Situation and Outlook,* 94th Congress (Washington, D.C.: Government Printing Office, 1976).
24. U.S. House of Representatives Committee on the Budget, *Hearings before the Task Force on Entitlements, Uncontrollables, and Indexing,* 3 December 1981 (Washington, D.C.: Government Printing Office, 1981).
25. U.S. Department of Energy, *National Energy Plan II, Appendix C* (Washington, D.C.: Government Printing Office, 1979).
26. Philip Handler, "Exaggeration: The Other Peril," *Business and Environment: Toward Common Ground,* H. Jeffrey Leonard et al, eds. (Washington, D.C.: Conservation Foundation, 1977), p. 147.
27. *Not Man Apart*, August 1976.
28. "Getting Rid of Scary Words," *Mother Jones*, December 1981: 5.
29. Environmental Industry Conference, *New Initiatives in Environment and Energy: Proceedings of the Environmental Industry Conference* (Canoga Park, California: NILS Publishing Co., 1978), p. 65.
30. Henry M. Peskin, "National Income Accounts and the Environment," *Environmental Regulation and the U.S. Economy,* H. Peskin, P. Portney, and A. Kneese, eds. (Baltimore, MD: Johns Hopkins University Press, 1981), p. 80.
31. "Air Isn't Free," editorial in the *Wall Street Journal*, 14 July 1981.
32. John Maddox, *The Doomsday Syndrome* (New York: McGraw-Hill Book Company, 1972), p. 114.

33. Gottfried Haberler, "The Challenge to the Free Market Economy," *Business and Government: Toward Common Ground,* H. Jeffrey Leonard et al, eds. (Washington, D.C.: Conservation Foundation, 1977), p. 390.
34. Joseph Kraft, "Who Profits from Profits?" *Washington Post,* 25 October 1979.
35. Ibid.
36. *Business Week,* 30 June 1980: 146.
37. William Serrin, *The Company and the Union* (New York: Vintage Books, 1974), pp. 161-62.
38. Harry Johnson, *Man and His Environment* (London: British-North America Committee, 1973).
39. Robert W. Searby, "Nuclear Energy and the Radical Agenda of Environmentalism," *The Carpenter,* January 1980: 12.
40. Mobil Corporation advertisement, *The Washington Post,* 6 December 1981.
41. Iver Peterson, "Cancer Studies Only Reinforce Fears."

5

1. *Wall Street Journal,* 22 November 1978.
2. Mark Green and Norman Waitzman, *Business War on the Law: An Analysis of the Benefits of Federal Health/Safety Enforcement* (Washington, D.C.: The Corporate Accountability Research Group, 1979), Appendix A.
3. Ralph Miliband, *The State in Capitalist Society* (New York: Basic Books, 1969), p. 1.
4. John Quarles, *Cleaning Up America: An Insider's View of the Environmental Protection Agency* (Boston: Houghton Mifflin Co., 1976), p. 174.
5. Andrew Carnegie, *Problems of Today* (Darby, PA.: Quality Library, 1908), p. 48.
6. James Weinstein, *The Corporate Ideal in the Liberal State* (Boston: Beacon Press, 1968), p. 105.
7. G. William Domhoff, *Higher Circles: The Governing Class in America* (New York: Random House, 1970), p. 280.
8. Gabriel Kolko, *The Triumph of Conservatism* (Chicago: Quadrangle Books, 1967), p. 266.
9. John Roche, *Sentenced to Life* (New York: Macmillan, 1974), p. 205.
10. William E. Simon, *A Time for Truth* (New York: Berkley Books, 1979), pp. 65–66.
11. U.S. Senate Committee on Governmental Affairs, *Study of Federal Regulation, Volume VI,* "Framework for Regulation," 96th Congress, 1st Session, December 1978.
12. Weinstein, *The Corporate Ideal,* p. 105.

13. John G. Burke, "Technology and Government," *Technology and Social Change in America,* Edwin T. Layton, Jr., ed., (New York: Harper and Row, 1973), p. 18.
14. Ibid.
15. Kurt Wetzel, "Railroad Management's Response to Operating Employee Accidents, 1890-1913," *Labor History,* Summer 1980: 351.
16. Ibid.
17. Ibid.
18. Gus Tyler, *Scarcity: A Critique of the American Economy* (New York: Quadrangle Books, 1976), p. 13.
19. Kim McQuaid, "The Roundtable: Getting Results in Washington," *Harvard Business Review,* May–June 1981: 118.
20. J. C. Turner, *The Business Roundtable and American Labor,* (Washington, D.C.: AFL-CIO, 1969), p. 6.
21. McQuaid, "The Roundtable," p. 118.
22. Paul G. Rogers, Keynote Address to the Third Annual Conference on Health Policy sponsored by the *National Journal,* 22 May 1978.
23. Turner, *The Business Roundtable,* p. 1.
24. David M. Gordon, "Capital vs. Labor: The Current Crisis in the Sphere of Production," *The Economic Crisis Reader,* David Mermelstein, ed. (New York: Vintage Books, 1975), p. 393.
25. Lester Thurow, *The Zero-Sum Society: Distribution and the Possibilities for Economic Change* (New York: Basic Books, Inc., 1980), pp. 45–46.
26. Edward A. Grefe, *Fighting to Win: Business Political Power* (New York: Law and Business, Inc., 1981), p. 69.
27. Telephone conversation with Elmer Fike, 12 September 1981.
28. Robert Lindsey, "Tax-Exempt Foundations Formed to Help Business Fight Regulation," *New York Times,* 12 February 1978: 1.
29. *Democratic Left,* November 1977: 2.
30. J. W. Marriott, Jr., address to American Marketing Association, St. Louis, Missouri, 24 February 1978.
31. Ruth Jordan, "Labor Law Reform: Battle in the Class War," *Newsletter of the Democratic Left,* September 1978: 1-2.
32. Ibid.
33. Stephen Lagerfeld, "To Break a Union," *Harper's,* May 1981: 16.
34. Industrial Union Department, AFL-CIO, *IUD Digest,* July–August 1981: 1.
35. Ibid.
36. U.S. Department of Commerce, Regulatory Policy Committee, *Toward Regulatory Reasonableness* (Washington, D.C.: U.S. Government Printing Office, 1977), p. 67.
37. Murray L. Weidenbaum, *The Future of Business Regulation* (New York: Amacom, 1980), p. 1.
38. Arthur Andersen and Company, *Cost of Government Regulation*

Study for the Business Roundtable (Chicago: Arthur Andersen and Co., 1979), p. 1.

39. Margot Hornblower, "Major Industries Map New Attack on Clean Air Act," *Washington Post*, 15 January 1979.

40. Merrill Brown, "Regulatory 'Balance' May Shift to Dismantlers" *Washington Post*, 11 January 1981: L5.

41. Joanne Omang, "Reagan Criticizes Clean Air Laws and EPA as Obstacles to Growth," *Washington Post*, 9 October 1980.

42. Elizabeth Drew, "Secretary Watt," *The New Yorker*, 4 May 1981: 107.

43. Cass Peterson, "Executive Notes," *Washington Post*, 3 December 1981.

44. Joanne Omang, *Washington Post*, 23 August 1981: A10.

45. Howell Raines, "Reagan Reversing Many U.S. Policies," *New York Times*, 3 July 1981.

46. Warren Brown, "Donovan Selection Prompts a 'Who Is He?' Chorus by Labor Leaders," *Washington Post*, 17 December 1980.

47. Caroline E. Mayer, "Deregulation Will Attack Different Targets Under Reagan, Adviser Says," *Washington Star*, 4 February 1981.

48. Joanne Omang, "Strip-Mining Office Revamped: Crippling of Agency Charged," *Washington Post*, 22 May 1981.

49. Memo from William Drayton, Jr., to Save EPA Working Group, Arlington, Virginia, 16 November 1981.

50. David Osborne, "State of Siege," *Mother Jones*, February/March 1982: 27–28.

51. Letter to the Editor, *Washington Post*, 9 November 1981.

52. Warren Brown, *Washington Post*, 28 October 1981: A23.

53. Warren Brown, "Former Labor Spokesman Speaks His Own Mind," *Washington Post*, 9 November 1981.

54. Felicity Barringer, "OMB Accused of 'Backdoor' Policy Role," *Washington Post*, 29 July 1981.

55. Brown, "Former Labor Spokesman," *Washington Post*, 9 November 1981.

56. Martin Carnoy, "Why Reaganomics Will Fail," *Plowshare Press*, January–February 1982: 3.

57. Winston Williams, "Saving Jobs by Cutting Wages," *New York Times*, 25 January 1981.

58. William Serrin, "Unions Yielding 'Givebacks' to Employers at Rising Rate," *New York Times*, 12 October 1981: A16.

59. Ibid.

6

1. Lester Thurow, *The Zero-Sum Society: Distribution and the Pos-*

sibilities for Economic Change (New York: Basic Books, Inc. 1980), pp. 43–44.

2. Barry P. Bosworth, "The Economic Environment for Regulation in the 1980s," *Environmental Regulation and the U.S. Economy*, Henry M. Peskin, et al., eds. (Baltimore, Maryland: Johns Hopkins University Press, 1981), pp. 9–10.

3. Ibid., p. 9.

4. James C. Miller, III, "Lessons of the Economic Impact Statement Program," *Regulation*, July/August 1977: 15.

5. Hearings before the Subcommittee for Commerce, Science and Transportation of the U.S. Senate, *Cost of Government Regulations to the Consumer*, 95th Congress, Second Session, 21-22 November 1978.

6. Kenneth H. Bacon, "President Vows Big Budget Cuts in Inflation Fight," *Wall Street Journal*, 30 January 1981.

7. Data Resources, Inc., *The Macroeconomic Impact of Federal Pollution Control Programs: 1981 Assessment* (Washington, D.C.: U.S. Environmental Protection Agency, 1981), p. 18.

8. Paul R. Portney, "The Macroeconomic Impacts of Federal Environmental Regulations," *Environmental Regulation in the U.S. Economy*, Henry M. Peskin, et al., eds., (Baltimore, Johns Hopkins University Press, 1981), p. 34.

9. Ibid.

10. Gus Speth, "A Small Price to Pay: Inflation and Environmental Controls," *Environment*, Vol. 20, No. 8, October 1978: 26.

11. James C. Miller, III, "Lessons of the Economic Impact Statement Program": 15n.

12. James C. Tanner, "Name Change Brings Excedrin Headaches and Costs Approximately $100 Million," *Wall Street Journal*, 9 January 1973: 44.

13. Data Resources, Inc., *The Macroeconomic Impact of Federal Pollution Control Programs*, p. 1.

14. Telephone conversation with Citizens' Clearinghouse for Hazardous Wastes, Arlington, Virginia, 21 January 1982.

15. Samuel S. Epstein, "Cancer, Inflation and the Failure to Regulate," *Technology Review*, December/January 1980: 42.

16. Lester Thurow, *The Zero-Sum Society*, p. 41.

17. John Blair et al., eds, *The Roots of Inflation* (New York: Burt Franklin and Co., 1975), p. 28.

18. Ibid., pp. vi–vii.

19. Seymour Melman, *The Permanent War Economy* (New York: Simon and Schuster, 1974), p. 34.

20. Keynote Speech before the Second National Labor Conference for Safe Energy and Full Employment, Gary, Indiana, 22 November 1981.

21. U.S. Congress Joint Economic Committee, *Achieving Price Stability through Economic Growth*, 93rd Congress, 1973, pp. 41–42.

7

1. Rosabeth Moss Kanter, "Make 994. (Q. Why?)" *New York Times*, 7 November 1981.
2. Ibid.
3. Lester Thurow, "The U.S. Productivity Problem," *Data Resources U.S. Review*, August 1979.
4. David M. Gordon, "Capital vs. Labor: The Current Crisis in the Sphere of Production," *The Economic Crisis Reader*, David Mermelstein, ed. (New York: Vintage Books, 1975), p. 396.
5. Peter Behr and Joanne Omang, *Washington Post*, 26 March 1981.
6. Mark Green and Norman Waitzman, *Business War on the Law: An Analysis of the Benefits of Federal Health/Safety Enforcement* (Washington, D.C.: The Corporate Accountability Research Group, 1979), p. 52.
7. Council on Environmental Quality, *Environmental Quality—1979* (Washington, D.C.: U.S. Government Printing Office, 1979), pp. 434–35.
8. U.S. Congress Joint Economic Committee, *Environmental and Health/Safety Regulations, Productivity, Growth and Economic Performance: An Assessment*, 96th Congress, 1st Session, p. 34.
9. Edward F. Denison, "The Puzzling Setback to Productivity Growth," *Challenge*, November–December 1980: 8.
10. Joint Economic Committee, *Productivity*, p. 35.
11. Ibid., p. 36.
12. Ibid., p. 5.
13. "A Productivity Drop That Nobody Believes," *Business Week*, 25 February 1980.
14. Lester C. Thurow, *The Zero-Sum Society: Distribution and the Possibilities for Economic Change* (New York: Basic Books, 1980), p. 89.
15. Lester C. Thurow, "Death by a Thousand Cuts," *New York Review of Books*, 17 December 1981: 3.
16. Paul Nyden, "Miners, Mr. President, Are Not Slag," *New York Times*, 24 January 1982.
17. Conversation with United Mine Workers Research Director Michael Buckner, 3 February 1982.
18. Joint Economic Committee of the U.S. Congress, *Productivity: The Foundation of Growth: Special Study on Economic Change*, Vol. 10, 96th Congress, 2nd Session, December 1980: 20.
19. Conversation with Joe Frantz, Steelworkers Local 1010, 22 November 1981.
20. Rosabeth Moss Kanter, "Make 994."
21. *Wall Street Journal*, 16 January 1981: 1.
22. Thurow, "Death by a Thousand Cuts": 4.
23. Thurow, *Zero-Sum Society*, p. 86.
24. Steven Pearlman, "Are EPA's Clean Air Rules Worth Their Cost?" *Nation's Cities Weekly*, 5 January 1981: 5.

25. Institute for Labor Education and Research, "Labor Unions in Transition," *U.S. Capitalism in Crisis* (New York: Union for Radical Political Economics, 1978), p. 290.

8

1. United States Senate Select Committee on Small Business, *Small Business and Innovation*, 96th Congress, 1st Session, June 1979, p. 12.
2. Ibid., pp. 33–34.
3. *Wall Street Journal*, 22 November 1978.
4. Sumner Myers et al., *Why Innovations Falter and Fail: A Study of 200 Cases* (Denver, Colorado: Denver Research Institute, 1980), p. A-8.
5. Ibid., p. 22.
6. Ruth Ruttenberg, "Regulation is the Mother of Invention," *Working Papers*, May–June 1981: 43.
7. U.S. Environmental Protection Agency, Office of Pesticides and Toxic Substances, *Supporting Innovation: A Policy Study* (Washington, D.C.: U.S. Government Printing Office, 1980), p. 34.
8. Ibid., p. 32.
9. Michael G. Royston, "Making Pollution Prevention Pay," *Harvard Business Review*, November–December 1980: 6.
10. Ibid.: 8.
11. Lewis Lehr, "Preventing Pollution Pays Better Than Controlling It," *Financier*, December 1980: 19–20.
12. James M. Fallows, "American Industry: What Ails It, How to Save It," *Atlantic Monthly*, September 1980: 44.
13. Robert H. Hayes and William J. Abernathy, "Managing Our Way to Economic Decline," *Harvard Business Review*, July–August 1980: 72.
14. David T. Kearns, "Let's Take Risks Again," *Newsweek*, 5 May 1980: 13.
15. Ibid.

9

1. Linda Greenhouse, "Justices Decide U.S. Must Protect Workers' Safety Despite High Cost," *New York Times*, 18 June 1981: A1.
2. Douglas M. Costle, "Defense by Disaster," remarks to Women's National Democratic Club, Washington, D.C., 29 March 1979.
3. U.S. House of Representatives Subcommittee on Oversight and Investigations of the Committee on Interstate and Foreign Commerce, *Cost-Benefit Analysis: Wonder Tool or Mirage?*, 96th Congress, 2nd Session, 1980, p. 5.

4. Ibid.
5. Samuel S. Epstein, "Cancer, Inflation and the Failure to Regulate," *Technology Review,* December/January 1980: 47.
6. Mark Green and Norman Waitzman, *Business War on the Law: An Analysis of the Benefits of Federal Health/Safety Enforcement* (Washington, D.C.: The Corporate Accountability Research Group, 1979), p. 24.
7. Ibid., pp. 24-25.
8. Ibid.
9. House Subcommittee on Oversight, *Cost-Benefit Analysis,* pp. 13–15.
10. "The Cost-Benefits Argument—Is the Emphasis Shifting?" *Occupational Hazards,* February 1980: 59.
11. Murray C. Weidenbaum and Robert De Fina, *The Cost of Federal Regulation of Economic Activity* (Washington, D.C.: American Enterprise Institute, 1978).
12. Green and Waitzman, *Business War,* p. 29.
13. William K. Tabb, "Government Regulation: Two Sides to the Story," *Challenge,* November–December 1980: 48.
14. Green and Waitzman, *Business War,* p. 29.
15. Tabb, "Government Regulation," p. 48.
16. "Executive Notes," *Washington Post,* 16 October 1981.
17. House Committee on Oversight, *Cost-Benefit Analysis,* p. 9.
18. Arthur Andersen and Company, *Cost of Government Regulation Study for the Business Roundtable: Executive Summary* (Chicago: Arthur Andersen and Co., 1979), p. 11.
19. Joseph P. Biniek, *The Status of Environmental Economics: An Update* (Washington, D.C.: Library of Congress Congressional Research Service, June 1979), p. 1.
20. Council on Environmental Quality, *Environmental Quality—1980* (Washington, D.C.: U.S. Government Printing Office, 1980), p. 146.
21. Ibid.
22. Ibid., Chapter 4.
23. Douglas M. Costle, "A Law in Trouble," remarks to the Air Pollution Control Association, Montreal, Canada, 23 June 1980.
24. National Commission on Air Quality, *To Breathe Clean Air* (Washington, D.C.: U.S. Government Printing Office, 1981), p. 11.
25. Council on Environmental Quality, *Environmental Quality—1980* (Washington, D.C.: U.S. Government Printing Office, 1980), p. 146.
26. U.S. Environmental Protection Agency, Office of Planning and Evaluation, *National Accomplishments in Pollution Control: 1970–1980* (Washington, D.C.: U.S. Government Printing Office, 1980), p. 10.
27. Ibid.
28. Ibid., p. 54.

29. Ibid.
30. Ibid., p. 56.
31. United States Senate Committee on Labor and Human Resources, *Occupational Safety and Health Improvements Act of 1980,* 96th Congress, 2nd Session, 1980, p. 69.
32. Industrial Union Department, AFL-CIO, "OSHA Saves Lives," *Viewpoint,* Winter 1980: 9.
33. Bureau of Labor Statistics, U.S. Department of Labor, press release 81-526, 18 November 1981.
34. "Study Rates Expense of OSHA's Rules to Chemical Firms," *Wall Street Journal,* 23 June 1981.
35. A. Myrick Freeman, III, *The Benefits of Air and Water Pollution Control: A Review and Synthesis of Recent Estimates: Executive Summary* (Washington, D.C.: Council on Environmental Quality, 1979).
36. Ibid., p. xi.
37. Council on Environmental Quality, *Environmental Quality—1979,* p. 655.
38. "The Cost-Benefits Argument—Is the Emphasis Shifting?" p. 59.
39. Steven Pearlman, "Are EPA's Clean Air Rules Worth Their Cost?" *Nation's Cities Weekly,* 5 January 1981: 5.
40. "The Cost-Benefits Argument—Is the Emphasis Shifting?" p. 59.
41. Felicity Barringer, "Nader to Stockman: U.S. Rules Saved Economy $5.7 Billion," *Washington Post,* 11 August 1981: A13.
42. National Academy of Sciences, *Saccharin: Technical Assessment of Risks and Benefits* (Washington, D.C.: National Academy of Sciences, 1978), p. 3–72, table 3-8.
43. Deborah Sheiman, *The Dollars and Sense of Environmental Regulation* (Washington, D.C.: League of Women Voters Education Fund, 1980), p. 5.
44. "Stockman Asks Benefit Panel to Refine Economic Estimates," *Air Waves,* December 1979, Bulletin of the National Commission on Air Quality, p. 1.

10

1. Herbert E. Meyer, *The War Against Progress* (Middleton, New York: Storm King Publishers, Inc., 1980), pp. 93–94.
2. Ibid., p. 29.
3. Thomas Donahue, assistant to president of AFL-CIO, at Black Lake Conference on "Working for Environmental and Economic Justice and Jobs," 2–6 May 1976.
4. Bayard Rustin, "No Growth Has to Mean Less is Less," *New York Times Magazine,* 2 May 1976.
5. Office of Public Affairs of the Department of Energy, press release, 9 December 1977.

6. Richard Grossman and Gail Daneker, *Energy, Jobs and the Economy* (Boston: Alyson Publications, Inc., 1979), p. 112.
7. Ibid.
8. Ibid., p. 36.
9. Ibid., p. 35.
10. Frank Swoboda, "Automation Shifts Bode Bleak Future for Labor," *Washington Post,* 24 April 1981: E1, E3.
11. Stanley Aronowitz, "The Labor Movement and the Left in the United States," *Socialist Review,* No. 44, March–April 1979: 15.
12. "Changing 45 Million Jobs," *Business Week,* 3 August 1981: 62.
13. Ibid.
14. Ibid.
15. Colin Norman, *Microelectronics at Work: Productivity and Jobs in the World Economy,* Worldwatch Paper 39 (Washington, D.C.: Worldwatch Institute, October 1980), p. 31.
16. Colin Norman, "Chips and Jobs," *Environment,* December 1980: 18.
17. Ibid.: 15.
18. Ibid.: 16.
19. Melvin Humphery, "Minorities in the Energy Industries" *Energy and Equity: Some Social Concerns,* Ellis Cose, et al, eds., (Washington, D.C.: Joint Center for Political Studies, 1979), p. 66.
20. Carl Pope, "Growth and the Poor," *Sierra Club Bulletin,* April 1975.
21. H. V. Hodson, *The Diseconomics of Growth* (London, Earth Island Limited, 1972), p. 27.
22. Ibid.
23. Philip Shabecoff, "Protecting Environment and Economy," *New York Times,* 28 May 1977.
24. Lester C. Thurow, *The Zero-Sum Society* (New York: Basic Books, 1980), p. 204.

Introduction to Part III

1. Leonard Woodcock, keynote address, "Working for Environmental and Economic Justice and Jobs," conference, Black Lake, Michigan, 2 May 1976.
2. Labor History Slighted, "Experts Say," *New York Times,* 8 September 1981.

11

1. U.S. Department of Labor, "Child Labor Laws," *Growth of Labor Law in the United States* (Washington, D.C.: U.S. Government Printing Office, 1967), p. 507.

2. Jeremy Brecher, *Strike!* (Boston: South End Press, 1972), p. 45.
3. Richard O. Boyer and Herbert M. Morais, *Labor's Untold Story* (New York: United Electrical, Radio and Machine Workers of America, 1955), p. 144.
4. Ibid., p. 40.
5. United States Senate, *Report of the Committee of the Senate Upon the Relations between Labor and Capital* (Washington, D.C.: U.S. Government Printing Office, 1885), p. 759.
6. Brecher, *Strike!*, p. 27.
7. Ibid., Chapter 2.
8. Ibid., p. 37.
9. Ibid., p. 39.
10. Ibid., p. 45.
11. Ibid., p. 53.
12. Ibid., p. 63.
13. Ibid., p. 84.
14. Ibid., p. 94.
15. Richard Edwards, *Contested Terrain: The Transformation of the Workplace in the Twentieth Century* (New York: Basic Books, Inc., 1979), pp. 43–44.
16. David Montgomery, *Workers' Control in America* (New York: Cambridge University Press, 1979), pp. 13–14.
17. Frederick Winslow Taylor, *Principles of Scientific Management* (New York: Harper and Row, 1911), pp. 31–32.
18. Frances Fox Piven and Richard A. Cloward, *Poor People's Movements: Why They Succeed, How They Fail* (New York: Pantheon Books, 1977), p. 100.
19. Boyer and Morais, *Labor's Untold Story,* p. 184.
20. Montgomery, *Workers' Control,* p. 96.
21. James Weinstein, *The Corporate Ideal in the Liberal State* (Boston: Beacon Press, 1968), p. 40.
22. Philip Foner, *History of the Labor Movement in the United States, Volume III. The Policies and Practices of the American Federation of Labor: 1900–1909.* (New York: International Publishers, 1980), p. 22.
23. U.S. Department of Labor, "Child Labor Laws," pp. 8–9.
24. Joseph A. Page and Mary-Win O'Brien, *Bitter Wages* (New York: Grossman Publishers, 1973), p. 51.
25. Weinstein, *The Corporate Ideal,* p. 43.
26. Ibid., p. 51.
27. Daniel M. Berman, *Death on the Job: Occupational Health and Safety Struggles in the United States* (New York: Monthly Review Press, 1978), p. 104.
28. Ibid., p. 24.
29. "Fumes Kill Laborer Cleaning Tank at Chemical Firm in Baltimore," *Washington Star,* 16 February 1981.
30. Richard Engler, *Oil Refinery Health and Safety Hazards: Their Causes and the Struggle to End Them* (Philadelphia: Philadelphia

Area Project on Occupational Safety and Health, 1975), p. 1.
31. Fred W. Thompson and Patrick Murfin, *The IWW: Its First Seventy Years* (Chicago, Illinois: Industrial Workers of the World, 1976), p. 118.
32. Ibid., pp. 118–119.
33. Montgomery, *Workers' Control*, p. 96.
34. Ibid., p. 95.
35. Ibid., p. 99.
36. Ibid., p. 96.
37. Ibid., p. 98.
38. Ibid., p. 96.
39. Sidney Lens, *Radicalism in America* (New York: Thomas Y. Crowell Co., 1966), p. 259.
40. Alvin W. Gouldner, *Wildcat Strike* (New York: Harper and Row, 1965), p. 34.
41. Alice and Staughton Lynd, *Rank and File* (Boston: Beacon Press, 1973), p. 52.
42. Page, *Bitter Wages*, pp. 60–61.
43. Ibid., pp. 62–63.
44. James R. Green, *The World of the Worker: Labor in Twentieth Century America* (New York: Hill and Wang, 1980), p. 138.
45. Ibid., p. 138.
46. Piven and Cloward, *Poor People's Movements*, p. 112.
47. Ibid.
48. Ibid., p. 120.
49. Ibid., p. 123.
50. "Industrial War," *Fortune*, November 1937: 108.
51. Edwards, *Contested Terrain*, p. 128.
52. Brecher, *Strike!*, p. 206.
53. Thomas Brooks, *Toil and Trouble: A History of American Labor* (New York: Delacorte Press, 1971), p. 198.
54. "Manifesto: American Iron and Steel Industry," *Fortune*, May 1937: 91.
55. Montgomery, *Workers' Control*, p. 165.
56. Joseph C. Rayback, *A History of American Labor* (New York: Free Press, 1966), pp. 365–371.
57. Ibid.
58. Green, *World of the Worker*, p. 18.
59. Ibid., p. 205.
60. Ibid., p. 203.
61. Ibid., p. 208.
62. Dan Georgakas and Marvin Surkin, *Detroit—I Do Mind Dying: A Study in Urban Revolution* (New York: St. Martin's Press, 1974).
63. David M. Gordon, "Capital vs. Labor: The Current Crisis in the Sphere of Production," in David Mermelstein, ed., *The Economic Crisis Reader* (New York: Vintage Books, 1975), p. 395.

64. Harry Braverman, *Labor and Monopoly Capital* (New York: Monthly Review Press, 1974), p. 179.
65. "Interview with William Winpisinger," *Challenge,* March–April 1978: 50.

12

1. Brock Evans, "The Wilderness Idea as Moving Force in American Cultural and Political History," *Idaho Law Review,* as reprinted in *The Congressional Record,* Vol. 127, No. 61, 97th Congress, 1st Session, 27 April 1981: 1.
2. Ibid.
3. Edward Dalton, "The Metropolitan Board of Health," *American Environmentalism: The Formative Period 1860–1915,* Donald Worster, ed. (New York: John Wiley and Sons, Inc., 1973), pp. 142–143.
4. Ibid., p. 143.
5. Ibid., p. 143.
6. Ibid.
7. J. Clarence Davies, III, *The Politics of Pollution* (New York: Pegasus, 1970), p. 33.
8. Booth Tarkington, *Growth* (Garden City, N.Y.: Doubleday, Page and Co., 1927), p. 1.
9. Alice and Staughton Lynd, *Rank and File* (Boston: Beacon Press, 1973), p. 152.
10. James Ridgeway, *The Politics of Ecology* (New York: E. P. Dutton and Co., 1970), p. 36.
11. Stephen Fox, *John Muir and His Legacy: The American Conservation Movement* (Boston: Little Brown and Co., 1981), p. 299.
12. Ridgeway, *Politics of Ecology,* pp. 43–44.
13. Fox, *John Muir,* p. 300.
14. Evans, "The Wilderness Idea," p. 2.
15. Gifford Pinchot, "The Fight for Conservation," *American Environmentalism: The Formative Period 1860–1915,* Donald Worster, ed. (New York: John Wiley and Sons, Inc., 1973), p. 85.
16. Samuel P. Hays, *Conservation and the Gospel of Efficiency* (New York: Atheneum, 1969), p. 266.
17. Fox, *John Muir,* p. 112.
18. Ibid., p. 103.
19. Eric Seaborg, "The Battle for Hetch Hetchy," *Sierra,* November/December 1981: p. 62.
20. Fox, *John Muir,* pp. 145–47.
21. Ibid., pp. 167–68.
22. C. Wright Mills, *The Power Elite* (New York: Oxford University Press, 1956), p. 101.
23. Grant McConnell, *Private Power and American Democracy* (New York: Vintage Books, 1970), p. 271.

24. Hobart Rowen, *The Free Enterprisers* (New York: G. P. Putnam, 1969), pp. 61–62.
25. Joseph A. Page and Mary-Win O'Brien, *Bitter Wages* (New York: Grossman Publishers, 1973), p. 116.
26. Daniel M. Berman, *Death on the Job: Occupational Health and Safety Struggles in the United States* (New York: Monthly Review Press, 1978), pp. 138, 119.
27. Curtis Seltzer, *Surveying and Analyzing the Field of Employee Rights Related to Occupational Disease* (Washington, D.C.: U.S. Department of Labor, 1979).
28. Ridgeway, *The Politics of Ecology*, p. 45.
29. Fox, *John Muir*, p. 283.
30. Ibid., p. 285.
31. Frank Graham, Jr., *Man's Dominion* (New York: M. Evans and Co., 1971), p. 301.
32. Barry Commoner, *The Closing Circle* (New York: Alfred A. Knopf, 1971), p. 168.
33. James Fallows, "American Industry: What Ails It, How to Save It," *Atlantic Monthly*, September 1980: 43. Used by permission of James Fallows.
34. Commoner, *Closing Circle*, pp. 67–68.
35. Morton Mintz and Jerry S. Cohen, *America, Inc.* (New York: Delta Books, 1971), p. 6.
36. Rice Odell, *Environmental Awakening: The New Revolution to Protect the Earth* (Cambridge, MA: Ballinger Publishing Company, 1980), p. 132.
37. Ibid.
38. Beatrice N. Vaccara and Patrick H. MacAuley, "Evaluating the Economic Performance of U.S. Manufacturing Industries," *Industrial Economic Review*, Summer 1980 (Washington, D.C.: U.S. Department of Commerce, Bureau of Industrial Economics, 1980), pp. 6–19.
39. Environmental Action Foundation Waste and Toxic Substances Project, *A Review of Chemical Industry Economics and Statistics* (Washington, D.C.: Environmental Action Foundation, November 1980).
40. *Business Week*, 11 May 1974.
41. Peter Behr, "Controlling Chemical Hazards," *Environment*, Vol. 20, No. 6, July/August 1978, pp. 25–27.
42. Robert Hoover, "Environmental Cancer," *Public Control of Environmental Health Hazards*, E. Cuyler Hammond and Irving J. Selikoff, eds. (New York: New York Academy of Sciences, 1979), p. 50.
43. Ibid.
44. Environmental Defense Fund and Robert H. Boyle, *Malignant Neglect* (New York: Vintage Books, 1980), p. 21
45. United Steelworkers of America, *Post Hearing Brief of United Steelworkers of America on Standard for Coke Oven Emissions,*

(Pittsburgh, PA: United Steelworkers of America, 1976), p. 11.
46. James M. Fallows, *The Water Lords* (New York: Grossman Publishers, 1970), p. 48. Used by pemission of Viking Penquin Inc.
47. Lynton K. Caldwell, Lynton R. Hayes and Isabel M. MacWhirter, *Citizens and the Environment* (Bloomington, IN: Indiana University Press, 1976), p. 199.
48. Fox, *John Muir*, pp. 327–328.
49. Ibid., p. 295.
50. Berman, *Death on the Job*, pp. 130–31.
51. Paul Brodeur, *Expendable Americans* (New York: Viking Press, 1974), p. 8.
52. United Steelworkers of America, *Post Hearing Brief*, p. 11.
53. Odell, *Environmental Awakening*, p. 5.
54. Fox, *John Muir*, p. 315.
55. "A Call to Survival," *Environmental Action*, 14 May 1970: 3.
56. Richard N. L. Andrews, "Class Politics or Democratic Reform: Environmentalism and American Political Institutions," *Natural Resources Journal*, April 1980: 224.
57. Llewellyn King, "Washington Energy Report," *Power Engineering*, December 1977: 26.
58. Louis Harris, "Substantial Majorities Indicate Support for Clean Air and Clean Water Acts," *The Harris Survey*, 11 June 1981.

13

1. Interviews with Vernon McDougall, Workers Institute for Safety and Health, Washington, D.C., 9 January 1981; and George Lambertson, International Representative for United Paperworkers International Union, 16 January 1981.
2. Leonard Woodcock, keynote address, Working for Environmental and Economic Jobs and Justice Conference, Black Lake, MI, 2 May 1976.
3. "Dying for Work: Occupational Health and Asbestos," *NACLA Report on the Americas*, March–April 1978: 37.
4. United States Senate, Subcommittee on Air and Water Pollution of the Committee on Public Works, *Economic Dislocation Resulting from Environmental Controls* (Washington, D.C.: U.S. Government Printing Office, 1971), p. 301.
5. James C. Oldham, "Organized Labor, The Environment, and the Taft-Hartley Act," *Michigan Law Review*, April 1973: 959.
6. Ibid.: 961.
7. William Schweke, *Plant Closing Strategy Packet* (Washington, D.C.: Progressive Alliance and Conference on Alternative State and Local Policies, 1980).
8. "Words and Deeds," *Wall Street Journal*, 23 November 1979: 20.
9. Barry Bluestone and Bennett Harrison, *Capital and Communities: The Cause and Consequences of Private Disinvestment* (Washing-

ton, D.C.: The Progressive Alliance, 1980), p. 260.

10. Ibid., pp. 256–59.

11. Joint Report of Labor Union Study Tour Participants, *Economic Dislocation: Plant Closings, Plant Relocation and Plant Conversion* (Washington, D.C.: United Auto Workers, United Steelworkers of America, International Association of Machinists, and Aerospace Workers, 1979), p. 7.

12. Ibid., p. 8.

13. *Occupational Safety and Health Reporter,* 12 February 1981.

14. Toxic Substances Strategy Committee, *Toxic Chemicals and Public Protections: A Report to the President* (Washington, D.C.: U.S. Government Printing Office, 1980), p. 3.

15. Barry Commoner, "Labor's Stake in the Environment/The Environment's Stake in Labor," keynote address before the Conference on "Jobs and the Environment," San Francisco, CA, 28 November 1972.

16. Ed Bloch, "PCB, UE and GE," *Monthly Review,* October 1981: 19.

17. Donald Janson, "Hooker Chemical in Jersey Struck on Toxic Gas Arrival," *New York Times,* 28 February 1981.

18. Mary Melville, "Risks on the Job: The Worker's Right to Know," *Environment,* November 1981: 13.

19. Ibid.

20. Robert Howard, "There is Life After Auchter—At Least in Philadelphia," *In These Times,* 16–22 September 1981: 8.

21. Caron Chess, "In One City, at Least, You Have a Right to Know," *In These Times,* 28 January–3 February 1981: 4-5.

22. Phone conversation with John Yolton, United Auto Workers International staff, Detroit, MI, 10 March 1982.

23. John Robinson, "Firms Oppose EEC Plan for Union Rights," *Washington Post,* 10 February 1982.

24. Ibid.

25. Howard, "Life After Auchter," p. 5.

26. Robert Cahn, *Footprints on the Planet: A Search for an Environmental Ethic* (New York: Universe Books, 1978), p. 252.

27. Paul Dalby, "He Said No to the Boss—Now He's a Hero," *Toronto Star,* 17 October 1980.

28. "Lifesigns," *Quest/81,* April 1981: 8.

29. Samuel Epstein, *The Politics of Cancer* (Garden City, New York: Anchor Books, 1979), p. 441.

30. Letter from Jordan Barab, Environmentalists for Full Employment, 15 April, 1980.

31. Alan S. Miller, "Towards an Environment/Labor Coalition," *Environment,* Vol. 22, No. 5, June 1980: 23.

32. Mike Cooley, "Design, Technology and Production for Social Needs," *The Right to Useful Work,* Ken Coates, ed., (Nottingham, England: Spokesman Books, 1978), p. 200.

33. Mike George, "Lucas Aerospace Workers Campaign," *Labour Monthly*, July/August 1978: 275–276.
34. Interview with Jack Mundey in Sydney, Australia, 2 October 1977.
35. Marion Hardman and Peter Manning, *Green Bans* (Melbourne, Australia: Australian Conservation Foundation, 1976).
36. Interview with Jack Mundey, 2 October 1977.
37. Jack Mundey, *Green Bans and Beyond* (Sydney, Australia: Angus and Robertson Publishers, 1981), p. 147.
38. Pete Thomas, "The Green Bans in Australia," *The Right to Useful Work*, p. 100.

14

1. Interview with Mike Olszanski, Environmental Committee, Local 1010, United Steelworkers of America, Gary, Indiana, 22 November 1981.
2. James C. Oldham, "Organized Labor, The Environment and the Taft-Hartley Act," *Michigan Law Review*, April 1973: 936.
3. Ibid.: 951.
4. Ibid.: 957.
5. Ibid.: 971-973.
6. Ibid.: 958.
7. Ibid.
8. Ibid.
9. Ibid.: 963n.
10. Interview with Brock Evans, Vice President, National Audubon Society, Washington, D.C., 24 February 1982.
11. Interview with Franklin Wallick, United Auto Workers Washington Representative, 9 March 1982.
12. Tom Alexander, "It's Time for New Approaches to Pollution Control," *Fortune*, November 1976.
13. Jeanne Briggs, "Environmental Backlash Begins," *Forbes*, June 1977.
14. Letter from Robert A. Georgine, President, Building and Construction Trades Department, AFL-CIO, Washington, D.C., 26 June 1979.
15. "The Coalition Behind Full Employment," *Business Week*, 12 July 1976: 76.
16. Interview with an official of the United Paperworkers International Union, Flushing, N.Y., 7 October 1976.
17. Letter from Lane Kirkland, President, AFL-CIO, Washington, D.C., 12 August 1981.
18. David Moberg, "Unions Are of Three Minds on Clean Air," *In These Times*, 11-17 November 1981.
19. Press Release, OSHA/Environmental Network, Washington, D.C., 6 February 1981.

20. Liv Smith, "Labor and the No-Nukes Movement," *Socialist Review*, No. 54, November–December 1980: 147–148.
21. Ibid.: 138–139.
22. Richard Grossman and Jordan Barab, "An Exercise in Power," *Environment*, Vol. 22, No. 9, November 1980.
23. Walt Anderson, "Jobs vs. the Environment: The Fight Nobody Can Win," *Cry California*, Summer 1977: 3.
24. "Ruckus in Redwood Country," *International Woodworker*, 20 February 1981: 4-5.
25. Marc Reisner, "The Tragedy of Redwood National Park," *Natural Resources Defense Council Newsletter*, July/August 1977: 14.
26. Alan Cline, "Redwood for Lumber Is Almost Gone," *San Francisco Examiner*, 11 May 1977: 1.
27. Ibid.
28. Phone conversation with Jay Power, Legislative Office, AFL-CIO, 29 January 1981.
29. Phone conservation with Ron Karp, Department of Labor, 27 August 1981.
30. Phone conversation with Al Lasley, Carpenters Union, Eureka, CA, 5 February 1981.
31. "Ruckus in Redwood Country," p. 4.
32. Ibid., p. 5.
33. Phone conversation with Tim McKay, North Coast Environmental Center, Arcata, CA, 3 March 1981.
34. Al Martinez, "California Redwood Park Leaves Timberbeasts Jobless, Bitter," *Washington Post*, 26 November 1981: F1-2.
35. This case study is drawn from two interviews with Michael Olszanski and Joe Frantz, 22 November 1981 and 14 March 1982, and from the Local 1010 newspaper.
36. Ibid.
37. "Inland State Boiler Permit Is Challenged," *Hammond (Ind.) Times*, 7 July 1978.
38. Olszanski interview.
39. Ibid.
40. Ibid.
41. Brenda Frantz, "Two First-Hand Accounts of the Bailly Fight," *Critical Mass Energy Journal*, November–December 1981: 8, 15.
42. Olszanski interview.
43. National Commission on Air Quality, *To Breathe Clean Air* (Washington, D.C.: U.S. Government Printing Office, 1981) p. 5.59.

Index

Index